HOUGHTON MIFFLIN REPRINT EDITIONS

SANDWICH

The Town That Glass Built

HARRIOT BUXTON BARBOUR

*Illustrated with Drawings by Robert Hallock
and with Photographs*

001231

AUGUSTUS M. KELLEY · PUBLISHERS
CLIFTON 1972

First Published 1948
(Boston: Houghton Mifflin Company)
Copyright 1948 by Harriot Buxton Barbour

RE-ISSUED 1972 BY
AUGUSTUS M. KELLEY · PUBLISHERS
Clifton New Jersey 07012
By Arrangement with HOUGHTON MIFFLIN COMPANY

. . . .

ISBN o 678 03564 4
LCN 72 153175

. . . .

PRINTED IN THE UNITED STATES OF AMERICA
by SENTRY PRESS, NEW YORK, N. Y. 10013

To T. V. B. in grateful memory

ACKNOWLEDGMENTS

I WISH HERE to express my deep appreciation to the many persons whose generosity with source material and patience and kindness in sharing their memories with me have made the writing of this book not only possible, but a very pleasant experience. To Wilmon B. Chipman, Jr., of Reading, Massachusetts, for use of the very rare and valuable *Constitution of the Flint Glassmakers of Massachusetts* discovered by him among the effects of his great-uncle William Talbot of the etching department at the old Boston and Sandwich factory, and to him and Mrs. Wilmon B. Chipman for access to documentary material used in *The Romance of Sandwich Glass* by Frank W. Chipman. Also to Mrs. Ruth Webb Lee for her kind permission to quote from her *Sandwich Glass* and for use of valuable illustrative material, as well as to Miss Dorothea Setzer, author of *The Sandwich Historical Society and Its Glass*. I am particularly grateful to Miss Flora Jarves of Kingston, Rhode Island, for her invaluable help with information concerning the Jarves family and to Mr. Francis Steegmuller of New York for sharing with me some of the fruits of his own research; to Mr. and Mrs. Charles S. Lloyd of Sandwich for access to the old company store book and other priceless material; also to Mr. George E. Burbank, Treasurer of the Sandwich Historical Society, Mrs. George E. Burbank, Librarian of the Weston Memorial Library, Sandwich, the late Mr. John Liberty and Mrs. Liberty, Mrs. Christopher Brady, Miss Alice Grady, Miss Nellie Kelleher, Mrs. Charlotte Chipman, Mrs. Lillian Tangney, Mrs. Thomas, Mrs. Bradford Shaw, Mr. J. N. Leonard, all of Sandwich, and Mrs. Jessie R. Rogers of South Dennis, whose memories of "Uncle Billy Kern" were instrumental in getting the book under way in the beginning. I am also deeply indebted to Miss Margaret P. Hazen, Associate Research Librarian, Massachusetts Institute of Technology, Miss Annette B. Kelley of the *Yarmouth Register,* Miss Elizabeth Nye, Librarian, Sturgis Memorial Library, Barnstable, Miss Eleanor Gow, Thomas Crane Public Library, Quincy, Massachusetts, Miss Elizabeth Driscoll, Town Clerk, Sandwich, and Mr. Donald Trayser, Clerk of Court, Barnstable County.

H. B. B.

SOUTH DENNIS, MASS.

CONTENTS

ILLUSTRATIONS

SANDWICH
The Town That Glass Built

Individual Enterprise

EARLY IN 1824, the industrial revolution arrived in Sandwich, Massachusetts, aboard the packet *Polly* from Boston.

The first founders of Sandwich had hewn from the wilderness a new town with church and school and mill and tavern and all that they felt man would ever need, and they believed that they were building a world of unchanging and firm foundations. Surplus sons might go and build new towns, or someone might forsake the soil to preach and teach, or grind the corn for his fellow men. At times, the quiet years might be disturbed by some prophet showing new ways to God or by some new war to tear men from their fields. But always after the vision and the strife, there would be the earth, and men would tend their creatures and watch their weather and plow and plant and reap. So, it could not be doubted, life would go on for the common man until the end of time. And thus nearly two centuries had passed in Sandwich.

Of course, in the passing years, Nature had taught the uni-

1

versal lesson that few men or towns can best live wholly to themselves. As had been true for other men and communities since the beginning of time, commerce started here first with a shortage which could be supplied only by the exchange of some surplus with a more favored community. Wheat would no longer grow in Sandwich fields because of a persistent blight. Therefore, the lack had to be made good by trade of corn, timber, and sheep — the last two of which were, in 1824, the town's chief articles of commerce. Small boats loaded with firewood and building timber skimmed across the bay to Boston and great dun flocks of sheep trotted along the sandy, hilly cartpath carrying their mutton to market. Still, the town could have lived quite well in immemorial ways without trade or the city.

Revolution slipped in unnoticed in the guise of just one more jaded businessman down from Boston for what was then termed the Sporting. There had been many other men from the city before him, alighting from the coach or walking up from the packet with rod and gun to rest for awhile and warm themselves without and within by the wide fireplace in the taproom at Mr. Fessenden's tavern.

The inn itself stood as monument of a sort to one of the first men to come from the city to Sandwich — the Reverend Roland Cotton, one of the preaching Cottons, well known for his ability to deliver "a Gospel sermon, a long one, full of meat." To induce him to stay, the town, in 1690, had offered all the favors in its power, the privilege of pasturing his horse in the "bury-ground," "all such drift whales as shall be driven or cast ashore within the limits of the town," and "land to be held by him, his heirs and assigns forever if he remain among us until God take him away by death *or otherwise*. But if he die without issue or if he remove to better himself, the lands shall revert to the town."

On this grant of land, Mr. Cotton proceeded to build quite the grandest house Sandwich had seen. It was perhaps the first in town to be fitted with the tiny diamond-shaped, violet-colored panes brought so carefully across the sea, since, in the words of an old jingle:

> The Window Glass is with us here
> Exceeding scarce and very Dear
> So that some in this Way do Take
> Isinglass Windows for to Make.[1]

There was an elegantly graceful staircase down which Mistress Cotton might swish to greet her flock. Mistress Cotton was no homespun country dame, but a Saltonstall of Boston, used to living among gentlemen who hired others to care for their horses and never handled a tool heavier than a pen, ladies who did not bake or sweep or spin, but sat in brocade-curtained drawing rooms and selected from rich stuffs spread at their feet. Mistress Cotton wore her gowns of silk and satin over an impressively firm foundation of English stays. Her trim shoes were never home-cobbled. Each afternoon, she had her tea in a fragile china cup, stirring the lump sugar delicately with a thin silver spoon.

It speaks a great deal for Mistress Cotton's essential Christian humility of spirit that her husband's ministry endured for thirty years during which the church prospered and the brethren dwelt together in unwonted unity. However, if the sight of the finery of the pastor's lady did not actually tempt parishioners' wives into breaking the Tenth Commandment, it did give them new ideas. The more prosperous farmers' wives had their Sabbath silks. Even the humblest developed a taste for a mug of tea while her man liked his nip of Jamaica rum against the cold, and sometimes more than a nip when he gathered with his fellows.

Though Mr. Cotton made no miraculous ascension, as the townspeople had seemed half to believe in the wording of

[1] Beard and Rogers, *5000 Years of Glass.*

the land grant, he and his lady did pass from the scene in the normal way, leaving the mansion to become the parsonage of his successor, the Reverend Benjamin Fessenden. Mr. Fessenden's heirs had cared more for men's bodies than their souls, and Mistress Cotton's mansion became the town tavern.

It seemed fitting enough that the house where worldliness and godliness had appeared to the town hand in hand should be the connecting link with the world outside. Here the farmer folk drove in for their mail and weekly paper, to refill their jugs of rum, and to hear the tales of travelers returned. As was the case with most towns by the sea, some sons had gone forth in ships, carrying furs from the west coast, silks and spices from the Orient, manufactured wares from Britain, or whale oil from wild ocean wastes. On their visits home between voyages, they would swap stories of storms and sharks and mutinies. Old Captain Handy could even tell of an encounter with a polar bear from which he escaped only by running over the snow crust through which the heavier bear broke and floundered with every step.

With such colorful yarns from native sons, it is not much wonder that little heed was paid to the outsiders who came and went, or those who came and stayed. It had always been the humble men who stayed, flotsam picked up by mine host, William Fessenden, or stranded when some cattle caravan passed through. There was Gilbert Lewis, drifted over from Caermorthen in Wales, whose home was with horses wherever they were. At the end of his life, his obituary was to read, "a faithful domestic in the family of William Fessenden for 21 years, and the care he took of the weary beast will long be remembered by many a traveller." More famous was the ancient Irishman known simply as John Trout whose real name had been lost in his wanderings.

"This second name, like Scipio Africanus," William Tudor had said, "was the reward for most distinguished services" — services to the grand gentlemen from Boston who passed like shadows across the Sandwich scene.

No one knows how early men from the city had found the unbounded fish and game of Sandwich. It had slowly become quite the fashion for the Boston Brahmins to turn to the countryside in a pseudo-philosophical search for simplicity or a more genuine quest for relaxation.

"Wee had good sport," wrote one traveler simply in 1770 of the visit to Sandwich and sojourn at Fessenden's.

About fifty years later, the town had become the subject of an essay in a diluted Addisonian manner for the *Monthly Anthology*. This was the literary effort of William Tudor, merchant-shipper who had made his fortune by converting the wealthy planters of Martinique and South America to cold drink and then supplying the necessary ice from his own pond in Saugus. He was as ingenious and energetic in purveying culture to his native land, being the founder and leading spirit of the Anthology Society through which at monthly supper parties, merchants and ministers turned their minds to the problem of fabricating a national literature.

"To persons fond of fishing, sporting, or riding," Tudor began, "Sandwich offers greater resources than any other spot in the country." He followed with a somewhat coy account of the arrival at Fessenden's, the call for "everything in the house," and the summoning of "John Trout as outrider." After a pleasant day spent in trout-catching and snipe-shooting at Deacon Nye's brook, the party would "dine at four on the proceeds of the day's sport aided by tautog and Sandwich mutton. The latter is worthy of all praise. It resembles exactly the mutton of the Downs of England." As a final judgment, the town was called "one of the most pleasant villages in Massachusetts. Some parts of Sandwich resemble districts in Surrey and Sussex in England." This, from Federalist Boston, was praise indeed.

The genteel publicity made Sandwich a fashionable male
paradise for those weary of the close-packed houses and cob-
bled streets of Boston or the inescapable swish of skirts
among the carefully clipped shrubbery of the great estates at
Swampscott and Nahant. John Trout became a celebrated
character whose portrait was preserved "among the embellishments of the Athenaeum" and whose Irish wit was
quoted at the meetings of the Anthology Society.

"When asked what was due for his services," reported
Tudor, "he told us that his wages were $1.25 a day; this was
the price when grain (Indian corn) was $2.00 a bushel, and
he should not increase the price. Although corn was now
selling at 50 cents, he would not charge more." John, moreover, shared with his patrons a contempt for the natives
(which word he disdainfully rhymed with knives) who were
to be outwitted by poaching or any other chicanery at every
opportunity.

The Bostonian view of the outlanders was voiced some
years later by Henry Adams, who asserted that though the
Saxon farmers of the eighth century could not read or write
and did not receive a weekly newspaper, their customs and
habits were not so greatly altered and improved by time that
they would have found much difficulty in accommodating
their way of living to that of their descendants of the early
nineteenth century.

This was a favorite view. But the Sandwich Saxons and
their brethren elsewhere did have weekly newspapers as well
as wits sharpened by theological discussions and a firm conviction that the country belonged to the farmer folk who had
first won it from the wilderness. Such qualities caused alarm,
as well as contempt, in the minds of men who, like the wiz-
ened little Federalist, Fisher Ames, were convinced that all
power should be in the hands of the "wise and good" or
those whose estates reached the value of two thousand dollars.

As Ames skirted the Sandwich marshes, he was rather dis-

turbed by the casual offhand greetings of the farmers who
were seemingly quite unimpressed by his store of wisdom
and virtue banked in Boston. "What is to become of our
country he who made it best knows," he scolded in 1803. "It
is too big for union, too sordid for patriotism, too democratic
for liberty. A democracy cannot last."

But, after all, why should Sandwich be excited over city
men? Except for mine host, William Fessenden, and John
Trout, no one in town really needed them or anything they
had to offer. It was pleasantly convenient for the farmer to
supply some of his wants at the general store on the fruits of
trade, but if need be, he could live completely to and by
himself — which was more than could be said of the gentlemen whom he saw dependent on such a zany as John Trout
to find them birds to shoot and fish to catch.

Mr. Deming Jarves, arriving on the *Polly* and making his
way up to town, certainly did not seem worth any particular
attention. Here, anyone who gave him an extra glance
would have said, was simply one more Bostonian with rod
and gun, a tall sandy-haired man of about thirty-five who
walked up from the shore to Fessenden's with the neat
measured steps of one whose feet generally fall on city pave-
ment. His blue eyes did not have the far-seeing sweep of
some who had in times past briefly stirred Sandwich by
heavenly visions or tales of fortunes beyond the seas. They
scrutinized the world at hand with a quizzical calculation
from beneath brows already slightly furrowed by a shrewd,
half-humorous frown. Of course, to John Trout and Mr.
Fessenden, it was apparent from the set of the shoulders and
the cut of the clothes that this was a man among the wise
and good. As a matter of fact, his stock of essential wisdom
and virtue had been quite materially augmented within the
year by a legacy of twenty-five thousand dollars from his
father, John Jackson Jarves, Gentleman.

2

The elder Mr. Jarves had begun his career as cabinet-maker in London at the time when there were drifting about the city a number of North American loyalists whom the recent successful rebellion had left without a country. Not a few of these had honestly believed that they were serving the best interest of a well-loved land in fighting to prevent the breach. Among these was Samuel Seabury, a clergyman who had fought his battle so ably with pro-British pamphlets signed A. W. Farmer (a Westchester farmer) that he goaded Alexander Hamilton into reply.

Now that the political separation which he had tried to prevent had been forced by blood, he still sought to preserve a religious tie by becoming first bishop of the mother church in the new nation. However, his weeks in a Connecticut prison in 1775 whither he had been rushed by a "mob of lawless Whigs" and his turn as chaplain of the King's American Regiment in 1778 could not counterbalance his present refusal to take the British oath of allegiance. Hence, England denied him the consecration which he eventually received in Scotland, but not before his daughter Hannah had met and married the young London cabinetmaker. When the new bishop sailed back home, Hannah persuaded her husband to accompany him.

The first builders of Sandwich and sister towns had come laden with pots and pans, kettles and cranes, axes and nails, and other needful things which could not be made by men hewing homes from a wilderness, but might be fashioned only in an old, settled land where some few had left the soil to live by the skill of their hands. In time, craftsmen began to find it more profitable to take themselves and their skills across the sea than to pay the exportation duties by which the mother country profited from her monopoly of manufactured wares.

It was certain that cabinetmakers and their wives, like John and Hannah Jarves, would be of more social consequence in the New World than the Old. Besides, the Seabury influence was not inconsiderable with the Federalists and a few forgiven Tories who were, as a class, those with the most money to spend on the Jarves wares. Thus, the Boston weeklies of 1787 carried the quite genteel advertisement of John Jackson Jarves, Cabinet, Chair, and Clock Maker from London, now of 76 Newbury Street who "respectfully informs Gentlemen and Ladies that he makes the following Mahogany Furniture on reasonable terms." Then followed a quite overwhelming list of articles, forty-nine in all. Besides all common and uncommon varieties of desks, tables, chairs, and beds were such luxury items as "Balance, Pole, Face, and Hand Fire Screens, Cellerets, Butler's Trays, Knife Trays, Oval Tea Trays, Tea Chests and Cadys, Ladies' Urn Stands, Gentlemen's Wardrobes, Weight and Spring Clock Cases, Watch Cases, and all kinds of Picture Frames." [2]

Ties with the Old World were not completely severed. At intervals, the young couple bobbed back across the ocean for lengthy visits, so that it has taken interested research workers some years and a few mild disputes to decide whether their only son was born in Boston or in London. Be that as it may, young Deming was christened with fashionable correctness on December 9, 1790, in the Old South Church, Boston.

To the small boy growing up in the solid, over-lavishly furnished house on Beach Street, no place in the world was as fascinating as his father's workshop which gradually expanded into three buildings. Here was all the bustle and stir of trade. There was a constant coming and going of fine gentlemen and ladies with fashionable clothes and polite manners for whom the clerk would deferentially bring forth treasures usually hidden from young eyes and fingers.

2 Ruth Webb Lee, *Sandwich Glass*.

Weathered sea captains appeared from time to time reporting cargoes of mahogany from the tropics or rich stuffs from
the Orient and were never too busy to chuck Bub under the
chin and tell him a story.

In the workshop was also to be found the thrill of creation,
the conversion, as Deming himself later put it, of something "shapeless and apparently uncontrollable into some
elegant article" — rough mahogany sticks into graceful curves
and fluted pilasters of chaste federalist design, with surfaces
mirror-smooth and as alluring to the touch as the jewel-
toned upholstery fabrics to the eye. And the child was mad
about color.

He loved to paint — a trait which was surely distressing to
his father, for the country was still too new for any art which
could not be lived in or sat upon or in some way harnessed
to everyday living, and artists were generally ne'er-do-wells.
To be sure, Mr. Gilbert Stuart had earned a respectable
fame and modest fortune, but his art fulfilled the noble
function of preserving the lineaments of substantial citizens
for a presumably admiring posterity. However, young Deming had not the slightest interest in the florid faces of Boston
burghers. He cared only for pictures of sea, forest, or flowers
or anything that would give an excuse for splashing on color
— color — and more color, and this was an occupation surely
more suitable for his sister Sally.

The father need not have worried. From his environ-
ment the boy had been thoroughly impregnated with what
was to become the prevailing American doctrine — that comfortable living was the symbol of civilization, and that purveying the means for this civilization should be pressed with
missionary zeal. On holiday sails around the harbor in the
family pleasure boat, he saw great ships from all parts of the
world. These spoke not so much of adventurous voyages and
strange romantic ports as of bulging cargoes of good things
to be added to the lives of solid men. To young Jarves, the

tallest tales of sea captains could not hold a candle to the accounts of pioneer manufacturers over their cups of claret in his father's drawing room.

One of these, Robert Hewes, made a lasting impression on the listening boy. There was adventure aplenty in all attempts to establish manufacturing in the New World, but in none more drama or catastrophe than in glassmaking.

Legend has it that the ill-fated Jamestown colonists in 1608 brought glassmakers with them for the purpose of making glass beads to trade with the Indians. There is no doubt that England would have liked to foster in the colony an industry which she was obliged to shut down at home because the insatiable need of her navy for timber left no surplus to feed glass furnaces. But in 1635, with the introduction of coal instead of wood as fuel, the British policy was reversed. All competition — whether colonial, French, or Venetian — was suppressed by a government bounty to manufacturers of from twenty-five to fifty per cent of the actual cost of manufacture on any glass for export, or what amounted to "dumping" to drive competitors from the field.

Thus it was that most of the early glassmakers in America, from Wistar and Stiegel to the more prosaic manufacturers of window glass in Quincy, Massachusetts, were Germans, who considered wood the proper fuel for glassmaking and were using furnaces for wood-burning as in the old country. Robert Hewes was attempting to establish a window-glass factory on the German system and, following the common custom of "carrying his works to the fuel," had erected his factory in the virgin forest of New Hampshire. Young Deming could never hear enough of glassmaking and glassmakers. There seemed magic in the process whereby "elements derived from the earth — earthy, opaque, apparently incapable of being transmuted" — could become "a transparent and brilliant substance." There was added excitement in Mr. Hewes's personal experiences. He told the wide-eyed boy of tracks of bears to be seen every morning in and around his works. Unfortunately for Mr. Hewes, flames proved' more voracious than bears, and his project fell to a common fate of glasshouses when it went up in smoke.

From this and other ventures conceived, worked out, carried to success or failure before his very eyes, young Jarves was so imbued with the constant adventure of business life, the sense of struggle and achievement, that years of being bound to books at Harvard or Yale seemed a wicked waste of youth. Few went to college except to prepare for a profession. Deming had not the slightest desire to follow in the footsteps of his august grandfather, and teaching and the law seemed equally musty. Consequently, in 1813, the *Boston Directory* listed "Jarves, Deming, dry goods, 11 Cornhill."

John Jarves had not yet retired to the life of a gentleman on the fruits of his life's labor, and no doubt he would have liked to have his only son prepare to carry on his very prosperous business. But there was no more possibility of expansion. After all, mahogany furniture was distinctly durable goods which, once purchased, seldom needed replacement, and the class of purchasers was strictly limited to men of substance. Deming would have had only to fall into a long-established routine, and he preferred to strike out for himself.

He soon showed his initiative by seeking to ride a wave to prosperity on the flood of English manufactures which came in at the close of the War of 1812. Finding a partner, he formed the firm of "Henshaw and Jarves, Dealers in Crockery Ware, Belknap St.," and with Webster's voice warding off an adequate protective tariff, began to supply fine English porcelain dinner sets, Holland salts, and Irish wineglasses to add their luster to the dark mahogany surfaces of his father's dining tables.

More than ever, he was brought into contact with the masters of ships, and one of them became his particular friend

— Captain William Stutson, a young man with a beak of a nose and a sharp eye under commanding brows. Like all sea captains, he had his tale to tell — a tale of privateering in the war and long months in Dartmoor prison. He also had a goodly supply of sisters, and the young businessman proceeded to fall in love with as much prudence as passion, for the Stutsons were decidedly substantial citizens. The father, Captain Levi, had been a local hero of the Revolution. Cousins, uncles, and relatives more remote were intricately and profitably involved in Boston's great shipping trade. There was a smart town house and a rococo summer estate in Swampscott. And on May 29, 1815, in the *Boston Independent Chronicle* appeared the item: "In this town, Mr. Deming Jarves mar. to Miss Anna Smith Stutson."

It was not long before young Mr. Jarves became corporation clerk to the Boston Porcelain and Glass Company of East Cambridge and found himself in a position to enjoy some fruits of his family connections. The company was about to go the mushroom way of most early American glasshouses, and one of the first duties of the new clerk was to sign a call for a meeting to wind up its affairs. Already, in his mind, the meeting was to mark a beginning rather than an end.

This firm had come by a devious way from an early window-glass company. During the period of the Embargo Act and War of 1812 when few ships could slip in with the little violet panes so desired for the mansions of Boston, Massachusetts had given strong protection to the infant industry — a fifteen-year monopoly of manufacture and five-year exemptions of capital from taxation and workmen from military service. For the proprietors, life would have seemed without a care if the workers had not persisted in the very human trait of trying to better themselves.

The success of the Boston Window Glass Company had induced plenty of rivals to try their luck beyond the limits of

the Massachusetts monopoly, and these were forever persuading the workmen with offers of increased wages "to
leave their employ and break their indentures." One such
band of workmen, en route to an embryonic plant in Utica,
New York, was arrested just before reaching the state line
and brought back to face expensive lawsuits. Another group,
"seduced" by a Doctor Adams of Richmond, Virginia, actually "succeeded in reaching Richmond to try their fortunes
under the auspices of the Doctor." But the deserters were
soon "convinced" of what Jarves calls the "fallacy of increased pay," for "after very heavy losses, the works were
abandoned and the workers thrown out of employ." They
came back to Boston only to find that the company had filled
their places with "workmen engaged in the meantime at a
very heavy expense from England."

During the years when the country was still a British colony, English glass blowers could find no refuge here from
the stringent industrial restrictions of their native land.
Now that independence had been won, a mechanic or craftsman was safe once he had smuggled himself and his precious
skill beyond the seas. There were always New World merchants as ready to deal in human contraband as in any other
forbidden ware. More and more workmen were coming in
from Manchester and Birmingham, Sturbridge and London
in England, Dublin and Waterford in Ireland.

According to *Reminiscences of Glass-Making,* "the excess
of window-glass blowers brought into this country by the
enterprise of the Boston Window Glass Company led to the
introduction of the manufacture of flint glass, so called from
the English use of crushed flint as an ingredient of their
finest ware." Since window glass at that time was made by
blowing huge spheres, like enormous bottles, from which,
while the glass was still warm enough to be flattened, the
tiny panes were cut, many of the blowers had been recruited
from flint-glass works, for "a good flint glass blower with

manual strength could fill the part of window-glass blower exceedingly well."

Thus the Porcelain and Glass Company was an offshoot of the early manufacture of window glass. Its ownership repeatedly changed with circumstances and finally the firm came to grief because of managers who, to quote Jarves, "proved in no way qualified for the task."

"The Porcelain Company, discouraged by so many failures," he continued, "agreed to wind up their concern, and in November 1817, they disposed of their entire property at public auction. As one manufactory dies out, only to give place to another, so the New England Glass Company was formed." This terse account neglects to mention that the auction was arranged by Deming Jarves, and the company of successful bidders included his brother-in-law, Captain Stutson; his sister Sally's husband's nephew, Daniel Hastings, a well-to-do merchant and importer; and Anna's cousin, Edmund Munroe, a very wealthy banker; to say nothing of Deming himself, at least to the extent of nineteen hundred dollars contributed, as proved by a note found after his death, by Father Jarves. Thus the new concern was to be a cozy little family affair, and Deming became agent, or active manager.

For a time, he was as happy as a small boy with a hobby. To the intricate and interesting game of buying and selling was added the joy of creation, and glass was as fascinating to him as when he had first hung on the words of Mr. Hewes. He had an absorbed interest in everything from the Portland Vase to glass bugles on "the wrappers of mummies." He brushed up half-forgotten Latin to plow through the "technological literature of the ancients — Pliny, Theophrastus, Strabo, Petronius Arbiter, Berzelius, Neri, and others." He found new delight in Vergil who had compared crystal glass to "the clearness of the waters of the Fucine Lake." He exercised his French to dig up information about mediaeval furnaces and the working habits of the lordly glass blowers. There was a certain wry comfort in learning that glass-makers had changed their ways so little throughout the ages, for he had inherited the labor troubles of his predecessors. He was just enough to give brief credit where credit was due, and when some of the workmen left in 1820 to build a factory in New York City, he paid restrained tribute to their "skill and success."

However, it was much more satisfying to the self-esteem of the solid man to be able to report that:

> another secession of workmen from the New England Glass Company took place to embark on their own account their savings of many years in the doubtful enterprise of establishing flint-glass works in Kensington, Philadelphia, under the title of the Union Flint Glass Company. The proprietors, being all workmen, were enthusiastic in the project, happy in the belief that they could carry it on successfully, work when convenient, and enjoy much leisure. All was *then* to them sunshine. Ere long, they realized the many inherent evils attendant on flint-glass works; the demon of discord appeared among them, and they discovered, when too late, that they had left a place of comfort and ease for a doubtful enterprise.

Now he found his commercial experience useful not only in little matters like arranging to have ships come ballasted from France and Africa with fine sand and from British Guiana with pot clay; but in selling the company to that rare bird, the desirable worker. Hearing of the exceptional mechanical ability of one James B. Barnes, he stalked his prey warily and finally pounced as Barnes, in a mellow mood, was strolling with his children on the Common. After a casual greeting, and no doubt some kind and condescending words for the little Barneses, Jarves succeeded in persuading this complete stranger to exchange his current occupation for the incomparable "comfort and ease" of the New England Glass Company.

Moreover, invention was in the air, and the *Zeitgeist* seized young Jarves. For more than a generation, preachers like Cartwright and teachers like Whitney, barbers like Arkwright and painters like Fulton had been spending hours tinkering with wheels and gadgets in the service of the new gods, speed and quantity. In 1821, Deming Jarves registered his first patent — a labor-saving contraption for opening glassmaker's molds. The next year, he obtained his second on an improvement in the tubes of glass lamps.

He plunged into the mysteries of the "batch," mixed according to immemorial custom from secret formulae behind locked doors. Now he could revel in color more gorgeous and glowing than the most exuberant daubs of his childhood. One of the ingredients of flint glass — perhaps the most costly — was litharge or red lead which "should be perfectly pure, for the presence of any other substance or metal will be shown in the color of this glass." Only the finest quality of litharge would produce the crystal clarity so prized in itself and as a basis for pure colors not muddied by a greenish or violet tinge. At that time, England was trying to keep a stranglehold on certain manufactured products, like litharge, as well as raw materials and human skills, and the need of economic self-sufficiency was challenging American ingenuity. Deming Jarves was one of the first to meet the challenge.

With characteristic understatement he related:

> The writer believes he was the first person in the U.S., aided by a director of the New England Glass Co., to build a lead furnace. His only guide was a volume of *Cooper's Emporium of Arts and Sciences* which furnished a plan on a very limited scale. The furnace proved successful and enabled the company to continue their manufacture of glass at a period when no foreign red lead was to be procured.

They enlarged their works until they have become the most
important in the country, monopolizing the business in all
its branches from the highest qualities of pure Galena and
painters' red lead to common pig lead. By experiment, he
found the cost of manufacture of one batch to be $169.50
and the market value $250, thus showing a satisfactory profit
to the company for their outlay in this branch of the business.

And so he went on making more and more money for the
proprietors.

In 1823, John Jackson Jarves died, leaving, in accordance
with the English custom of primogeniture, his house and
shops and sailboat and twenty-five thousand dollars in the
hands of his son and trusting him to provide for widow and
daughter, although the latter had by her marriage quite
capably provided for herself. Deming became conscious of a
vague dissatisfaction with life. True, he was quite generally
recognized as a man of substance, had served two terms on
the Cambridge Council, and had recently been elected representative to the General Court. But the vista of long years
devoted to piling up profits for his relatives, even though he
also enriched himself thereby, was no longer alluring. Besides, here was the new problem of putting twenty-five thousand dollars to work, for idle money was considered as sinful
as idle hands.

He decided to take time off for a tour of American glass
factories to see what stimulation he could derive from an
inspection of his competitors. So he took a packet to New
York and thence bounced along by stagecoach to the smoky
little sheds straggling and struggling along the seaboard. He
found nothing at all impressive until he reached Pittsburgh
and met Mr. Thomas Bakewell of the flint-glass firm of Bakewell and Pears. Here he listened to an experience which in-
fluenced him as profoundly as the earlier tales of Mr. Robert
Hewes.

The Bakewell manufactory had been founded, characteristically, by a few wandering English workmen from a defunct German window-glass company in Maryland who were attracted by the near-by coal and became the first in the country to use this fuel in glassmaking. "The persons engaged in the enterprise, however," wrote Jarves in *Reminiscences of Glass-Making,* "were deficient both in requisite knowledge and capital, the effort proved abortive, the parties quarrelled, and the establishment in an incomplete condition was offered for sale."

Mr. Bakewell and a friend "were induced to purchase the concern under the representation of one of the owners that he possessed the information and skill for the proper pursuit of the business." But Mr. Bakewell soon discovered the incompetence of the erstwhile owner and found that he must rely on his own efforts if his venture was not to go the way of its predecessor.

"The fortunes of his family and friends were, of course, deeply involved, and he therefore set himself to the accomplishment of his task most manfully," recorded Mr. Jarves as he related with sympathy the various and almost insurmountable difficulties to be encountered and overcome.

The Bakewell workmen, like all the rest, were fully aware of the value of their skill as a marketable commodity and, in their effort to turn the law of supply and demand to their benefit, fell into what Jarves called "the great evil of a determination to prevent the instruction of apprentices by the most arbitrary and unjust means, and, so far as it was in their power, endeavoring to prevent competition by not only controlling the hours of work but the quantity of manufacture; in fact, doing the least amount of work possible for the largest amount of pay that could be coerced from the proprietors."

Mr. Bakewell counteracted these "oppressive acts of the workmen" by supplanting them with more workmen brought on from England at a time when the prohibitory laws in regard to mechanics leaving there were in full force — "an undertaking requiring great secrecy and at the risk of imprisonment, if detected." But he also resorted to the more typically American expedient of counterbalancing the heavy cost of labor by cheapening the cost of production with an improvement in the construction of furnaces and the discovery of "better materials in his immediate vicinity."

Nowadays, there seems to be an epic quality in Mr. Bakewell's struggles for raw materials at a time when the sea furnished the only cheap and convenient means of transportation. Mr. Bakewell had to procure his pearlash and red lead from Philadelphia, the pot clay from Burlington, New Jersey — "the whole being transported over the mountains in wagons to Pittsburgh." As for saltpeter, Bakewell was obliged to have it dug in a crude state in the caves of Kentucky, pulled by straining horses over boggy and rocky roads to Pittsburgh where it still had to undergo an extensive refining process before it was capable of being used. After a settled peace with Britain, it was found simpler and cheaper to ship saltpeter from Calcutta. "At length his arduous and untiring labor was crowned with the desired success," Mr. Jarves closed his saga of a new world and age.

Success brought a dream to many of these early businessmen — the great American dream of founding an industrial dynasty to be handed down to one's sons and sons' sons. With Mr. Bakewell this dream was realized, and years later Deming Jarves, a brokenhearted old man, was to write that "his sons still carry on a profitable business on the premises originally occupied by their father. By father and sons, this has covered a space of forty-four years, a length of time rarely finding a business in the same family in America."

In 1824, however, future disillusionment was unforeseen by Deming Jarves. The dream seized him, too, driving the undefined feeling of lack from his life and offering the illusion of permanency and continuity that men so crave. Why should he devote the best labors of brain and hand to developing a business for merely financially interested proprietors when he might be establishing a dynasty for himself? His Anna was maintaining a satisfactory production rate in the matter of sons. Surely, he could do the rest, especially with twenty-five thousand dollars at his command. But exactly what should he do? With this problem pressing on his mind, he came to the hunting ground advertised by the favor of Boston's "solid" men and their great god, Daniel Webster.

3

Although Deming Jarves had come to Sandwich to relax in the enjoyment of hunting and fishing, he found that he could not leave the crowding schemes and plans back in Boston with a faulty batch or refractory workman. As he followed John Trout in the usual rounds, he had only an absent eye for the beauty of the long, lovely millpond and the peaceful peninsula with the somber slates of the burial plot where sons were laid beside their fathers when they had plowed their last furrow and carried their last corn to the little gray grist mill across the narrow waters.

All along the shores and up and down the sandy country roads were snug farmhouses sending lazy whirls of smoke from broad chimneys. In the surrounding fields, men with oxen were harrowing the fresh-plowed earth as men before them had done for nearly two hundred years in this Sandwich and for untold centuries in an older Sandwich across the sea in Kent. What Mr. Jarves dreamed for his sons and grandsons was a way of life as enduring, but less static — not a following in one's father's furrows so much as a dynamic growth from old foundations.

Mr. Jarves was a determined man. Though relax he could not, shoot he would. He dutifully went the customary rounds. He squinted along his gleaming gun barrel. He glimpsed the dark pine forest, the deep blue bay, the shining sands — and a sudden vision.

Such visions were dazzling more and more of Boston's solid men as they turned their eyes inward from the sea and saw in the wooded hills and flashing streams not sermons in stones and books in the running brooks, but fuel here and water power there and factories and smokestacks everywhere. To do them justice, they were not consciously motivated by the sole desire for gain. They told themselves very convincingly that it was a patriotic duty to develop their country's resources, a sacred obligation to set in motion the wheels which — as everyone so fondly believed — were to whirl the world into Utopia.

Now Deming Jarves suddenly saw all dreams come true. The dark and spreading forest? An inexhaustible supply of fuel for his furnaces. The bright white sands? The bulkiest ingredient of glass right at his very door; for had not Plymouth Beach sands been used quite satisfactorily during the War of 1812? The blue bay with navigable creek threading in behind the dunes? Cheap and easy transportation for raw materials and completed goods so that there need be none of the costly trundling over rough roads in wagons which had so handicapped Mr. Bakewell. His enthusiastic eye could even see the uses of the waving marsh grasses as packing for his finished articles.

As for that most vexatious element, labor, the site also had evident advantages. "Secession" and "seduction" were the two most harassing problems of management, and off in the wilderness, with packet and coach more or less under control of the company, it would not be easy for workmen to "secede" in order to form an independent enterprise or to be "seduced" with the offer of higher wages by a rival firm.

The rest of the morning after the vision he spent wandering, gun in hand but birds forgotten. When, occasionally, he stopped to squint at a patch of tall timber or test the ground by stamping in a flat meadow near the marsh, the townsmen gave his actions little thought. Men from the city were always doing queer things — ask John Trout. And if he sat down at Fessenden's with a somewhat abstracted appetite, no one noticed. He carried his vision back to Boston without a word to anyone, and Sandwich slept peacefully on.

Other men came and went and after a due and discreet interval of time, a rather colorless Mr. Jabez Dame arrived one day by packet, presumably for the customary fishing and shooting. He was distinguished chiefly by his very unusual technique in following the sport. Streams and the lore of John Trout interested him not at all. He wandered briefly along the edge of the marsh, but lingered in the woods where the trees grew thickest and gave a particularly absorbed attention to cartpaths. Though he carried a gun, the sound of his shot was never heard, and as a farmer would be working on his land at the edge of the woods, the stranger would suddenly appear from among the trees and ask some seemingly casual questions about a near-by wood lot and its ownership. Before he really had grasped the import, the owner would have exchanged what he regarded as a not particularly valuable piece of land for the bit of cash always so hard for a farmer to find in hand.

The Sabbath after Mr. Dame's silent departure, Sandwich farmers swapped stories outside the meeting house and were amazed to find how their experiences tallied. It soon became apparent that a large plateau of meadowland by the winding creek — all of thirty acres in extent — as well as a full three thousand acres of woodland, had quietly passed into the hands of Mr. Dame, and at very low prices, for Mr. Dame had plainly not believed in letting his right hand know what his left hand was doing.

While the town was still buzzing over the matter, another

wonder came to pass. Early in 1825, Mr. Deming Jarves of Boston and Cambridge petitioned the selectmen that a special town meeting be called in the interest of the prosperity of the town. Curiosity, of course, prompted the granting of the request, as well as the desire for entertainment in any form, for there was little enough excitement in the town at any time, especially in the winter. But who was Mr. Jarves? John Trout and Mr. Fessenden answered the question as best they could. He was a businessman. He had something to do with a factory — a glass factory, wasn't it? Between Mr. Dame's mysterious visit and Mr. Jarves's request, there was as yet no discernible connection.

On the appointed day, the *Polly* deposited Mr. Jarves once more on Sandwich shores. A near-by neighbor had piled wood in the stoves of the big bare meeting house, and the farmers began to flock in from near and far, on horseback and on foot. Mr. Jarves stood before them, urbanely surveying the rude assembly with his shrewd blue eyes. He began, with his rather charming one-sided smile, by paying his compliments to the town — a fair town wherein he had spent many happy hours. The townsmen nodded concurrence. Most towns cherish a deep conviction of their own inherent superiorities, and the Sandwich opinion of itself had been substantially corroborated by the influx of city visitors.

But, Mr. Jarves continued, his feeling for Sandwich had been only augmented by a recent tour he had taken through the country. Then the travelogue became more and more entrancing to his hearers as section after section of the land was described to Sandwich's advantage. At last, he came to Pittsburgh where he dwelt long and lovingly — not on the place, but the exceptional prosperity of its inhabitants. There men did not break their backs over the soil. They earned from $2 to $2.50 a day at work "neither arduous nor dangerous" — work in a glass factory.

Sandwich was impressed. Two dollars for a mere day's

work was as much as one could get for the bushel of corn on which one had spent over half a year of toil and struggle, preparing the soil for the seed, guarding the growing plant against weed, worm, and bird, and praying against drought and blight.

Here, Mr. Jarves went on in a spirit of all-embracing benevolence, was his opportunity of showing his appreciation to the inhabitants of the town he loved so well. If the townsmen were "sufficiently interested," he would like to build a glass factory in Sandwich so that they might "profit by the employment." By this time, the connection between Mr. Dame's purchases and Mr. Jarves's plans was becoming plain to most of the assembly. However, spellbound by the Jarves charm, the farmers would hardly have been surprised to see the gentleman begin to pull gold pieces out of his tall beaver to toss to the crowd. They were in a mood to "grant him leave" for almost anything.

Industrial Revolution

WHEN TROUT SEASON HAD COME once more to Sandwich, Daniel Webster alighted from the stagecoach in front of Fessenden's with his trusty rod, Killall, and his young son, Fletcher. The arrival of the great Daniel from his estate, Careswell, in Marshfield, was an event which the few farmers clustered for their mail would duly report to their wives and children, or neighbors met along the homeward way. The smoldering black eyes under cavernous brows — "dull anthracite furnaces waiting only to be blown," as Carlyle described them, and what Emerson called "the eloquent thunder" of his voice, could make drama of the most casual greeting. Watching him ascend the graceful staircase to the chamber always reserved for him, the bystanders would grin expectantly as they listened for the mighty rataplan on the wall that sent his mug of rum creaking up on his private dumb-waiter.

Of all the city visitors, Webster alone was greeted by the townsmen with more than the usual faintly hostile indifference. In a way, they considered the great Daniel one of themselves — a farm boy who had worked and won his way until the big Bostonians were paying him fees aggregating twenty thousand dollars a year to handle their lawsuits and now had even elected him to represent them in Congress. What was the mere man of business with his money and his schemes beside the mighty statesman who, in guiding the country along the ways of freedom, had come to stand for the leadership earlier personified by the preacher and man of God!

Webster was one of the new generation of politicians who were finding it more profitable to manipulate the mob than to scorn it. His keen mind and mighty voice had brought him a long way from the Salisbury farm, but there was nothing cynical in his use of his talents. His country was his idol and ideal, and if he conceived a government resting principally with "the solid man," at least he hymned a nation in which the poorest and meanest might, like himself, by his own efforts achieve the requisite solidity.

On this day, he took unto himself the indispensable John Trout and fresh horses for the party and struck out through the woods toward the Indian village at Mashpee. And if he met an unusual number of woodsmen plying their axes, his busy mind took no note, although he was never too absent-minded to dispense the stately yet comradely greeting that would send many a man home that night with the great news that Dan'l Webster had passed his way. Once he was wading Mashpee Stream, his abstraction deepened. He paid no attention at all to the chatter of the boy and the gossip of the guide, and little, if any, to Old Killall. At last, even the lad, fishing only certain prescribed holes and bends at a dutiful distance behind his revered sire, noticed that the usual zest was lacking.

He would let his line run carelessly down the stream or hold his rod still while his hook was not even touching the

water, omitted trying the best places under the projecting
roots of the pines and seemed indeed quite abstracted and
uninterested in his amusement [wrote Fletcher]. This, of
course, caused me a good deal of wonder and, after calling
his attention once or twice to his hook hanging on a twig or
caught in the long grass of the river, and finding that after
a moment, he relapsed again into indifference, I quietly
walked up near him and watched. He seemed to be gazing
at the overhanging trees and presently advancing one foot
and extending his right hand, he began to speak, "Ven-
erable men, you have come down to us from a former generation. Heaven has bounteously lengthened out your lives
that you might behold this joyous day!"

The mighty voice flowed on, and before the eyes of the
wondering boy, a phantom battlefield rose in the quiet wood
with "roll of hostile cannon," "volumes of smoke and flame,"
"ground strewn with dead and dying," and "a thousand
bosoms freely and fearlessly bared in an instant to whatever
of terror there may be in war and death." Thus rang forth
the words that were to honor the laying of the cornerstone
of Bunker Hill monument.

After the apostrophe to the bloody glorious past came
Webster's call to the future! "The great trust now descends
to new hands. We can win no laurels in a war for independence. Earlier and worthier hands have gathered them.
Nor are there places for us by the side of Solon and Alfred
and the other founders of state. Our fathers have filled them.
But there remains to us a great duty. *Let us develop the
resources of our land, call forth its powers.*"

The orator who catches the most ears is not he who utters
new truths, but he who glorifies existing forces. Webster's
invocation simply supplied words to the rhythm of the axes
in the woods, heralding the businessman who would replace
minister and statesman as the dominant figure on the American scene.

Mr. Jarves's own account of these busy months showed his characteristic terse understatement, "Ground was broke in April, dwellings for the workmen built and manufactory completed, and on the 4th day of July, 1825, they commenced blowing glass — three months from first breaking ground."

It was boom time in the old town, with work for every hand that could be spared from the farms to wield spade, axe, or hammer — not, to be sure, for the fabulous $2.00 or $2.50 a day, but, as set forth in the expense sheets — "labor, $6.00 a week." The marshy land was leveled and filled. The box-like wooden factory was erected, with its squat little tower for the bell which would govern the weekdays far more arbitrarily than the church bell had ruled the Sabbath.

Building did not stop there. A number of little low houses sprang up around the factory, and the strangest thing in the eyes of the townspeople was that several were elongated, with doorways in a row — sometimes two, sometimes four. Of course, everyone had heard of the brick houses of Boston, laid end to end for lack of room. Those who had made the trip to Boston by packet had even seen them. It was said that Mr. Jarves himself lived in such a house. But with all God's green country round about, it surely was no way for men to live — in stalls like cattle, without land to call their own.

The implication of the new tenements in signifying that all the promised $2.50-a-day jobs might not be for Sandwich men was quite lost in the excitement.

Never in the world had there been so much to see and do and talk about. Mr. Jarves came and went from city to town, and no one could tell when he would suddenly appear around the corner of a woodpile just as a man had straightened up for a minute to watch some scows loaded with sand being poled up the creek from the dunes. There was little enough chance for loitering anyway, for Captain Stutson was staying at the Fessenden to superintend the work and was here, there, and everywhere with his sharp eyes and sea voice.

Several times a day, the bull wagons, drawn by four oxen and a horse and piled high with wood, would swing out of sandy cartpaths through the town to the plateau by the factory. This wood, it was told by those who had seen, was split into sticks no thicker than a woman's wrist and dried before a fire in a brick arch until it was the color of coffee and could be lighted from a candle.

The *Polly* came down from Boston loaded low with queer cargo — bricks, clay, red lead, saltpeter, kegs of broken glass — and at last, even men, women, and children, but mostly lusty young men full of high spirits and horseplay.

Skilled workers still came from overseas, and few but the young had had the fortitude to break old ties. Some of the Irish, thrust from home by perpetual famine and an English excise tax that was squeezing the life from the glass factories of Dublin and Waterford, had succeeded in bringing loved ones along to the promise of better living. So James and Michael Doyle came with wives and children, and Daniel Fogarty brought his old mother.

England, however, was jealously guarding her supremacy in mechanical manufactures, as highly industrialized nations would do for ages to come, and had taken drastic measures to keep her craftsmen and trade secrets from seeping out to lands which, it was feared, would become rivals instead of markets. Thus, many of the young English blowers could tell tales of hairbreadth escapes, of climbing over English factory walls on the shoulders of their fellows, of being smuggled aboard ship in hogsheads. Most had come unencumbered, like Thomas Lloyd, from Birmingham. But with his brother Samuel of the Welsh taffy hair and humorously quirked mouth, it was already "Yes, dear" and "No, dear" and "Just as you say, dear" to a dark-eyed, tight-lipped Ver-

mont bride who was to bring up her family grimly on a fortnightly two ounces of castor oil.

Very few had come directly from the old countries. In
spite of Mr. Jarves's words against the seduction of workmen, he had succeeded in luring the ablest away from the
New England Factory in Cambridge and smaller South Boston concerns. Just as he had once sold the idea of work in a
glass factory to the mechanic, James Barnes, so he now persuaded Barnes and his brother and all the other workmen
he wished, that there was no place like Sandwich with its
new factory in the sweet sea air, the new village of houses
waiting for occupants, the countryside teeming with fish and
game.

From the deck of the *Polly,* this land seemed as good to
them as it had to the first settlers who had seen all they
needed to build their way of life in forest and fertile land,
bay and pond, marsh hay and millstream. Now mothers saw
a country good for growing children, wives a spick and span
little village very different from the workers' dingy quarters
in the city. The men saw themselves enjoying sports considered fit for Boston's best. Lanky young Charles Lapham,
from England by way of Campbello, Ireland, and East Cambridge, was so excited by the prospect that he could not wait
for the *Polly* to warp her passage up the shallow tortuous
channel to the dock. With a shout, he splashed overboard
and swam ashore.

Mr. Jarves, in his discreet way, was hardly less stirred as
he stood by the rail of the *Polly* with Mrs. Jarves and the
young ones, coming down for the public blowing of the first
piece of glass. He pointed out to them the fat feather of
smoke floating over the empty shoreline, the great conical
chimney poking above the dunes, and the long, bare, wooden
structure with its wart of a belfry from which clanged the
voice which was to rule the town. All this had sprung from
his vision and substance and effort, and all was his very own.

And it was, he told Anna, but a beginning of the realization of his dream.

He always had a sense of high destiny. He had chosen April 19, the anniversary of the first blow for freedom struck by the embattled farmers, as the day for taking the first shovelful of earth to mark his emancipation from his service to the rich Boston relatives and some not too congenial directors of the New England Glass Company. Now on the Fourth of July, it seemed even more fitting to celebrate his country's independence by the formal beginning of his own. As for the workers themselves, idleness was a vice not to be encouraged in the laboring classes. How could they make better use of a holiday than by devoting it to the enterprise from which they were all to draw sustenance? Besides, to most of the recent foreigners, the Fourth of July would have no patriotic significance.

For nearly two days now, the smoke plume had hung over the town night and day while the furnaces were being heated and the mysterious "batch" set to boiling and foaming. Most of the preparations, as the tempo of activities increased, had been performed by newcomers. A free farmer would not wheel hods or carry burdens like a beast for six dollars a week. So most of the common labor was performed by Irishmen brought in from South Boston. Other work required special skills. Word was passed around town about one of the "foreigners" who trod damp clay with his bare feet and then formed it into viscous ropes which he laid in layers to build great pots — eight of them — for the brick furnace.

But Braddock Fish, the village carpenter, was knocking together casks in the carpentry shop for the packing of the glass, and Ebenezer Chamberlain, the mason, was continually at work on the brick furnaces. As men of the town watched them and other fellow townsmen in labors around the factory — driving the bull wagons of raw lumber in from the lots and cutting it to size, hauling salt hay from the marsh, they felt the mingled pity and envy that men always feel for those who forsake a time-tried way of living for something new.

On the glorious Fourth when the first glass was to be blown, pity prevailed. Once the farmer folk had cared for their creatures, they could arrange their chores at their own sweet will and make the day their own. The labor of these others, jerked from their homes at the clang of a bell, was just a show for them. After they had eaten their good country picnic lunches, they crowded around the great open door at the 12.45 bell which called the workers to the afternoon shift. All morning one set of workers had cooled and skimmed the melt to just the right clearness and consistency. Now the glass blowers would begin their magic.

Mrs. Jarves looked out at the assembled crowd of rustics gawking at the frilly pantelettes of small Miss Anna Maria and her own sprigged silk gown and pastel bonnet strings so different from sober Sandwich homespuns and wear-for-a-lifetime bombazines. She certainly found distasteful the mocking glances of ruddy farmer lads in rugged jeans or grubby glasshouse boys with their forked carrying sticks as they gazed upon the spotless little light pantaloons, bright buttoned jacket, and snowy linen frills of seven-year-old James. It was good that this rabble kept at a respectful distance and even better that she did not have to live among them like her brother who was to be superintendent of production.

How fortunate it seemed that Mr. Jarves would have to spend as much time handling business in Boston as here at the works, so that she not only could keep her Hancock Street home, but could anticipate something bigger and better to match her husband's expanded prospects. She was determined that her darling James should not be sucked into the heat and grime of a glasshouse and had plans for him quite different from those of his father. Woman and child

shared an unexpressed but ever growing contempt for anything as crass and material as a businessman or a glass factory. Probably mother and precocious small boy were the
only ones in the assembly less than completely enthralled
when, at a nod from Mr. Jarves, the "shop," or group of
three men and two boys selected for producing the first piece
of glass, was set in motion.

"No branch of mechanical labor possesses more of attrac-
tion for the eye of the stranger or the curious than is to be
witnessed in a glass-house in full play. The crowded and bee-
like movements of the workmen with irons and hot metals
present a scene apparently of inextricable confusion," wrote
Mr. Jarves years later.

> The business of the glass-blower is literally at his fingers'
> end. It is most interesting to witness the progress of his
> labor from the first gathering of the liquid metal from the
> pot and the passing of it from hand to hand until the shape-
> less and apparently uncontrollable mass is converted into
> some elegant article. Equally interesting is it to witness
> with what dexterity he commands and with what ease he
> controls the melted mass; the care with which he swings it
> with force just enough to give it the desired length, joins it
> to other pieces or with shears cuts it with the same ease as
> paper.

While the crowd gaped at the doorway, the gatherer
twirled his five-foot pipe with a virtuoso flourish and plunged
it into the seething pot of molten glass. After twisting and
turning it a moment, he pulled it out and swung it upward,
tipped with a glowing orange fireball, "like a royal trum-
peter sounding a fanfare."

The crowd let out a long breath and pressed closer to the
open door. As the glass ball cooled, it changed in color from
orange to rose red. Once more the gatherer plunged it into
the pot for a second coating of the metal.

Now a second workman took over the pipe and with a puff

expanded the orange-red ball into a glowing bubble of molten glass and, still attached to the blowpipe, rolled it on an oiled marble slab or marver to give it an even thickness all over. The rich crimson bubble of glass swayed lazily as the pipe was twisted about, making it ready for the master blower, or gaffer, Charles Lapham, who now assumed a grave manner as befitted one whose skill had been chosen to produce the first article in the new factory. The artist of the occasion, he stood on a bench about three feet high.

The crowd began to bulge in through the doorway within range of the swing of the long pipe. Lapham frowned and shook his head at Mr. Jarves who nodded assent.

"Oot — all of yez! Oot — all of yez!" cried one of the workmen with his outlandish twist of tongue.

With the apprentice lads shoving importantly at some of the straggling urchins, the townspeople were shooed out, and the heavy factory doors closed on the final magic which was to produce a crystal tumbler, an article many of them had never owned.

For hours, the crowd stood outside, awaiting it knew not what dramatic announcement or display. There was none. At last, the people drifted off to their powder crackers and their bonfire. A very few saw a sobered Mr. Jarves lead his family back to Stutsons' for supper.

If the trial blob of yellowish glass had been doubtful, the finished article was hopeless. It was carried to a window for full inspection by Lapham, Captain Stutson, and Mr. Jarves. Each in turn held it to the strong light which showed every fleck and flaw. Each in turn shook his head.

"The sand is at fault," said Mr. Jarves finally. "The pebbles did not flux."

It was a stunning blow to find that the tempting value of all that fine and shining sand had been only a mirage. However, the calamity was not fatal. Other advantages were still at hand — the proximity to the fuel which was the most bulky raw material needed, the access to water transportation, the isolation of the workers from evil influence. After all, sand could always be brought in by vessel as it had been to the Boston factories, and arrangements were made for this immediately.

One of the first steps, of course, was to get the product of Mr. Jarves's Sandwich Manufacturing Company on the market. On September 24, 1825, one of that era's discreet and genteel advertisements appeared in the Boston *Columbian Centennial*:

> The inscriber informs his friends and the public that his Flint Glass Manufactory in Sandwich is now in full operation and is ready to receive and execute orders for any article in that line — particularly Apothecaries, Chemical and Table Wares, also Chandeliers for Churches and Halls, Vase and Mantel Lamps, Glasses, and all other articles usually made in similar establishments and on as favorable terms.
>
> Orders directed to Sandwich, Mass., will receive prompt attention.
>
> Deming Jarves.

Soon he was producing a variety of articles. Less than a month after the starting of the factory, articles manufactured on the day of July 30, 1825, had been listed as "chamber and high-blown stem lamps, lamps on foot, peg lamps." During the next few months, the wares were expanded to include "six inch round dishes, heavy plain inks, button stem short lamps, moulded salts for cutting, liverpool lamp glasses, small and large rose foot lamps, oval moulded 9 inch dishes, tulip lamp glasses, cylinder lamp glasses, flint liqueurs, cologne bottles, flint champagnes, 5 inch moulded patty pans, center dishes, 38 pound bowls, 21½ pound bowls, and bird boxes." [1] These were articles hardly dreamed of by the simple citizens of Sandwich who fingered and wondered at

1 Ruth Webb Lee, *Sandwich Glass*.

the defective or broken pieces their youngsters snitched from the cullet pile.

In November of 1825, the Jarveses made the move, which Anna had planned as suitable for a flourishing industrialist, from the old home at 47 Hancock Street to a more stately mansion at 71 Summer Street. One result was that the son of the furniture maker found himself sorely in need of more furniture.

"I find the house we have taken is so large it will require a great deal of furniture. Am sorry we parted with so much," he wrote on November 23, 1825, from Boston to Captain Stutson, his brother-in-law, who was sheltering his family during the upheaval and apparently had taken over some of his household goods as well. "Wish to have the yellow chairs sent. Send all the wash tubs, noggins [small mug or cup], piggins [small wooden pail or tub with an upright stave as handle] and those milk bowls. I can not replace them easily, tried to get some today. We have worked hard and done but little. Furniture is higher than I expected. Should be glad of some of my old furniture.

"I long to see the children. Dear George, I hope he will not take cold. How soon does Mother mean to come up?" And in view of the fact that most of Jarves's brood was hardly beyond infancy, he supposed Stutson would be "very glad to get rid of the folks at last."

Most of the rest of the lengthy letter was concerned with business:

> I hope the winter has not yet set in and believe it will continue fair enough to send up goods until 20 next month. The weather here this day Tuesday commenced with light North wind and snow which has continued falling through the day. It now [the evening] clearing up and hope the weather fair enough for my family to come up — if the *Polly* has not sailed, wish you to send the yellow chairs as the present house is large and shall want them. Do not wish

the *Polly* detained a moment for my account as it is more important to get the goods up for those who orders — as the business is now over [for the season], do not expect to get any more orders of consequence [until spring, as at that time most sales were on a semi-annual basis].[2]

There was an order for eleven dozen glasses of various types from Messrs. Sumner and a recommendation of types to be made for the spring market:

> Expect to be down shortly, Shall then bring down some patterns for best articles which will please the men — flint wines will be wanted in the spring.
> Have all made light as possible and as many made each week as convenient.
> Have Mr. Lapham add to all the batches about 10 lbs. lead to a pot. Please send me a memo of what articles the store will require for the fall and winter — also lumber, lime, or any other articles.

There followed some of the matters which a proprietor in Boston was called upon to adjust. "Messrs. Waldron has white salts instead of blue sent him. They ordered blue. They are also charged for 2 ring Decanturs. . . . A. T. Hall, Summer, and Hay and Atkins have had many of their rose foot lamps broke by bad packing. Hall had one-half of his broken — little or no straw being between them and laying acrost."

Just as Deming Jarves found his newly acquired mansion too large for his stock of furniture, he soon discovered his growing plans too grandiose for the state of his finances. It was not wholly a question of expansion. There was the unforeseen expense of having sand shipped from the Morris River in New Jersey as well as the fact that his agent, Mr. Dame, had been carried away by the ease of his mission and instead of the directed two thousand acres had, before finally

[2] Ruth Webb Lee, *op. cit.*

being checked, purchased twenty thousand acres of Sandwich woodland.

Confident of the value of his enterprise, Jarves applied to Anna's wealthy cousin, Edmund Munroe, for funds and received one of the great shocks of his life. The forty-five-year-old broker and ship owner was capitalist pure and simple, manipulating money as Jarves dealt in materials and skills. He caught the enthusiasm for the Jarves dream, but he could not see a straight loan for the purpose of establishing an individual industrial enterprise for the sole benefit of one Deming Jarves. He wished a larger stake both in the Jarves genius and the Jarves empire. At the same time, he saw that for a proper fulfillment of Mr. Jarves's plans, more capital would be needed than even a Munroe personally could furnish.

So under the chill Munroe eye, Mr. Jarves found himself faced with a heartbreaking dilemma. Either he could keep his Sandwich Manufacturing Company to himself as an "individual enterprise" in its present small and uncertain status or he could reorganize the concern as a corporation with his backers as joint stockholders and have all the money he needed for expansion. In other words, he could either possess or create. He was still young enough to prefer creation.

2

In the spring of 1826, events marched along both for Deming Jarves and his Sandwich Manufacturing Company. First, the New England Glass Bottle Company "for the purpose of manufacturing black and green glass wares in the city of Boston and town of Cambridge" was organized by Jarves and Munroe. The manufacture would be a coarser, cheaper ware, requiring less expensive materials and less skilled workmen than the Sandwich product which was fine table and ornamental ware of flint glass — so called because in

England, one of the ingredients of the finest glass was flint. Thus, the product of the new factory would supplement, rather than compete with, the line made in Sandwich and would make the later company a corporate affiliate in the most modern sense of the word.

Then on April 3, an Act of Incorporation was formally registered:

> that Deming Jarves, Henry Rice, Andrew T. Hall, Edmund Munroe and such persons as may become associated with them and their successors and assigns be and therefore are made a corporation by the name of the Boston and Sandwich Glass Company for the purpose of manufacturing glass in the city of Boston and town of Sandwich in the county of Barnstable, and for that purpose shall have all the powers and privileges and shall be subject to all the duties, requirements, and disabilities prescribed and contained in an act defining the general powers and duties of manufacturing corporations, etc.
>
> That the said corporation in their corporate capacity shall and may lawfully hold and possess such real estate not exceeding $100,000 and personal estate not exceeding $200,000 as may be necessary and convenient for carrying on the manufacture of glass in the place aforesaid. As of February 22, 1826.[3]

The chief stockholders besides Jarves and Munroe had already had dealings with the Sandwich company and fully realized that they were buying into a promising venture. Hall, a retailer, had handled the Sandwich ware. It was he who had been mentioned in the Jarves letter to Stutson as receiving the shipment in poor condition because of faulty packing. Rice, a wholesaler, had supplied goods for the company store and already stood on the company books along with:

Mitchell and Freeman for their bill, Cigars — $12.80
Henry Rice and Co. for their bill, sundries — $10.01

3 Ruth Webb Lee, *op. cit.*

On April 19, 1826 — exactly a year from the taking of the
first shovelful of earth for the foundation of the "individual
enterprise" — the incorporators met at their office in the Exchange Coffee House in Boston for a choice of officers and
the adoption of by-laws. They chose Samuel Hurst as clerk,
Samuel P. P. Fay as director and president, Edmund Munroe as director and treasurer, Benjamin Sewall and Andrew
T. Hall as directors, and Deming Jarves as agent.

The new treasurer recorded all the transactions in his
books: "Deming Jarves by E. M. [Edmund Munroe] for
transfer of his factory, etc. April 3, 1826 as per voucher accepted by the company for the sum of $62,713.68." Munroe
had it figured to the last penny.

And "Real Estate, To Deming Jarves for all the real estate
and wood lots, transfer by deed dated April 3, 1826 —
$31,125.00."

Thereupon, the new corporation proceeded to take over
the individual enterprise of Deming Jarves, lock, stock, and
barrel, including the company store "for the convenience
and supply of the workmen" with its "West Indian, domestic, and foreign goods."

The next transaction in Mr. Munroe's account book is
the item: "E. Munroe-Treasurer, to Capitol Stock — For 150
shares of said stock at $500 per share, in his hands, to be
issued under the company certificate and seal to the respective stockholders — $75,000."

Thus, Deming Jarves at least was allowed a chance to buy
back a share of the enterprise he had created, but as far as
independence was concerned, he was no whit better off than
when he had first had his vision upon the Sandwich marshes.
His fortunes were once more interwoven with those of Anna's rich relatives, and others as well. He may have broken
intimate connection with certain directors of the New England factory at Cambridge who are said to have cramped
some of his plans for invention and expansion, but the for-

tunes of his Sandwich creation were, through Mr. Munroe's interests in both companies, hopelessly interwoven with the older concern.

His red lead for Sandwich had to be shipped from the Cambridge plant which held a monopoly on the furnace and formula which he himself had invented. Even the sale of finished ware was handled in the large cities by a joint "Agency of the Boston and Sandwich and New England Glass Companies," the one in Philadelphia coming eventually into the hands of a son and nephew of Munroe who had a way of caring for his own.

What is more, not even his time was at his command, for he had on his hands the affairs of the so-called "bottle-house," the New England Glass Bottle Company which Munroe had conceived for the orders for coarser ware which might come through the Boston and Sandwich and New England factories.

"Black Bottles — 50 groce heavy Porter Bottles, 100 do. Wine Bottles, 50 do. Pint Bottles, 20 do. Oil Bottles, 160 do. half pint and pint Pocket Bottles," reads an old advertisement.[4] "The above are offered at factory prices and any article in the Black Glass line will be made to pattern and on the most favorable terms at the New-England Glass Bottle Works.

"Also, packages of glass for exportation, together with an extensive assortment of Cut, Plain, and Moulded Flint Glass Ware manufactured by the Boston and Sandwich Glass Company, constantly for sale by Deming Jarves, No. 3 Phillips Building."

And again, "Orders addressed to the agent at the Manufactory, left at the store of Deming Jarves, 93 Water Street, A. J. Hall's, Milk Street or at Edmund Munroe's office, Old State House (at which places specimens of the ware may be seen) will meet prompt attention."

4 Lura Woodside Watkins, *Cambridge Glass.*

Deming Jarves, Proprietor, had become once more Deming Jarves, Agent. Mr. Munroe had shoved him abruptly through the era of individual enterprise and possession into the as yet hardly realized age of corporate ownership and industrial management when nothing that a man did or had was wholly within his own control.

In his *Reminiscences of Glass-Making,* Mr. Jarves compressed his personal tragedy into a few dry sentences:

> It [the "individual enterprise"] was purchased of the proprietor, a company formed and incorporated under the title of Boston and Sandwich Glass Company. They commenced in a small way, beginning with an eight pot furnace, each holding 800 pounds. The weekly melts at that time did not exceed 7000 pounds, giving employment to from 60 to 70 hands. From time to time, as their business warranted, they increased their capital until it reached the present [1852] sum of $400,000 dollars. Their weekly melts have increased from 7000 pounds to much over 100,000 pounds, their hands employed from 70 to over 500.

Hypnotized by Mr. Munroe's juggling with figures and futures, he could almost persuade himself that he had not lost a dream, but gained an opportunity. The Munroe books recorded a brilliantly satisfactory state of affairs. As long as the accounts showed a profit, Deming Jarves was allowed a free hand with ideas, and he proved adept at snatching ideas from here and there to turn to his own uses at Sandwich, shaping them with a magic that dazzled and often enraged their innovators. To him ideas were like natural resources to be used by those best able to develop their utmost possibilities, and who was more able than he? The waste of a good idea was as sinful as waste of good money or material.

It might be that, visiting the Cambridge factory to arrange for his supply of red lead, he would be attracted by the experiments of Enoch Robinson, a locksmith, who, with the blessing of Mr. Whitney, the present agent there, was devising a machine for pressing glass doorknobs. Immediately, he recalled that a dozen years before, his firm of Henshaw and Jarves had imported "from Holland salts made by being pressed in metallic molds and from England glass candlesticks and table center bowls, plain with pressed square feet, rudely made." He hastened to Sandwich to try to make a more efficient machine for better doorknobs and beat out a Robinson and Whitney patent.

Or in an odd corner of the carpentry shop at Sandwich, he would come upon one of the villagers who worked there hammering away at a queer contraption. What was he trying to do? Make something of glass which the glass blowers said couldn't be done. But why not, Mr. Jarves? If you made a mold, poured hot glass into it, and then pressed the glass down with a plunger shaped like the inside of the article you wanted to make, the glass would be forced into all the indentations of the mold and the plunger would make the article as hollow as it could be blown by the glass blower's breath.

On this occasion Mr. Jarves abruptly broke off his indulgent laughter. Molded glass, or glass blown into fancy molds held and opened by the apprentice boys, was very common, especially in the making of fancy bottles where a design was to be impressed in the glass. In 1821, while agent at the Cambridge factory, Deming Jarves himself had taken out a patent for a new and improved method of opening glassmakers' molds. Now if elaborate molded articles could be pressed by machine without benefit of glass blower, one of the heaviest costs of glassmaking, skilled labor, would be cut to a bare bone. All at once, the Cape Cod carpenter did not seem so crazy.

For some weeks thereafter, Mr. Jarves spent hours closeted in the carpentry shop at the Sandwich factory, with occasional consultations with the blacksmith, while the glass blowers snickered in their sleeves. Nothing could be more entertaining for them than to see the fizzle of one of Mr. Jarves's grandiose ideas. Even the outgoing shift lingered for the show when the strange machine was finally brought into the furnace room for a try-out. At Mr. Jarves's command, the gatherer fetched his gob of glass out of the pot and plumped it directly into the mold, while the blowers stood aside with faces frozen into faint mocking smiles.

"Of course," reflected Mr. Jarves, "we may later be able to ladle the melt from pot to mold."

Down pressed the plunger; out came the article which in time emerged from the cooling oven as a not quite perfect, but very passable tumbler. There was silence while the glass blowers gazed — then no guffaws, but a muttered curse that swelled to a threatening roar as they broke out of their trance and began to surge toward the machine and the man whose money and brains had devised it.

Mr. Jarves hastily removed himself and his tumbler to a position of comparative safety. The carpenter and his fellows rushed the press back to the carpentry shop. But the news traveled on the *Polly* to the glass blowers around Boston. Knowing the Jarves ingenuity, they realized that here was only a beginning. Besides, tumblers for ships' cabins and tavern taprooms formed the largest item of the flint-glass trade.

"The glass-blowers on discovery that I had succeeded in pressing a piece of glass were so enraged for fear their business would be ruined by the new discovery that my life was threatened," Deming Jarves wrote to a friend, "and I was compelled to hide from them for six weeks before I dared venture in the street or in the glass house and for more than six months there was danger of personal violence should I venture in the street after nightfall." [5]

Premonitions of disaster were driving the glass blowers toward violence. From the days when men had dwelt in

5 Ruth Webb Lee, *Sandwich Glass*.

tents and kept cattle, there had always been in tribe or village some few set aside by special skills to create for the use or pleasure of the others — the weavers and sandal makers, the "cunning artificers" in brass and iron. These skills, like fat flocks or ancestral acres, were passed from father to son. At Sandwich, there were father and son, brother and cousin, working at their trade, Laphams and Kerns, Doyles and Lloyds, the nobility of the craft.

As tribes and villages grew to towns, these craftsmen formed associations or guilds to protect the secrets of their skills which, in case of a widening market for their use, were imparted or sold to a few carefully chosen apprentices. No craft required greater natural endowments — strong back and lusty lungs, quickness of foot and a practically asbestos skin — than glass-blowing, and none was the fruit of a more intricate apprenticeship. Aside from the manual dexterity involved, the gaffer or master glass blower, in the words of Mr. Jarves, "must understand the science of chemistry sufficiently well to mix and purify his materials in the best possible manner, removing all crude or foreign matter and combining the proper substances into a homogeneous mass." In the New World up to now, glass blowers had had matters quite under their control. Though they had no formal guild or union, Mr. Jarves was wont to complain bitterly of the way they agreed to limit the number of apprentices to keep up wages and to adjust the tempo of their work for the protection of the least capable or, as he put it, "act as one body, the lazy controlling the efforts of the more intelligent and industrious."

"Even in our own democratical land with all the tendencies of its institutions," he wrote, "workers in glass claim a distinctive rank and character among the trades, and in the prices of labor and the estimate of the comparative skill involved are not controlled by those laws of labor and compensation which govern most other mechanical professions."

Their wages were many times those received by laborers, even by skilled workmen like carpenters and blacksmiths, and in most cases surpassed the salaries of teachers and preachers. They could sell their services from factory to factory to the highest bidder, and even hope for a fling at playing manufacturer, for a clever gaffer with the gift of gab could almost always lure some over-optimistic capitalist into partnership.

Hours of labor were necessarily dictated by the needs of the furnace. The workmen put in two five-hour shifts a day, one set working from seven to twelve and the alternate set from one to six, while the *tiseurs,* or teasers, as the furnace tenders were called, worked in twelve-hour shifts, night and day. But at Sandwich, as in most old-time glasshouses, the fires were banked Friday morning and revived Sunday night, leaving a long week-end for rest and recreation.

In summer, the gaffers decided when the temperature of the day was better for fishing than glass-blowing. And when too many at the same time showed up too tipsy to wield blowing iron or punty rod, there was nothing a harassed superintendent could do but have the melt ladled from the pots and pray for a fresh crew of more reliable or unspoiled workmen to be fetched from the Old Country.

And now glass blowers, like most other artisans trained in the ancient skills, saw not only privileges, but livelihood itself menaced by the machine. It was a natural reaction of self-defense to cry out, "Smash the machine! Kill its maker before he can do us more harm!"

There had, a generation before, been an angry surge of Lancashire weavers when the Reverend Edmund Cartwright had devised a power loom whereby their work could be done for a pittance by little girls under twelve years old. While the glassmakers could not believe that any machine would be able to place the manipulation of molten glass wholly in the hands of little children, they were terrified lest no longer on the sloar or account books would stand the item: "Gaffer — $17.00 per week," but only "Labor — $6.00 per week." Since Mr. Munroe's accounts showed that wages amounted to about fifty-three per cent of the operating costs of the Boston and Sandwich Company — and approximately the same figure was true of other companies — the workers, as well as Messrs. Munroe and Jarves, could grasp the full possibilities of the pressing machine.

The frenzied English weavers had succeeded in burning the Manchester mill of the Reverend Mr. Cartwright, but Mr. Jarves was a prudent man, and rocky-knuckled Irish guards spoiling for a brawl came cheap in South Boston. There were no casualties to life, limb, or factory, and in time, familiarity with the deficiencies of the machine relieved the glass blowers of much of their fear and Mr. Jarves could safely show his face in the glasshouses again.

To begin with, no machine possessed the mystery of the batch, the secret formulae which each gaffer held for making clearer or more richly colored glass. However, the most reassuring limitation was that neither the blowers, nor for that matter Mr. Jarves, could see how any article, such as bottle or lamp, in which the opening was smaller than the interior could ever be pressed by plunger. In a country growing by leaps and bounds, there was still plenty of work left for the glass blowers.

Other defects of the machine, though more spectacular, were not so insuperable. At first, if the molds were overfilled, the pieces would be heavy and clumsy, sometimes as much as a half inch thick. Or if the plunger came down slightly off a true level, the article would be as much as a quarter inch thicker on one side than the other. These faults were soon remedied by the invention of a rim or ring for the mold to control conditions with mechanical exactitude. Then there were ridges in the cruder early molds which caused seams to run across almost all of the early cup plates, larger bowls, and other pressed ware, but these were called "straw marks" and generally attributed to Mr. Jarves's sagacity in making the articles more breakable to boost the trade.

In blown-in-mold articles, the molds were usually of pear or apple wood, kept from burning by being dipped in cold water just before each blowing. In spite of this treatment, the molds for pressing charred, and it became necessary to make them of brass or iron, a much more costly process. But if metal molds were costlier, they were also more durable and could be made in far more intricate patterns, developing an entirely new line of skilled artisans, the moldmakers, who were artists and machinists combined. As the simple rays of lines in the earliest pressed articles grew into more elaborate design, artists from the old countries devised variations of the traditional Gothic cathedral arch and the trefoil, rose, or thistle, while young Americans produced native and contemporary patterns of a homespun vigor.

In 1826, young Hiram Dilloway, handsome in a poetic Poe-like manner, and his voluptuously beautiful blonde wife were added to Sandwich society. Hiram Dilloway raised moldmaking to a degree of artistry and craftmanship equal to the manual and chemical mastery of the glass blower. It was Dilloway who evolved the lacy patterns of frostlike delicacy which have made the name of Sandwich stand for the ultimate in pressed glass. Of an old Uxbridge family, he was a pioneer in the trend for native sons to develop and expand new careers opened by the machine age while the older crafts were kept in the hands of men from the old countries and their kin. Clerical and managerial positions, too, were generally filled by Americans like Charles C. P. Waterman, friend of Mr. Jarves, who came to be head bookkeeper and paymaster of the factory which grew mightily along with the craze for pressed glass.

Patterns grew ever more beautiful and intricate and

rivaled those of the best hand-cut glass, thus showing the tendency characteristic of American mass production to bring cheap imitations of luxury articles within reach of the low-income consumer. Now Sandwich farmers could give up their wooden and pewter mugs for the glassware, hitherto used largely by city folk, which would let a body see the color of his drink. Sandwich housewives could set their cups on pretty little pressed plates while elegantly sipping their cooling tea from their saucers, for with cup plates listed in 1827 as Nos. 1, 2, and 3 at four, five, and six cents each, almost any family could afford them and not worry too much about breakage.

Then, too, Deming Jarves saw that each topical trend was reflected in some ware to catch the popular fancy. The visit of the French hero of the Revolution, Lafayette, was the sensation of the time. Congress granted him two hundred thousand dollars and a township of land. Cape Cod children studied their grammar from *The American Instructor,* published in 1825, which took care that the rising generation should not forget by impressing on the infant mind as example of apposition, "The Marquis De La Fayette, the Hero, Statesman, and General, was loved by Washington, the President, and the Americans, the people of the United States." And Mr. Jarves put out "Lafayet" lamps, salts, and cup plates, together with cup plates impressed with the American eagle alternating with the ship *Cadmus* which had brought the hero to the scene of his triumphs. With the salts at sixteen and a half cents each and the cup plates even cheaper, who couldn't have them? And if you broke "Lafayet," you had, as far as Mr. Jarves and the Boston and Sandwich Company were concerned, only to wait for another hero or heroine to come along — Henry Clay or maybe Jenny Lind.

Thus, the pressing machine actually brought about the benefits claimed for the machine age in general by its most

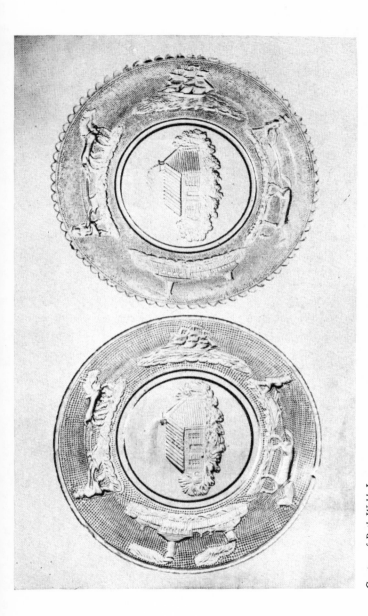

Courtesy of Ruth Webb Lee

These "Industry" bowls were campaign literature for the Harrison and Tyler campaign of 1840. They represent the growth of America from a log-cabin civilization to a land of smoking factories, and the model for the factory is the Sandwich Glass Company.

Courtesy of Ruth Webb Lee

These pressed glass cup plates, for holding cups while tea cooled in saucers, show the evolution of design at Sandwich in the period 1827–1830. Pieces like these were produced so cheaply they were soon replacing pewter on poor men's tables.

ardent supporters — the opening up of new lines of work and new markets.

America can claim the credit [reported Deming Jarves with patriotic modesty] of great improvements in the needful machinery which has advanced the art to such a degree of delicacy and fineness. More than three quarters of the weekly melt is now worked up into pressed glass. When we consider the difference in cost between pressed and blown ware, this rivalry in beauty of the former with the latter becomes all the more important to the public as it cheapens one of the staple necessaries of civilized life. Great credit therefore is due for success in overcoming difficulties well understood by glass-makers and doing away with the prejudice of the skilled blowers who naturally were not inclined to put the new and more mechanical process of manufacturing glass on a par with the handicraft of the old.

3

The figures mounted steadily in Mr. Munroe's books. Total business year by year: 1827 — $31,722.39; 1828 — $55,-957.87; 1829 — $80,381.90; 1830 — $93,140.37

Translated into flesh and blood, this meant a steady flow of newcomers into town. There were, of course, more Irish for the`heaving and hauling, and the glassmakers came in clans as had the farmer folk centuries before. Charles Lapham was followed by his brothers, William, a blower, and Francis, an etcher, as well as a Henry and Joseph Lapham, said to be cousins. Samuel Kern attracted cousins, William and Theodore, brothers who were exceptionally able gaffers. They had come to America and started their own little glasshouse in the Berkshires for the manufacture of glass paving blocks to set in the sidewalks and light the basements of Boston's new business buildings — and hazard the bones of countless generations in slippery weather. After its failure, they came to the comparative security of the factory at Sandwich which was already one of the three largest glass manufactories in the country. There was also another cousin, Francis Kern, a glass cutter, for in addition to the cheap pressed ware, the Sandwich factory was developing a reputation for high quality cut ware.

Of course, this meant more money paid out in wages not only to the additional "shops" of glass blowers, as the working groups of gaffer, servitor, footmaker, and two boys were called, but also to cutters and engravers, carpenters and common labor, and the newly trained pressers, machinists, and moldmakers. More money spread out through town. The amount paid by the company for cutting wood, for example, in four years' time increased from $400 to nearly $4000. There was a proportionate flow of tax money into the town treasury, but the new prosperity brought added responsibilities. In a few years' time, the school appropriation increased from $500 to the incredible sum of $1200 in 1829.

Though the old town found it an inescapable duty to educate the children in Mr. Jarves's village along with Sandwich sons and daughters, in most respects Mr. Jarves provided for his own people. In view of the distance from Boston and the limitations of the few small shops in town, a "company store for the convenience of the workmen" opened its doors under the direction of Mr. Jabez Dame almost as soon as the factory stack began to smoke.

The company store was the one meeting place of farmer and mechanic — as all factory workers then were called. Here men gathered over their herring and crackers, 2¢, cheese and crackers, 3¢, beer and crackers, 5¢. Fishermen brought in their lobsters, clams, oysters, salmon, salt mackerel and plain "fish." Farmers came with cordwood, cabbage, squash, rhubarb, turkey, fowl, lamb. Children would carry in the whortleberries (our huckleberry) and wild craneberries they picked. Mr. Samuel Fessenden, the town shoemaker, turned in boots and shoes to be sold and credited to his account.

Goods were priced so reasonably that if the keeper of a little shop in the town unexpectedly ran out of supplies, he would send to Jarvesville for a "bbl. flower" or "16 yds. cossinet." Miss Rebecca Newcomb, the village schoolmistress, trudged over the marshy cartpath for "1 Flagg — $1.50." Roland Gibbs, the packet captain, bought his hard bread, pork, bacon, and bully beef by the twenty-five-pound lot for the galley of the *Polly*, and to the account of the *Polly* were also charged a spider, a bucket, a peg lamp, a broom, a coffee pot, and a gallon of sperm oil.

All sorts of services were performed through the agency of the company store — money loaned on note to Samuel Kern, a wagon mended for one Samuel Drody — 40¢, the hire of "½ horse and chaise" to Plymouth and dinner — $1.41 — charged to Mr. Waterman's account, and "supper — 18¢" and "drink for fishing" for Alfred Green, one of the first blowers. In the store was to be found everything a glassmaker might desire from lottery tickets, $1.00, to Bibles, $2.25 (only two of these sold during the fifteen months' record of the store still preserved and both to country folk). He might buy a three-cent rattan to discipline his child, senna and castor oil to dose him, or a glass toy to make him happy.

Standards of living and traits of character stand in the faded figures of the old calfbound volume. Ebenezer Chamberlain, the mason, purchased only the staples — flour, meal, molasses, pork, beans — but always including that prime masculine necessity, rum. Here was a man trying to raise a large family on his modest $9 a week. On the other hand, the Doyle brothers added to the basic supplies, candy and pickles, almonds, filberts, oranges, "chucklate," apples, pepper sauce, mustard, lobster, oysters, turkey, and — in the case of Michael such fancy items as a bird fount and a "parisol." As blowers, they were making good money, but sometimes their weekly bill exceeded their income. Obviously starved for the good things of life, they were now luxuriating in a land of plenty.

Stories lie in certain combinations or sequences of sales. "Needles and rum, 14¢" — a man on an errand for his wife. "Rum and peppermint" — self-evident! "1 oz. castor oil — 10¢, 1 toy, 6¢" — a bribe? When a glass blower who had hitherto spent his money only for rum and beer, tobacco and snuff, powder and shot suddenly squandered twelve cents in June for a string of beads, what could it be but love? "1 string beads — 12¢" was the favorite present for a lady, though some of the more open-handed would give "fancy box — 25¢." A purchase of cambric, lawn, and lace would be inevitably followed by "14 yds. diaper" and about a month later, the paregoric.

There was one great event in the life of every glassmaker, and that was his broadcloth suit. With broadcloth at from $6 to $9 a yard and the accompanying vest pattern, buckram, padding, linen for shirts, gingham for linings, buttons, and silk twist, his bill for that week would amount to several times his weekly pay. Then would come the accessories — the hat —$5.50, cravat, "Flagg handkerchief — $1.50," clothes-brush, blacking, pomatum, and cologne. Now the well-dressed glassmaker was ready to fare forth and show himself to the town, with an especial eye for the country damsels.

Handkerchiefs seem to have been strictly for ornament rather than use, being purchased no more than semi-annually at seventy-five cents to a dollar fifty apiece — though a David Benson once made history by buying eleven in one day. Toothbrushes were even rarer — implements equally unknown to the workmen fresh from England and the villagers whose forebears came from the same place two centuries before. Except in the case of the executive-class newcomers like Mr. Waterman and Captain Stutson, they were sold only to the Kenneys, Doyles, and Heffernans, and then only one to a customer which would make them seem like family affairs.

Incoming workers had always overflowed the living quarters provided. Relatives would take shelter with their kin, friends with friends. Then as more houses crowded the crisscross streets of the factory village, a family would find its own rooftree and the listed items in the store account would suddenly expand from the purely personal broadcloth and bombazine, rum and cologne to one great splurge (often soaring to $100 in one month) of china, glassware, and cutlery, shovels, tongs and firedogs, kettles and pans, spiders and skillets, pails and brooms, clotheslines and baskets and eleven-pound sad irons, sheeting and blankets, and finally the "1 bbl. flour" which showed that housekeeping had really begun. Then, come spring again, there would appear the cucumber seed and garden seed, early peas and late beans by which the men would celebrate the use of a corner of land.

Captain Stutson, living up in the town, came to the company store for all the usual staples, together with three milk pans and a mouse trap. When Mr. Jarves had settled his family for the summer on "the farm" where he could keep a sharp eye on the growing factory, his account at the company store showed his flour and bacon, eggs, lemons, ginger, mustard, raisins, rice, fowl, lamb, whortleberries. Sandwich town has long since forgotten the Jarves farm and remembers only the days when Mr. Jarves kept a suite of rooms at the inn always reserved for his periodic trips of inspection. In the midst of all the Jarves buying of real estate with a thought for future expansion, it is impossible to point a finger now at any one item in the tax assessments and say, "Here was the Jarves farm." But in May, 1826, his account at the company store says plainly "1 qt. turpentine for house, 20¢," "5 doz. screws for house, 25¢," and later, there is 1 Hearth Brush, 1 milk pan, 2 "Chambers" (one plain at 20¢, one blue pr. 70¢).

That his family was with him was certain from the sixteen and half yards diaper as well as the quantities of lace, lawn, muslin, and cambric with which Mrs. Jarves could ever beguile her boredom by sewing for the latest little biennial Jarves always recently arrived or on the way. Family memories of the farm are longer. Young James, completely the city child, reveled in "finding hens' nests, climbing the loftiest trees, tumbling into hay-cocks, and plucking the finest fruits and flowers for my mother."

To the father's chagrin, the small boy had no interest in the factory and village mushrooming on the marsh. Only one event connected with the erection of the works would have piqued his imagination. The first few shovel thrusts for the new foundation had unearthed a handful of human bones. After considerable town talk, it was decided that they were the earthly remains of Richard Bourne, the friend of the Indians, who had been laid to rest in this sunny corner of his own acres after his work was done. Under his active protection, his Indians had been assigned their own village, so guarded by laws that they were safe from the skulduggery of the white man even though their reservation included some of the richest land in town, teeming with game, fish, and shellfish. There they had lived, insulated from the bloody Indian wars which had laid waste so much of New England and eventually destroyed their race. There they lived still, separated by nine miles of forest from the white man's town and connected only when a Daniel Webster went to fish Mashpee Stream or an Indian lass plodded over to work in Sandwich kitchens.

In the year of publication of *The Last of the Mohicans*, a real Indian village within reach was a magnet to the extremely precocious eight-year-old. Under the spell of Indian lore, he ran off to join the Mashpees, dreaming of "sedate old chiefs around the council fires, war dances, the startling war whoop, the twanging bow, dark-skinned maidens grinding corn." He found a straggled scattering of unpainted board shacks in the midst of "famine-like looking potato patches and starved corn fields, mangy curs, and cackling hens." The Indians "wore petticoats and hats and had no more idea of fur aprons and feather head-pieces than my old nurse, Hepzibah. God bless us! They were *civilized* Indians, emasculated of all forest virtues and loving the vices and rum of the pale faces."

The disillusioned lad turned back to his own people, consoling himself with pranks on the staid villagers while he enjoyed the immunity accorded "the rich squire's son." Sandwich was finding itself for the first time with distinct social classes. There had, of course, always been wise men and foolish men, men with more land and men with less. But society still had one basis — the land. There was no one man who controlled the livelihood of masses of man, no landless without natural roots and without respect for land ownership. Mr. Jarves and his satellites the town could tolerate and, in time, respect. With "Mr. Jarves's village," it was a different matter. The town was to find that the problem of an obnoxious social class could not be solved as simply as that of the unrelished race by the well-proved methods of extermination and/or the reservation.

Unlike Mashpee, Jarvesville was not separated by miles of woodland from the town. The huddle of houses lay hardly a stone's-throw across the marsh. When Jarvesville glassworkers purchased their hooks-and-lines and skates, it meant that they would set forth to Sandwich streams and ponds. Almost to a man, they bought powder and shot, gun caps and shells, and went trespassing en masse over farmers' fields and into farmers' woodlots. It was not like the city gentlemen, coming and going singly or by two's and three's under the discreet guidance of John Trout. Here was an invading army, come to stay.

By late 1825, the great Dan'l Webster had mostly given up his hunting and fishing in Sandwich because his sacred haunts were increasingly violated by "the great number of glass-house operators and their dogs."

Webster could retire gracefully from a distasteful situation, but for the country folk, there was no escape or retreat. For the most part, they were inclined to blame Mr. Jarves for this alien settlement squatting at the edge of their nice neat little town. Likewise, the glass blowers themselves had held Mr. Jarves personally responsible for the new threat of the machine, while Mr. Jarves himself probably had moments when he attributed to Mr. Munroe's personal greed the swallowing up of his cherished individual enterprise into a vaster, more complex organization. Not villagers, nor workers, nor Mr. Jarves had the slightest realization that their planned and ordered ways had been upset by an impersonal power far greater than any the world had ever known.

Sandwich and Jarvesville

"WE LEARN that three young men belonging to the Glass Establishment at Sandwich were committed to the jail in this town on Wednesday evening last, charged with having cut off the teats and otherwise injuring a cow belonging to Mr. J. Tobey of that town which caused her death. We forbear making any comment on the inhuman way of getting revenge, but hope the perpetrators receive justice at the Sept. Court of Common Pleas."

So reported the *Barnstable Patriot,* the weekly which, in 1830, was started at the county seat. Here was climax to the long-continued friction between farmer, town, and factory village — the jeers and stones of glasshouse gamins flung at outraged farmers protecting their fruit trees, the strategic posting of snarling dog or misanthropic cow across the approaches to trout stream and woodland way, the suits for trespass, and the summons before local constables for disturbances of the peace.

The native viewpoint toward the newcomers had crystallized early. "One of the evils attendant on great corporations, and not the least important, is the great influx it occasions of foreigners of the lowest grade," the *Patriot* observed.

Any knowing resident of the Glass Factory Village could not have helped resenting the almost perpetual slurs. One story circulated was that "an independent company of militia had been formed in Sandwich at Jarvesville and were organized under the name Jarvesville Rangers." Jests on the supposed doings of this bibulous, raggle-taggle band were broadcast until it was discovered that the whole matter was a hoax, and no such company had ever been in existence.

Town men and factory men met in the regular militia, though it is doubtful to what extent the Jarvesville "foreigners" were represented. The Colonel was Ebenezer Chamberlain, the local mason in the employ of the company. The adjutant was Theodore Kern, one of the two Kern brothers who had come from the ending of their own factory to supervise various departments of the Boston and Sandwich Company under the general superintendency of Captain Stutson. But a squabble, well publicized in letters to the editor, between colonel and adjutant perhaps symbolized the feeling between old-timers and newcomers.

Drills were held near some inn, thus giving "the Innkeeper a chance to sell us a plumb pudding twice a year at ten times its cost." Notices were sent out for two drills to be held within two hours of each other, one at Swifts' tavern in West Sandwich, the other at Hatch's in West Barnstable. Even if two drills in one day had not been an unheard-of thing, it would have been an utter impossibility for men to march from one in time to attend another.

Colonel Chamberlain promptly blamed the error on his adjutant, Mr. Kern, in a lengthy and sarcastic letter to the editor. Mr. Kern soon found a defender among the townspeople. "We must exculpate Mr. Kern as we know him to be a correct businessman and the orders were not in his writing."

Colonel Chamberlain, who always insisted that the boys apprenticed to him at the factory to "learn the mason business" come furnished with written references as to their "good moral character." was before long in a rather less toplofty position. Early in 1832, he was "taken up and examined before Seth F. Nye, Esq., on a charge of being concerned in taking from the store of Hiram Durpee the sum of $400. Ordered to recognize in the sum of $1000 for appearance at the Supreme Judicial Court next to be holden, he was committed for the want thereof. Except about $12 of the money was recovered."

From the earlier account of Ebenezer Chamberlain in the company store, it is easy to imagine the temptation of Hiram Durpee's carelessly guarded till. Seemingly safe from suspicion in his place of authority in the militia, he had had little thought of a public trial "for breaking and entering store in Sandwich in the day-time and stealing therefrom a sum of money, about $400" or the bitter "one day's solitary imprisonment, 2 years in State's Prison."

"The prisoner had hitherto sustained good character and held positions of some responsibility and distinction among his fellow citizens. One slip deprives his amiable wife and six children of their husband and provider."

There was, of course, considerable town interest in Ebenezer Chamberlain's one slip and some sympathy with the circumstances. But the case of the three young men from the glasshouse and Josiah Tobey's cow was the sensation of the times. It crowded the coach from Sandwich to Barnstable and jammed the sandy road to the Court House with plodding horses and creaking carryalls. There were no feelings of mercy in the hearts of the farmer folk with whom "the house was thronged to hear the pleas of the Gentlemen who managed the case."

Even those who did not regard the act as deliberate and unspeakable sadism looked with horror on a new race of men, set in the ways of cities and machines, who apparently regarded the moans of a tortured animal as of no more consequence than the gasps of a dying trout.

"After a prolonged trial, the Jury found a verdict of Guilty. The defendants appealed for another trial at the Supreme Court and gave bonds of $700." Even a second trial could not save them from a sentence stiff enough to offer some protection to Sandwich cows.

Yet the minor incidents continued — the trespassing and pilfering, assault and battery and disturbances of the peace. Of the total of seventy-five people committed to the county jail during the three-year-period — 1833 to 1836 — twenty-one were from Sandwich, exclusive of the fifteen additional from Indian Mashpee which had its own brands of morals, religion, and firewater. Provincetown which supplied the jail with its next largest number could, for all its sailors and waterfront ways, contribute only eight. To Sandwich, the conclusion was obvious. No other Cape town had a Jarvesville. There was almost from the beginning a feeling that anything disreputable was sure to have its origin in the Factory Village.

Another local item in the *Patriot* reported that "Mr. Loring Holmes of West Sandwich committed suicide by cutting his throat and several stabs in the breast with a knife. He was a man of intemperate habits. A wife and child are left by this rash act." No one in Sandwich could have been greatly surprised when in a very short time indeed, "Mr. Loring Holmes's relict, Hannah," was married to Mr. George Hyde of Jarvesville — though store records of the Hyde family would make it seem that Mistress Hannah's second choice was not much more temperate than her first.

Mr. Jarves, who had given the habits and customs of the genus glassworker some study, did not rate temperance among the traditional virtues. In quoting an ancient writer, he stated:

It must be owned that those great and continual heats which these gentlemen are exposed to from their furnaces are prejudicial to their healths [an aspect of the business which Jarves in his own person always warmly counter-claimed, especially in seeking recruits]; for, coming in at their mouths, it attacks their lungs and dries them up, whereas most part are pale and short-lived by reason of dis-eases of the heart and breast which the fire causes, which makes Libarius say they were of weak and infirm bodies, easily made drunk.

"Such was the character and habits of noble glass-makers four hundred years since," Jarves went on with characteristic unconcern for singular verb and plural subject, "and whether their descendants still retain their blood or not, the habit of drinking believed at that time necessary as conse-quent upon the nature of the employment is, at the present day, confined to the ignorant, dissolute, and unambitious workman. Still, the conduct of the dissolute few affects the moral reputation of the entire body. They must not forget the old adage that 'One bad sheep taints the whole flock.' "

However much Mr. Jarves may have favored temperance as an abstract ideal, he was too practical a businessman to at-tempt to lure workmen off into a desert place. From the very first, the company store had offered the utmost variety in thirst quenchers — rum in three varieties, New England, Jamaica, and St. Croix, wine, beer, ale, flip, gin, brandy, cordial, lemonade, and a mysterious concoction listed sim-ply as "drink."

Thus, by the time the *Barnstable Patriot* was founded in 1830, Jarvesville gave the writers of dramatic letters plenty of opportunity to depict touching scenes — "the aged man, father of eight children, who found the street too narrow to accommodate him, bringing up alternately on either side," the little boy three years old carrying rum home to his father and "stopping three times to drink from the bottle in about

100 yards," the tot standing near the door, bottle in one hand, clutching a tattered coat in the other, tears flowing down cheeks — "I want some rum for uncle and I can't open the door."

Now some of the sober hard-working inhabitants of Jarvesville began to be disturbed at the way the bad sheep had tainted the flock. Someone complained through the columns of the paper that there was "not a place within my knowledge so devoted to scandal as the village of Sandwich. The least transaction is carried by word of mouth from one end of town to the other, growing as it goes, so that many an innocent person suffers severely."

Then, apparently believing that the best defense was attack, a group of so-called "Cold Water Men" of the Boston and Sandwich Glass Company wrote deploring the presence of "an arsenal in East Sandwich to furnish those who wish for the intoxicating draught." East Sandwich was quick and hot in denial. "We know that there is no dram shop kept in East Sandwich. As many of the readers are acquainted with the inhabitants of East Sandwich, we most cheerfully submit to their decision as to the moral standing of the inhabitants of that place as compared with the writers from the Sandwich glass house."

Perhaps the reputation of East Sandwich was cleared, but glassworkers could still point at the Monument section of Sandwich to prove that Jarvesville did not have any monopoly of disorderly conduct. One Joshua Avery bought a knife at the store of Elisha Perry. He declared that it was not sharp enough, took it outside to whet on a stone, and came back to thrust it into the storekeeper, through his vest and the waistband of his pantaloons into his body. Avery's defense was that he was "so groggy that he didn't know what he did." An indignant letter writer declared that Squire Elisha Perry should go to jail, too, for selling rum. Mr. Perry appeared at the newspaper office to protest that he had not sold Avery a drop of rum — although he did not commit himself as to rum-selling in general.

For the first time in a town which had always taken a discreet amount of rum as a commonplace commodity and from its earliest years had had its licensed "ordinary" — "only those who bought not to loiter unnecessarily" — the sale of intoxicants had become a moral issue. The company did nothing about drying up Jarvesville, perhaps judging that, with grog still obtainable here and there about town, such a course would have no appreciable results and would only stir up hard feelings. However, Mr. Waterman, the company clerk and paymaster, founded a Temperance Society and, under the appropriate pseudonym "Aqua Homo," conducted an ardent crusade against "King Alcohol."

"Unite in an effort to free the town of that notorious villain! Do your duty! Quit yourselves like men!" he would write before elections, appealing to the "friends of temperance in this town, long the byword and reproach of our neighbors."

His efforts had some success. Sabin Smith advertised that his tavern "kept in Sandwich for many years by Mr. Fessenden and more lately by the subscriber will now be open as a Temperance House." John Gibbs informed "friends and the public that he has abandoned the sale of ardent spirits. He hopes that those who would not patronize him while trafficing in ardent spirits will now give him a share of their patronage."

In 1835, it was "voted to have no distilled spirits or fomented [sic] liquors sold in this town the ensuing year, and the selectmen were instructed to recommend no one to the County Commissioners for license. Judge then of our surprise and astonishment," commented a writer from Sandwich, "to hear that the Commissioners had granted license to all who applied and that our town is to be deluged another year with liquid fire."

Perhaps the "no license" vote would not have passed except for the fact that a good part of Jarvesville had not attained citizenship and had no voice in the matter. On the other hand, if Jarvesville had not offered a certain number of good customers, there would have been no temptation to circumvent the law.

However, the sober, hard-working element of Jarvesville had sometime since made a mighty effort to free themselves from the ill repute attached to the Factory Village. On March 31, 1834, they drew up a petition:

> To the President and Directors of the Boston and Sandwich Glass Company: —
> The public journals are explicit and agree in their statements concerning the evils connected with the use of ardent spirits, and all is confirmed by facts which cannot be denied. We have made some attempt to reform. And we rejoice to say that it has not been without success. Still there is one hindrance in our way, one evil yet remains. We believe our duty to our fellow man requires us no longer to be silent. We believe it hard if the feelings of a virtuous community must be outraged and their attempts at reform hindered by the obstinacy of one man who has neither law nor decency to protect him in the course he pursues. [This was probably the man whose name was now serving as a dummy front for the company store.]
> The undersigned inhabitants of Jarvesville respectfully submit the above to the attention and consideration of those to whom it is addressed. We feel constrained to pursue the course we have adopted when we hear it repeatedly sounding in our ears that Rum is to be obtained only in the Factory Village, and also that you may know how we are divided in regard to temperance and intemperance.

A copy of this "address signed by 96 of the workmen of the Glass Factory in Sandwich" was sent to the *Barnstable Patriot*. Quite overwhelmed by the number of signatures,

Hiram Dilloway, among others, helped to evolve these complex "lacy" designs, including the native "Eagle" and, for export trade, the "Victoria" pattern to celebrate the coronation of England's Queen.

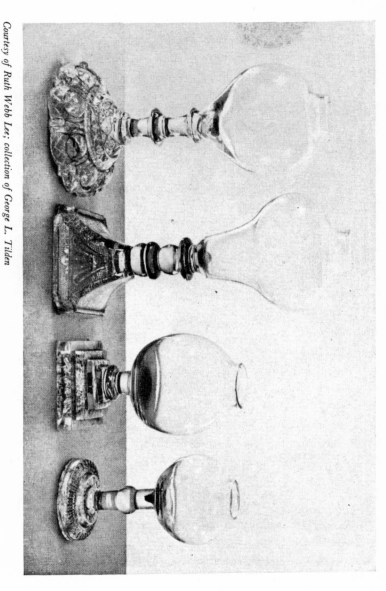

From ship's lanterns to electric light globes, Sandwich products marked each step of the progress toward better illumination in the nineteenth century. These are early whale-oil lamps.

and perhaps a little pricked by conscience at the part the paper had played in blackening Jarvesville's reputation, the editor hastened to give

> publicity to the voluntary act of so large a portion of the very respectable community and show the public the moral feeling that pervades it and the sensitiveness of those worthy citizens touching the reputation of that village. We cheerfully add our testimony, derived from frequent intercourse and observation, in favor of the urbane and gentlemanly deportment and the intelligence and morality generally of the workmen in the village. We doubt if another similar one is to be found in New England, employing so many men who have come together from different sections of the globe and under so many varied circumstances, and yet where such good order, fellowship, and exemplary conduct prevail as at Jarvesville.

Unfortunately, the names of the ninety-six who signed were not printed. However, there is not much doubt that this petition, as all other attempts to raise the moral standard of Jarvesville in particular and all Sandwich in general, was the work of that ebullient individual, the glass-blowing Reverend Joseph Mash.

2

Sometime before 1830, the Reverend Joseph Mash (as he then signed his name or Marsh, as it was later called) came out from Birmingham, England, with his wife Mary Ann and their growing brood to join his brother Thomas who had been a member of one of the first shops in operation at the Sandwich factory. He was a man in the early thirties — a little more mature than some of the first-comers. He came with an almost equal zeal for blowing glass and saving souls and he found what he considered a field ripe for the harvest. There was little or no social intercourse between Sand-

wich and Mr. Jarves's village. Few fresh from Old World
ways of worship strayed up into town to the bare little white
meeting houses for the local weekly dose of hell-fire or hope.
Any brave spirit who ventured would have returned to
Jarvesville frozen to the very soul by the chill of the atmosphere before and after meeting when the women huddled
away from the intruder to swap their recipes, scandal, and
symptoms and the men turned their backs for their weekly
discussions of crops, creatures, and the weather.

It took the Reverend Mr. Mash with his reformer's zeal to
round up the more or less ardent followers of Wesley and
Whitefield in Jarvesville and take over the meager handful
of native Methodists who for some thirty years had been
spasmodically served by a circuit rider. Soon the gathering
had a regular meeting place and a resident minister. Mr.
Mash even served his term in that official capacity until it
became time for the required biennial change. Then he
stayed with the glass factory, using his excess energy as sup-
plementary moral influence in his church and in the town.
If everyone within earshot could testify to a warmth in the
Reverend Mr. Mash's meetings which had not been heard in
Sandwich for many a year, he had the apt answer.

"As regards 'loud boisterous noise,' I am decidedly against
it, but still we might as well be troubled with a little wild-
fire as icebergs."

Since, in his official capacity, he could not be denied the
courtesies accorded the other ministers, he served as earliest
liaison between the old town and the new. He was not at
all backward about taking what he considered his rightful
place. He became an active and very vociferous director
of the Temperance Society. As a founder, he gave the chief
address at the opening meeting of the Sandwich Abolition
Society which spent most of its energy in arguments as to
whether slaves should be freed immediately or at some
vaguely later and more convenient date. Joined with the

Freemans, Tobeys, and Nyes of old Sandwich, he protested the sale of lottery tickets licensed by neighboring states when Massachusetts did not sanction lotteries of her own. Linked with names of another sort, he decried expensive public works — bridges, turnpikes, state's prison, etc. — with "money drained from the laboring classes."

From the very first issue of the county newspaper, his name appeared almost weekly at the foot of a column-long letter in four-point type, splitting theological hairs with New England orthodoxy. He had a wide vocabulary and a forceful means of expression which bespoke a vigorous self-education, if nothing more.

Mr. Mash and his Methodists, of course, gathered in only the purely English souls. That still left the fairly numerous Irish contingent and the Europeans, as yet very few indeed. During the earliest years, just one Frenchman appeared in the accounts of the company store — a Felelix (Felix?) Moren who bought his broadcloth suit, did not pay for it, and disappeared from the book. Lately, one or two German names had appeared in the records. None of these held any well-paid or prominent position. All the blowers were English with the exception of the Doyle brothers, James and Michael, who naturally assumed leadership of the outcasts. These assembled, it was rumored, at the home of James Doyle for their own outlandish Latin prayers which they muttered while fingering beads, like an abracadabra of more magic than meaning. They acknowledged supreme allegiance to a foreign power, the Pope. They were — in hushed and horrendous voice — CATHOLICS.

Separated by centuries from any personal contact with Catholics or the Catholic church, Sandwich citizens were, from the tales of their sea captains, rather more familiar with the mores of the Fiji Islanders. Nightmare stories aplenty had been handed down through the years of Old World tortures and martyrdoms, of New World raids by Indians swooping down from French Canada with bloody tomahawk in hand, crosses swaying against swarthy chests, and the blessing of black-skirted priests on their exertions.

At best, Catholicism, in New England eyes, seemed the religion of foreign royalty and rabble, and the sturdy old stock farmers felt that their country wanted neither. For generations, Puritan children had been brought up on the quatrain, supposedly delivered by John Rogers who was burned at the stake in the days of Bloody Mary:

> Abhor that arrant whore of Rome
> And all her blasphemies,
> And drink not of her cursed cup;
> Obey not her decrees.

Many old-timers were inclined to agree with John Adams. When the ancient Massachusetts charter giving toleration to all "except Papists" was amended to allow complete religious toleration, he had protested that "the barriers against popery erected by our ancestors are suffered to be destroyed to the hazard even of the Protestant religion." [1]

Fears did not seem unfounded when "the Catholics" — as they were called in damning tones — did not stop with private prayers. Next Sandwich knew, there appeared on its streets a priest— name with horrid paganish connotations to old New Englanders. The zealous young missionary in queer clerical garb, the Reverend William Barber Tyler, was as old New England as anyone, however. One of the Barber clan, he had been converted from chill New Hampshire parsonages to the warmth and color of the older faith.

Lean, bespectacled Father Tyler was seen again and again, and then one day the Bishop of Boston stepped off the packet — an enormously stout figure with apple-red cheeks, crisp black curls, and dark, commanding eyes. The Right Reverend Benedict Fenwick, from the plantation, Swamp

[1] Theodore Maynard, *The Story of American Catholicism.*

Island, Beaverdam Manor, St. Mary's County, Maryland, of
the Catholic Fenwicks who in 1632 had left England with
Leonard Calvert to escape persecution, certainly regarded his
church and himself as as truly American as any or anyone in
New England.

Both he and his young assistants, Father Tyler and his
cousin, the Reverend Virgil Barber, looked upon their Irish
brothers in the faith as hardly less foreign than did the Sandwichers and yearned for a more truly American following.
But it did not become a good shepherd to scorn any of his
sheep, however unwashed and wayward they might seem,
and here was a flock of seventy eager souls to be enfolded.

Soon the old town was buzzing with the news that "the
Catholics" had bought a lot of land and raised six hundred
dollars for a church. The little shell of a building, thirty by
forty feet, Bishop Fenwick had prefabricated in Boston and
sent down in sections on the packet, presumably because,
some Sandwich tongue was sure to remark, no unhallowed
hand of native carpenter was thought fit to touch the wood.

The Sunday set for the dedication was September 19, 1830.
After the tedious journey overland by coach, Father Tyler
had arrived in time to take charge of preparations. When
all was ready, the little church might be bare as a box outside, but within, so the town heard, were startling pictures
of bloody anguish, quaint and tortured images, a gleaming
crucifix, and an altar decked with velvet and gold.

The Bishop, Father Barber, a group of Catholic notables
from Boston, and part of the choir of the Church of the
Holy Cross were to sail Saturday morning on the packet
Henry Clay, which had replaced the smaller, slower *Polly.*
According to schedule, they were to arrive Saturday evening,
be parceled out among the faithful for the night, and proceed in procession to the church for the dedicatory service
next morning.

Bits of news were tossed from tongue to tongue. Sunday

morning saw men, women, and children in carriage and on
foot drawn from as much as eighteen miles around, not only
the sparse scattering of far-flung Catholics, but a throng of
Cape Codders avid for what the occasion might offer in the
way of excitement. After all, parades usually came only on
Fourth of July.

One of Cape Cod's own September gales was roaring over
the Bay, and as the people milled down the wind-raked
street toward Glass Factory Village and the shore, word was
passed along that no packet had landed, night or morning.
Therefore, there was no Bishop and no choir. There was
not even a sail to be seen — only the rising rage of waves
bursting into foam. Time dragged on in empty waiting
while the faithful grew panicky and the natives bored and
bone-cold. Could the *Henry Clay* have foundered in the
storm? Or have been driven aground on some sand bar? And
could the church be properly dedicated without blessing of
Bishop? No one wondered more anxiously about this than
Father Tyler. The Mass of dedication had been set for ten-
thirty. At eleven-thirty, he had about summoned courage to
carry on alone when a shout rushed along the street. The
Henry Clay had been sighted.

After more than twenty-four hours at sea, the greenish
delegation was hurried to the house of Mr. James Doyle to
get a firmer grip on storm-tossed stomachs and to don cere-
monial robes. At about noon, the procession set forth
through the main street to the church. Father Barber's as-
cetic pallor was now parchment. Bishop Fenwick's usually
ruddy face had turned to putty. All the dignitaries walked
gingerly as if surprised to find the ground so solid under
their feet. But few bystanders noticed the too frail human
flesh under the holy habiliments.

To the little band set down on foreign shores so far from
their loved native land, here were revered leaders whom they
might follow to the security of a spiritual home. Stiff in

their Sunday best, they fell in behind the procession to the little church which squatted solidly under its cross as if determined to outstay any storm. For spectators, here was sensation for gaping — cross bearer and crucifix, clergy in queer little caps, and silks, lace, and embroideries, with skirts flapping about their shins in the wind, and — most impressive to local onlookers, the black and white robed acolytes, grimy little glasshouse urchins scrubbed and turned cherub for the occasion.

The holiday seekers did not stop at the church door. In addition to the faithful, the little building was packed to bursting with "many persons of various sects in our town" who, according to "Observer" in a newspaper letter, were "led by curiosity rather than religious feeling" and displayed "much levity and a want of that respectful deportment usually manifested in places of worship."

The Bishop bore the commotion comparatively well during the mass of consecration, but the gaping and the giggling proved rather too much for Father Tyler, who in the evening attempted an "answer to some of the objections urged by Protestants against the Catholic customs."

From the very first day, the battle had begun — a battle of words wielded by the able Mr. Mash and others less persuasive, but equally passionate. If at times these communications reflected so "severely upon the rites and worship of the Catholics at Sandwich" as to "disturb the feelings of the officiating clergyman at that place," the editor of the *Patriot* stated firmly, "The followers of St. Peter shall receive at our hands the same favors as the disciples of Martin Luther." And Father Canavan, the resident priest, could not shout too loudly of discrimination as long as the same paper would occasionally publish an article headed, "All Universalists Go To Hell."

Rabble-rousing attacks were based on all angles. Alarm! "There is no place on the continent where the people are so much priest-ridden as on Cape Cod. We suffer here on account of the most degrading system of idolatry. Religion, liberty, and even life are in danger wherever it exists." Ridicule! "An Irish papist on this Cape was asked why he paid the priest one year in advance, seeing he might die before the year expired. He answered, 'Sure the praste will have to do his work whether I live or die." The fact is, according to the account given us of this pious work, more souls have been prayed out of Purgatory than ever were born." Pity! "O light of heaven! break! break! in upon all these poor deluded priest-ridden people."

But in the end, all the wielders of words had for their trouble was their pains. Far from being priest-ridden, these Sandwich Catholics had apparently caught freedom from the New World air. When they thought that Father Canavan was spending too much time out of town on missionary work, they refused to pay pew rent until they got more masses for their money. Yet to them, the ways and words that had expressed the faith of their fathers for centuries past could never be made to seem delusion or mummery by the rhetoric of a Reverend Joseph Mash. Small stout Saint Peter's stood as a sort of spiritual shelter and source of comfort to these socially despised and rejected of both the tight little town and their less alien factory fellows.

In time, of course, a brave lad or two would venture from the shadow of Saint Peter's to exercise a gift of gab and a rollicking eye among the village maidens. Results are inevitable "when youth and beauty meet," as the *Patriot* captioned the announcement in 1833 of the marriage of Miss Harriet Fish, daughter of Mr. Jonathan Fish of Sandwich, to Mr. Michael Hague of Ireland. However, victory was not all with the invading army of Rome. The ceremony, as was the case with all the very infrequent Catholic-Protestant marriages for the next twenty years, was performed by the minister of the orthodox meeting house,

3

Where youth and beauty met indeed — as well as the more than young and less than beautiful — were the Social Pick-Nicks. These great events occurred not oftener than twice each season and for years had been the highlights in the life of the town. For days beforehand, weather prophets called upon their powers of divination, the most famous cooks on their best talents. The great day would see folk coming by carriage from ten miles or more away. The picnic ground was a grove on the shores of the millpond, only a short distance from town. Here was an awning-covered pavilion, festooned for the occasion with greenery and surmounted by the Star-Spangled Banner.

In this pavilion, according to one who was present, tables displayed many tempting delicacies such as cakes of various names and shapes, cold ham, tongue, sweetmeats, fruit. At the head of the table we noticed a large frosted cake in the form of a cone whose apex was adorned with two imitation doves. From the beak of one a label was suspended, "Behold, how we love one another." At the foot of the table stood another of like shape, but smaller, on the top of which a minature swan sat with a strip of paper from his bill, "Cake for the unprovided." There were a brace of huckleberry cakes, adorned with a sprig of the shrub from which the name is derived, the shining luscious berries sparkling between the pretty leaves. At the upper part of the pavilion, a small bower afforded the sparkling mead, lemonade, apples, oranges, etc., which the managers received from the men who had charge of this and conveyed to the ladies. Several women were busily employed at the furnaces preparing tea and coffee. Occasionally a merry group of young ladies would come forth and take the healthful exercise of swinging.

"Laughter and frolic reigned," concluded the account,

"and old grudges were forgotten." But for a long time, the general good will did not extend to Jarvesville. Thus it probably was that "few of the members of the Mozart Union were present — a disappointment as we anticipated some of their fine glees, but those present did their best to gratify us."

This was the first public acknowledgment that the newcomers might upon occasion be a social asset, for in the days before the glass factory, there had been no Sandwich Mozart Union Society. The glassworkers had brought with them music as well as traits annoying to the townspeople. Both Saint Peter's and the Methodist chapel had flutes and viols. Eventually, this religious musical activity led to the formation of the Mozart Union.

Music proved to be a common meeting ground for Sandwich and Jarvesville. Among the officers of the society were a great-grandson of the founding Freeman who had first come to Sandwich with his queasy conscience and "much plate," as well as the Lapham brothers, William and Charles. Both farmers and factory men were among the "some dozen musicians and as many singers whose object is to improve themselves in vocal and instrumental music and contribute to their own and the happiness of others" — at twenty-five cents a single ticket, thirty-seven and a half cents for lady and gentleman, half price for children.

The program of their first "Concert of Sacred and Secular Music" testifies to something of a musical education on the part of at least one member of the society. Perhaps it was the Laphams who had come from England via the Irish glass works, for the first or secular half of the program contained works by Jonathan Blewitt, then organist of Saint Andrew's Church, Dublin, and composer and director of music in the Theatre Royal, and J. S. Smith, Chief Composer of State Music and Master of the King's Band in Ireland.

For the rest, there was a chorus by the German Marschner

— once joint *Kapellmeister* with von Weber at Dresden — whose operas were the rage in Europe just then, and there were catches and glees by England's famed Doctor Samuel Arnold, editor of Handel's works, and other musical notables who, at church organs and in opera and oratorio for Drury Lane or Covent Garden, were following English musical tradition developed by Purcell and brought to the peak of popularity by Handel. The second or religious portion of the program might have appealed even to the parishioners of Saint Peter's although they furnished no active members of the Union. It commenced with *Glorias* by Mozart and Pergolesi and continued with a wealth of excerpts from Haydn oratorios or Mozart masses until, after eighteen numbers, not including encores, the evening came to an appropriate close with a number entitled, "Now we are Nodding."

Even more to popular taste was the Sandwich Amateur Band, composed of "12 worthy young men," all glassworkers, and consisting of:

> 2 bass trombones, one Tenord [sic], 2 bugles, one Trumpet, 2 E flat clarinets, 3 B flat ditto, and one Bass Drum. They play 32 different tunes and are practicing more, all of them tunes of modern taste, except the old standards such as Yankee Doodle, etc.
>
> They send across the water and import their Paganinis, their Ostinellis and a great many other "nis" and "lis," and Boston folks boast of Kendall, etc. Why may not Cape Cod at some future time boast of her Kerns, her Laphams, her Collins, her Maher. We cannot own but feeling proud that we have among us two such societies as the Mozart Union and the Sandwich Amateur Band that the refinements and exquisite enjoyments of life are placed within our reach.

Slowly, even folk set so solidly in old ways began to admit that glassworkers could add zest and a certain tinge of urbane culture to community life. The newcomers possessed still

another winning quality and that was, according to a newspaper letter on the habits of glassworkers — perhaps by Mr.
Jarves — "the good nature which contributes to health and
you find it in none more than a glass-blower." More and
more of the band of jolly young men who could sing lustily
of love in the merry month of May found wives among local
maidens. Charles Lapham married Miss Eliza Fessenden,
daughter of William, one-time innkeeper. Francis Kern was
wed to Elmira Badger, a farmer's daughter.

Parental opposition dwindled to the vanishing point provided the suitor was not slave to King Alcohol or the whore
of Rome. Public opinion was changing. "Of all the pursuits of life," the *Patriot* now observed, "none more certainly ensures comfort and respectability than that of a
mechanic. The man who understands a useful trade, if
blessed with health, need never want food or clothing or
shelter, provided he is industrious and prudent."

The shelter provided by some of the glassworkers, even in
despised Jarvesville, was more than adequate, to judge from
the advertisement by which the Reverend Benjamin Haines
offered his house for sale:

> Situated in State St. at the Glass Factory Village, house is
> cottage build and finished throughout in superior style —
> 2 large front rooms with Fire Frame and Franklin Stove, 2
> handsome and convenient front chambers with fire-places
> and dormant [dormer] windows on the roof, front and
> back, also 2 convenient bedrooms, a convenient kitchen
> with Cooking-Stove, a sink room with Boiler set, a good
> well of water with pump in the kitchen, a convenient stable,
> carriage, and wood-house, all in complete repairs. Con-
> nected is a handsome garden with a choice variety of fruit
> trees.

Here was a home with every "convenience" to make a
wife happy, and from the records, the Reverend Benjamin

Haines seems to have been a marrying parson rather than a preaching or a praying one. First and last, he owned about a half-dozen such homes and made happy half as many wives.

Handsome, curly-headed young Reverend Mr. Haines had been at the factory from the first, gravely setting out for work each morning with his Bible under his arm. He was a minister probably chiefly because his father had been before him in the Methodist movement which had swept through England's artisans. He loved the Lord, but he also loved life as he found it, and he found it good in Sandwich. No one bought as much powder and shot. With his recorded purchases of "brandy and syrup," "rum and medicine," "cordial," "flip," and plain "drink," it is not likely that he was an ardent supporter of the Temperance Society unless he was converted later by his more zealous colleague, Mr. Mash.

So he might have been expected to be perpetually footloose like the traditional journeyman, accustomed to wandering with his skill to and fro over the face of the earth. But even as most of the other glass blowers who had found Sandwich pleasant, he satisfied his urge for change by moving from house to house about town.

Of course, some few did not stay in Sandwich. Thomas Lloyd, not finding the New World equal to its promise, started back to England. He either was lost at sea or died shortly after arrival, leaving the descendants of his brother Samuel perpetually tantalized by the thought of an unobtainable inheritance across the sea. Most of the others could find enough change of scene in Sandwich, and always the first move was out of Jarvesville into the town.

The Kern brothers, William and Theodore, having come to the factory as departmental supervisors, were uptown folk almost from the first. They were among the few newcomers to attend the Congregational meeting house along with the Dilloways, the Stutsons, and the more substantial of the natives. Theodore Kern was on the committee which presented a gift of cut glass to a departing minister. In 1836, Cousin Francis even became Americanized to the extent of being chosen delegate to the Democratic County Convention along with a Freeman, a Nye, a Fish and a Fessenden.

Samuel Lloyd, the Laphams, and the Haines brothers — the highly skilled and highly paid — soon went up into the town, and bought and moved, and built and moved again and again. For the most part, the permanent population of Jarvesville came to consist of those not prosperous enough to leave the company houses or reluctant to forsake the sheltering shadow of Saint Peter's and the fellowship of their brothers in the faith — a community of the humbler and more alien elements. There was one exception. The Reverend Joseph Mash could blow glass even more skillfully than sermons and stood on the company books among the seventeen-dollar a week élite. He and his brother Thomas early went to Barnstable Courthouse and there "renounced allegiance to King William IV." He had been almost the first to associate as an equal with the leaders of the town. Yet he stayed in Jarvesville to the end of his days, strenuously combating the Popery under his nose and doing his best to elevate the moral tone of the factory village.

Naturally, with all the coming and going, there was a brisk business in real estate, both in Jarvesville and that portion of Sandwich's Main Street nearest the factory. Advertised for sale was

> the Brick House — one of the best places for a mechanic or laboring man in the County, it being about ¼ mile from the glass factory where persons disposed to work can always find employ and is handy to mill, church, and P.O. To persons on the Cape who would like constant employment at good wages, this place offers a rare chance, as real estate is becoming more valuable each year.

By a typical transaction in 1836, Mr. William Fessenden,

one-time inn-keeper and now postmaster and auctioneer, advertised that the Nye farm in Sandwich had been purchased and a street would be laid out from the county road near the Methodist meeting-house to the Glass Manufactory. House lots would be offered for sale without reserve to the highest bidder:

> the most eligible Central house lots in this town, being in the immediate neighborhood of an active population where property for the last few years has been steadily increasing in value and forty Dwelling-houses can now find tenants. To the mechanics, it offers great inducement to settle near this place as an increasing demand for their industry will give them constant employ. Terms liberal and made known at the sale.

Provided that this process of expansion continued, soon workmens' cottages might be creeping across on either side until the marshy strip between would be filled in and obliterated. Then there would be no definite division between town and factory village. It was a prospect which the town fathers did not enjoy contemplating. If they had their way, it would never come to pass.

Accordingly, in 1838, addressed

> To the Honorable Court of County Commissioners: —
> The petition of the subscribers, inhabitants of the town of Sandwich, humbly shows that a town way leading from the County Road through the land lately purchased by Deming Jarves and Wm. H. Fessenden of Abraham Nye and through the land of Melatiah Tobey in the dark lane, so called, at the village of the Boston and Sandwich Glass Company Factory would be of great utility and is much needed by the inhabitants of said town, that they have petitioned the selectmen of said town to lay out said way, and they have unreasonably neglected and refused to do it.

This petition won the day over the last attempt to keep the factory village a pariah community at the end of its "dark lane, so called" across the narrow marsh. Henceforth, bound to town by a road laid out and maintained by public funds, Jarvesville folk were very definitely "inhabitants of the town of Sandwich."

Capitalist — American Primitive

To be a New England manufacturer in the early eighteen-thirties was to feel a little bit like Lord God Almighty. Probably such a blasphemous thought never crossed the mind of Mr. Jarves, even though he dared to say that he preferred remaining outside of the churches of his acquaintance so as not to be committed to either their heaven or hell. Perhaps it did not occur to any of the noble spirits who felt that they were redeeming from sinful sloth the nation's idle little waterfalls and idle little hands. But there was not one who did not realize that the manufacturer was distinctly the man of the hour.

His was the dominant voice in the land to which even the great Dan'l Webster now gave heed in reversing his position on the protective tariff. In a vain plea, John Randolph of Roanoke had likened the agriculturist to "the meek drudge, the ox" who is given the refuse of the farmyard, the moldy straw and mildewed shocks of corn while the manufacturer was "whirling in coaches and indulging in palaces."

On his now rare fishing trips to Sandwich, Webster cast a calculating eye at the changes which had come to the secluded little farming town going sleepily along its time-tried ways. Though he did not enjoy the occasional necessity of sharing his favorite spot in the trout brook with some glassworker on his off shift, he appreciated the significance of the smoke streamer heralding the new power in the land.

It was a power which many statesmen felt should be fostered as a weapon of self-defense. In spite of winning two wars for freedom from the mother country, most Americans felt that England was continuing the fight by commerce and trade and was seeking to keep the new nation an agricultural colony in fact, if not in name. As champion of the endless struggle, the American manufacturer was to be armed with all the protection his country could give him.

Accordingly, when South Carolina actively rebelled against the new order, it was Webster's thunder which had finally drowned out even the rousing opposition of Hayne and Calhoun, bringing about the compromise which had won the way for his "Liberty and union, now and forever, one and inseparable." To the manufacturer, this meant union of the country behind liberty for him.

Of course, Deming Jarves was not, properly speaking, a manufacturer, but only the agent of a corporation. But once he was on the packet with Boston behind him, he was his own man. He could disregard his occasional bickerings with Boston directors who preferred making money to making glass. He could forget Boston courts which had a way of deciding against him in countless lawsuits over patent priorities and patent infringements. Success was showing how well he could make use of ideas snatched from all sorts of sources.

The greatest engineering project in those years was the construction of the Bunker Hill Monument. After Quincy granite had been chosen as the ideal material, there had been the matter of finding a way to haul the massive blocks to some waterway, then the only easy means of transportation known. The civil engineer, Gridley Bryant, had solved the problem by a horse railway from the quarry to the Neponset River. After some heated discussion, the Massachusetts legislature in March, 1826, had granted a charter to the Granite Railway which had been the talk of New England ever since.

It did not seem at all revolutionary to Deming Jarves who was familiar enough with the English industrial scene to know that for two centuries such railroads had been used in the old country to carry coal from the mines to the waterways. But it suddenly and surprisingly offered him the solution of a problem of his own which was the risky awkwardness of lightering his fragile glass down the creek to the *Polly*, resting in deep water, with the dangers of careless handling in hoisting the clumsy casks over the side into the hold.

Why not his own railroad out across the marshes to a wharf where the *Polly* might stop? He would need no state charter since he would be crossing only his own land. If he could not get the sort of wagon he wanted sent down from Boston, Keith, the Sandwich blacksmith who was already branching out as carriage maker for the Cape, would be glad to exercise his ingenuity.

In October, 1833, the editor of the *Barnstable Patriot* had great news for Cape Cod:

> The enterprising Glass Company at Sandwich have just completed a Railway about a half mile in length extending from the Factory at Jarvesville to a wharf across a marsh hitherto inaccessible by carriages. Trial was made of the cars upon the railway last Saturday for the first time which we had the pleasure of witnessing. This Railway is constructed upon billets of wood which are driven into the earth at short distances, forming a very firm foundation;

upon this, the rails of wood are laid, the gravings being of iron. There are now but two cars attached to the railway, one for the transportation of passengers, the other for baggage, goods, etc. These are propelled by horse power at the rate of 12 miles an hour, but capable of moving at much greater rapidity. Everything succeeded beyond the most sanguine expectation of the proprietor, and the Railway promises to be a great auxiliary, both in saving of time and labor to the industrious citizens of Jarvesville, a name given to the factory village in honor of Mr. Jarves.

His urge for experimentation was even stronger within the factory walls, especially in the realm of the glowing jewel tones which glass with certain mysterious chemical compounds could achieve. Keeping in touch with developments in England, he caught wind of a Mr. Rice Harris who had devised a magic formula for a shimmering opalescent shade. Nothing would do but he must snare this rare bird for the Sandwich factory, although in the end, he had to offer the regal young gaffer five thousand dollars and expenses for a mere six months' period of instruction to Sandwich workers.

Mr. Jarves's publicity sense was shrewd, and Sandwich fame spread. About this time "A Traveller" wrote to "Mr. Editor" of the *Boston Traveler* that

> while on a journey to the Cape recently, I visited the Glass Works at Sandwich and was much pleased with the great improvement evinced in this important branch of manufacture. The work of this establishment is said to equal anything of the kind imported — What most attracted my attention was a window, stained and painted in the manner of the ancients, an art hitherto supposed to be lost. Here, however, is proof of its existence in this country, and the coloring is magnificent, the design chaste and on the whole beautiful. In the centre is the head of Christ after Guido, the coloring of which is equal to any oil painting of that master, though it has always been thought impossible to

produce the effect of an oil painting on glass in this manner. I think that this window has only to be seen to induce the rich and influential to avail themselves of one of the most brilliant and durable means of decorating churches and other public buildings. I made some few inquiries respecting this splendid specimen and was informed it was executed by a young man lately from England who was engaged by this company to stain cut glass, etc. and that he understands the making of all sorts of colors on glass or on the metal in the furnaces, but that he was about returning to England.[1]

Since patriotism then was almost a religion, the "Traveller" went on to recollect "seeing, not long since, a statement of the purchase of the picture of Washington painted by Stuart. Would it not be an honor to the city to have that copied for some of the public buildings in this imperishable style of painting?"

Perhaps it was well that Mr. Jarves did not share the "Traveller's" enthusiasm for the results of his experimentation, or there might have been a plague of stained-glass statesmen and politicians in public buildings up and down the land.

It has often been noticed [he reflected in his *Reminiscences of Glass-Making*] that old stained glass windows have a much richer effect than modern ones, and Mr. Chevreul (the distinguished French chemist) speaking of their superiority, attributes it to what moderns regard as defect. In the first place, much of the ancient glass is of unequal thickness and so presents convex and concave parts which refract the light differently and produce an agreeable effect. In the next place, old colored glass is not a colorless glass to which has been added the particular coloring material; such as protoxide of cobalt, etc. Old glass contains a good deal of oxide of iron which colors it green, and to this must be at-

[1] Frank W. Chipman, *The Romance of Sandwich Glass.*

tributed the peculiar effects of antique glass colored by
cobalt and manganese. M. Chevreul appears to think that
modern stained glass is too transparent to produce the best
effect.

However, the visit of Mr. Rice Harris was a great success,
for opalescent became a Sandwich specialty, and Mr. Lloyd
and others with New World ingenuity improved the Harris
opalescent by adding it to milk white, light blue, pale green,
and yellow to achieve effects he had never dreamed of.

In fact, New World ingenuity in the shape of the beautiful lacy patterns of Hiram Dilloway was about to turn the
tables against the old countries by enabling Mr. Jarves to
send forth such a flood of pressed ware as would, for the few
years the fad lasted, all but put foreign cutters out of the
business. Pressed lace patterns were lovely and pressed lace
glass was cheap. Thus, Mr. Jarves pioneered in what was to
become the characteristically American mission of industry.
With a sense of high destiny he wrote:

> It has been reserved for this age to render the art of glass-
> making tributary to the comfort of man and by its moderate
> cost to enable the poorest and humblest to introduce the
> light and warmth of the sun within, while excluding the
> storms and chilly blasts; to decorate his table with the use-
> ful and minister to his taste at a cost barely more than that
> of one of his ordinary day's labor. That which once was prized
> and displayed as the treasure and inheritance of the wealthy
> and which, with sacred carefulness, was handed down as of
> precious value, may now be found in the humblest dwell-
> ings, and is procured at a charge which makes the account
> of the former costliness of glass to partake almost of the
> character of the fabulous and visionary.

Not merely by mass production did Mr. Jarves act to extend the good things of life to the "poorest and humblest."
From his repeated visits to England, he was undoubtedly
familiar with social and industrial developments there. Thus,

his arrangements for his workers may have echoed to some extent Robert Owen's experiment in model housing and the well-ordered life for factory operatives at New Lanark — a success in contrast to Owen's later experiment in America with the too idealistic communism of New Harmony. More likely, though, Mr. Jarves was actuated by a shrewd idea of anchoring the proverbially foot-loose glassworkers to their jobs. Even articling workmen shipped from across the sea for a term of years did not insure that they might not jump contract when tempted by more money outside of state limits.

Mr. Jarves's Glass Factory Village was not the drab cluster of sun-scorched tenements surrounding many mills and factories in New England. He himself had seen to the planting of rows of young elms along the newly laid out streets and the pretty little park in front of the factory. Still slender and feathery, they would, in years to come, grow to arch the village with cool green shade. Mr. Jarves anticipated the financial arrangements of a coming age with a plan whereby any worker who, like the farmer or capitalist, wished his stake in the future, could own his own home free and clear by a series of rentlike fortnightly payments. Moreover, Mr. Jarves even made it possible for a householder to furnish his house by dollar-a-week instalments.

As Jarvesville began to spill over into the old town, Mr. Jarves would buy up farm land within suitable distance of the factory and give free house lots to workers who guaranteed to build homes. However, he cannily reserved for himself the corner lots in the newly laid out plots, advertising them for sale as ideal locations for blacksmith or wheelwright or any ambitious artisan wishing to settle in a thriving industrial community. Mr. Jarves's glassworkers took to his financial plans like spring herring to the creek. Some of the more affluent gaffers with their seventeen weekly dollars stuffing their pockets even went into the real-estate business on

their own, holding mortgages on the homes of their less
prosperous fellows. Had they realized that they were falling
in with Mr. Jarves's deep-laid scheme to root them to the
town, they might have shied off as hastily as they did from
the company store — the sole venture of Mr. Jarves's to go
awry.

Although company stores have generally been ostensibly in-
augurated for the convenience of workingmen in mines and
isolated manufacturing communities, they have too often
been turned into instruments of oppression, charging necessities up to the worker at profiteering prices and keeping
him in a state of perpetual serfdom. Even here the company
store seemed to stand as a mark of servitude to the worker,
and refusal to trade there whenever possible became a gesture of independence.

The prices in the company store of the Boston and Sandwich Glass Company were so reasonable that many times the
little local grocer or drygoods merchant would send over to
Jarvesville to replenish suddenly exhausted stocks. Many a
glassworker probably purchased up in the town the same
goods which he might earlier have bought at the company
store for the same price or even a penny or two less. Nearly
half of the men in the first "shops" of glass blowers never set
foot in the door. Hardly a quarter of the accounts carried on
the books were in such amounts as to keep the store on a paying basis.

If factory workers were psychologically set against any
company store, townsfolk were as unfavorably disposed toward the storekeeper, none other than Mr. Jabez Dame who
had so shrewdly stripped them of their wood lots.

The store lasted as a company store less than two years.
Then it failed, to be reopened at once under a presumably
independent proprietor. But everyone knew that it was operating only by "the arrangement and connection in business
existing between Deming Jarves, William Stutson, and

Nathan N. Crocker." Neither the bold black headline of Mr. Crocker's advertisement in the *Patriot* — "BE SURE YOU'RE RIGHT — THEN GO AHEAD — to Crocker's — Jarvesville" — nor the enticing list of goods under it drew enough customers.

Soon came the announcement that "Mr. Joel Powers takes over the Jarvesville store in place of Nathan N. Crocker. N.B. All kinds of country produce will be taken in exchange for goods." Again the change of faces fooled no one. Behind the personality of Mr. Powers and his string of successors was the power of Mr. Jarves and everyone knew it.

If the company store, however disguised, never prospered, the increased trade spawned a cluster of new stores at the end of the road where the old town and new town met. These were mostly run by outsiders drawn by the suddenly expanded market, together with an occasional native son seeking a way of living less arduous than the land, sea, or factory. In the mounting complexity of Sandwich's more industrial society, the class of merchant middlemen who live by distributing goods rather than producing them was rapidly increasing. Sandwich saw no more "general" stores, but a small shop for hats, another for saddles and harnesses, a third for clock- and watch-repairing. A villager, David Fish, opened a store for the sale of "Boots and Shoes, Hats and Caps, Neck Stocks, Linen Bosoms, Dickeys, and Silk and Cotton Umbrellas — One invariable price strictly adhered to." Because of the booming business in broadcloth suits, the plain "Jarvesville Tailor" had competition in Alfred Carter's "Emporium of Fashion" and "John Sutton, the Fashionable Tailor."

The old town, growing and prospering along with the factory community, started a few of its own plants. A cut-nail factory, capitalized by local money, was started in North Sandwich. Here, also, Mr. Keith, the blacksmith and carriage maker, had branched out from the shoeing of horses and oxen and the building of wagons and ox teams to the manufacture of stagecoaches, wheelbarrows, and sleighs.

Enriched beyond dreams by the tax money from all this enterprise, the town in 1834 built a new town hall — a white wooden structure, chastely plain, with lovely Doric columns in the neo-classic style so typical of the period when the nation regarded itself as heir to the virtues of ancient Greece. Columned porticos and carved pilasters gleaming whitely through shade patterns of leaf and branch, together with Wren spires reaching for the skies — here was beauty flowering from the wealth produced by factory wheels, just as the solid Georgian mansions of the shipping ports had sprung from the rich cargoes of far lands, and the silver-shingled farmhouses with the spare grace of their lines had grown simply from the needs of the soil.

Art and science paid periodic visits to town in the form of a lecturer on phrenology, a dentist with sample sets of teeth who could be consulted on Fridays at the Sandwich Inn, an itinerant portrait painter who inspired the ladies of the town with the idea of presenting to Doctor Leonard, the town physician, his own portrait as token of their esteem. Recognizing the part Boston and Sandwich Company money had played in all the expansion, townspeople gave Captain Stutson a part in dispensing philanthropy and culture by electing him Overseer of the Poor and one of the committee to select a Female Teacher.

There was no blinking the fact that the life of the town had come to center, not in the post office or tavern, but in the factory. Sportsmen from Boston were so rare that it was now great news when one got a deer — although even greater news, of course, when another, alighting from his carriage to take a shot at a robin, tripped over his gun and killed himself instead.

Sooner or later every man arrived at the factory door. A contractor could "bid at the Glass Factory for the building of a scow-boat of 50 tons burthen." The captain of a ship in search of a cargo would find the factory in need of "2 or 3 vessels to freight coal from Richmond to Sandwich for the present season — 15 cents per bushel freight paid and every dispatch to unloading at Sandwich."

Householders could receive twenty cents per bushel for their dry wood ashes at the factory. They could also deliver — "empty barrels of every description for which will be paid at the following rate. Flour bbls. full hooped and two heads — 18 cts. each — 1 head, 12 cts. Beer, pork, cider or any other of that description with 2 heads, 25 cts. The same with one head — 18 cts." If a man wanted to buy a boat, he could bid at auction on seven-sixteenths of the schooner *Caroline* "as she now lies at the Glass-House in Sandwich, also sail-boat for shore fishing." If he wished a cow, he could apply "to Josiah Gifford at the Glass Manufactory" for a "good new Milch Cow."

Those building a house or repairing a foundation or chimney could answer the advertisement "For Sale — A large lot of Well Brick, Face and Common Brick, and Tile which will be delivered on board of any vessel in the vicinity or at any of the adjoining towns at short notice by D. Jarves. Sandwich Aug. 18, 1835."

Mr. Jarves had started his own brickyards at a certain clay pit in town to supply the needs of the factory furnaces and the new construction. He was aiming at an industrial empire as complete as that of Henry Ford a century later. He had planned company ownership of all sources of raw material, all means of transportation, and control as far as possible of all necessities and conveniences for both factory and workmen. Little by little, he was adding to the Jarvesville store a "bake house and shoe shop," to the factory a "hammer and pattern shop, planing and grist-mills, and stave mill." Informed of the erection of two or more large stores in Jarvesville, Sandwich, the *Patriot* now reported "That village has not its equal in our country." Whenever, mentioned, Mr. Jarves never figured as mere company agent, but always "the enterprising proprietor."

2

In his glowing satisfaction at watching the growth of this organism rooted in his creative genius, Mr. Jarves could fairly well submerge the disappointments of his family life — particularly his relationship with his oldest son and first hope.

Already, as seen through the eyes of this son, James Jackson Jarves, Mr. Jarves's marriage and family life had taken on the pattern which novelists of a later time were to depict as typical of the American businessman. In the days of living upon the land, the wife was man's partner in every way, forming out of the raw stuff he provided all the household needs from coats to candles — and lending a knowing mind and hand, when necessary, to the care of the crops and the creatures. With the development of "big business" as a masculine world from which women were excluded as much as possible, the position of the wife came to have a slightly Oriental character.

"Never was a household more perfectly conducted than my mother's," wrote young Jarves. "Every want had been anticipated — the warm slippers, the punctual meals, the silence, order, and neatness, the subdued, yet cheerful welcome that ever greeted him, the quiet presence that listened when he talked, the active mind that gathered the pleasant daily chit-chat to amuse him where newspaper failed."

It was part of the new pattern of family life among the more well-to-do that the dominant influence over the men-children was now the mother's. On the farm, a lad worked into the ways of adult life bit by bit at his father's side. Now a boy was a child, educated in a home which had become a sort of harem, until it was time to be thrust quite suddenly into the world of men. The devotion which developed between Anna Jarves and her oldest living son held at least a trace of the abnormal, and from time to time he unconsciously bared the relationship with a nakedness that amounted almost to indecency.

"Surely, it was no fault of mine that my mother found in my nature more to attract and develop hers than in her husband." And again, "There is no reminiscence of her more dear to my mind now than of a whipping she once gave me with my favorite horsewhip. It was smartly done and so unexpected a display of vigor that, should she now call upon me to prepare for another, my reverence would impel me at once to unbutton."

These statements, it is true, appeared in his *Why and What Am I? or the Confessions of an Inquirer,* a book which drew such howls of protest from relatives and friends that he was impelled to express an injured surprise that his "lay figures" were "held to be live persons, the book an autobiography." He uttered no such disclaimer, however, when a lady admirer compared the so-called memoirs to the *Confessions* of Rousseau in "honesty, charming language, and exquisite pathos, but emanating from a purer soul, they appeal, unlike Rousseau, only to the pure in heart."

Moreover, the almost unnatural intimacy between mother and son has been corroborated in blunt terms by others in the family. She was "crazy about her oldest son," he was "completely spoiled by his mother." She stuffed him with stories of old heroes and old cultures until, as he said, "this vicarious life seemed more real to me than my own." She encouraged the craze for collecting anything that came to hand — old stamps, old coins, old books, Indian arrow heads, mineral and biological specimens, even human bones — the gathering and gloating which compensated in some measure for activities from which he was barred by ill health. She held up for his future Harvard and the prestige of a scholarly career as historian. She stiffened his opposition to all attempts of his distraught father to interest him in some useful pursuit, particularly the manufacture of glass.

Young James had no objections to Sandwich itself. After "Boston's ugly brick houses, tiled and slated roofs, a chaos of heights and depths, right and acute angles," the beauty-loving lad reveled in the spaciousness of greenery and blue sky, the sweetness of new-mown hay, the color and fragrance of fruit and flowers, the tinkle of cowbells, and the faraway music of flutes and viols from the little churches. He had the innate good taste to prefer the low gray farmhouses among their orchards and lilac clumps to more pretentious architecture.

But he found little except ugliness in his father's factory and the bulk of his product. So he kept away from the heat and confusion of the glasshouse as much as possible, aided by his mother who could always plead his delicate health. The lack of sympathy between Mr. Jarves and his oldest son must have been a cruel blow to the father. Probably no effort on his part could have bettered the situation. In the beginning, no one could have been hard-hearted enough to oppose Anna's complete absorption in James who had arrived so providentially after little Billy, the first-born, had, as his brother rather unfeelingly put it, "been forwarded to heaven on the croup express." Now it was too late. There could be no forcing the situation — even had Mr. Jarves been the type to coerce another's will. Young James could count not only on his mother's help in any event, but on considerable moral support from a grandmother and bevy of aunts who would prudently back the views of their well-to-do sister.

Though James always saw his parents and their marriage through his mother's eyes, an impartial observer could find considerable sympathy for Mr. Jarves's position. If he was harried by Anna's rich relations in Boston, he was saddled with the poor ones in Sandwich. From the first, Abby Stutson Thayer, a widow with one daughter, was settled in Sandwich keeping house for the aged Grandma Stutson — perhaps in the so-called Jarves farm. A second sister, Mrs. Charles Southark, also came to town so that her husband might be given work in the glass factory. The last and most colorful of these family arrivals was the oldest, Mrs. Lydia Stutson Bacon, with her dear Josiah.

"Auntie Bacon," as she liked to be called, lived so piously that a collection of her letters was published in 1852 by the American Sabbath School Society. Her husband Josiah, an infantry captain in the War of 1812, was for some years a commission merchant until "a great commercial pressure affected his interests most unfavorably. He would not eat the bread of idleness or dependence, but anxiously sought a situation for honest and comfortable livelihood." An honest livelihood Mr. Jarves afforded him in Sandwich in 1829. There were other opinions as to its comfort.

"My dear Josiah's time is too much occupied for him to write," Auntie Bacon was soon saying in a letter to an old friend. "His hours of business are from six in the morning to seven in the evening, and the business such as to require his constant presence."

Auntie Bacon found Sandwich "one of the loveliest villages that the sun ever shone on" and wrote quite lyrically of the springtime with "the bleating of the lambs and the sweet notes of the birds." But she also found cause for alarm in the "fearful strides Popery seems to be making in our happy land. Should not Protestant Christians soon awake and make commensurate efforts, we shall see Romanism gain the ascendancy. What an awful result to contemplate!"

Auntie Bacon met the challenge strenuously. As a result of her efforts, the First Parish Sabbath school was "sustained through the winter for the first time in its history. My dear

Josiah is superintendent, and I have charge of the female department. — One of my scholars, a colored girl [2] about 16 is a hopeful subject of grace. When she told me that her heart loved Jesus, I could have hugged her, black as she was. She is a dear child and seems like a 'new creature.' Others in my class are thoughtful." Auntie Bacon not only kept the Sabbath School alive during the months of chill winds and all but impassable roads and gathered an occasional dusky lamb into the old fold; she — or rather dear Josiah under her guidance — even offered brave, if somewhat futile competition to Father Canavan and the Reverend Joseph Mash with another Sabbath school "at the close of afternoon service in the Factory Village."

Amongst lengthy platitudinous homilies, Auntie Bacon let fall a very few allusions to life in Sandwich in the restricted social circle which consisted almost exclusively of the Stutson clan and "old lady Fessenden and her husband." The first blow of the scourge of the Stutsons fell. "The daughter of my sister (Thayer) died the first of April. It was sad to see such a young creature (just 18) sinking to an early grave. She was a pleasant and we trust a pious child."

Another vignette shows Auntie Bacon doing her duty as a poor relation. "Boston, April 24, 1834 — I am visiting the city. My sister has taken a journey to the South accompanied by her husband and oldest son. Knowing that she would not like to have her younger children without some person more suitable than the servants to look after them, I offered my poor services. So here I am, and mother to four children. The youngest is but two years old and a very lovely docile little creature."

She also referred to Sister Anna's many social engagements which perhaps accounted for the fact that the long Sandwich summers were definitely no more. Now there were only Mr.

---

[2] Probably from Mashpee where a certain number of fugitive or free Negroes had settled among the native Indians.

Jarves's necessary business trips to the factory and an occasional visit of Anna and the children to Mother Stutson.

Unfortunately for Mr. Jarves's dynastic longings, that meant less intimate acquaintance with the glass factory for his sons. He was reluctantly giving up hope of James. The worst of it was that he could not be much surer of the others. George was an amiable little lad without any marked abilities or interests. He was obediently polite, but not enthusiastic about glassmaking.

Sadly enough, the boy could not be set to work in a glasshouse at the age of nine like the son of a gaffer. Even Mr. Jarves could agree with Mrs. Jarves there. But he could do the next best thing. In 1836, he purchased the Mt. Washington Glass Works in South Boston. Authorities state that he bought it "for his son, George," but as George at that time proves to have been about eleven years old, he cannot immediately have taken any very active part in the management. He was more a sort of apprentice in ownership. A small boy who owned a glass factory should surely grow up with an interest in glassmaking.

Young Johnny alone seemed to show a natural liking for glassmaking as he trotted through the works at his father's heels, watched the exploits of the gaffers, and peered through the bye-hole of the furnace for a glimpse of the Salamander coiled on his glowing bed and glaring with fiery eyes at the intruder. His father had great stories to tell of this mythical monster of glassmakers who was always waiting to seize some unwary victim and drag him back into the flames. Thus many workers, carried off by the Salamander, disappeared. Gallant knights of old, armed *cap-a-pie,* often challenged the fiery dragon in combat. They were always driven back because — Mr. Jarves combined legend with science — they did not know or overlooked the fact that steel armor, being a rapid conductor of heat, would be more likely to tempt a ready approach of the fabled monster.

Whether John was really interested in glassmaking or merely liked the excitement of the glasshouse and the petting of the men was still not certain. Mr. Jarves could only hope for the best. He was far more the arbiter of human destiny outside of his own family.

3

No power over the lives of Jarvesville and Sandwich was more forceful than that of Mr. Jarves. Every loafer from nine to ninety leaning lazily in a sunny doorway would flee as from the wrath of God at the sight of the tall figure with the neat decisive step. There was not much chance to escape a forcible redemption from a pleasant but wicked idleness by being dragged off willy-nilly to work in or around the factory.

No one was turned away. The mason, Ebenezer Chamberlain, upon his release from state's prison, found work in the factory and once more became the support of his "amiable wife and six children," though the limelight of the militia had gone forever. It was literally true that the factory offered "constant employ at good wages" and the newspaper spoke of the "vast number of Cape people resorting to a town where they were supported by the enterprise and public spirit of capitalists."

Glass-blowing, of course, was still clannishly kept as a hereditary craft, and few apprentices were accepted outside of glassmaking families. But native Americans were particularly drawn by the machine shop where the molds were constructed according to the designs of Hiram Dilloway and machinery for operating them was devised and improved. Here were to be found Hoxies and Bassetts along with Sweeneys and Haleys.

Men with old town names were by this time working beside Kerns and Laphams in the cutting department. They soon found that they had not left all danger behind with a fractious bull in the farmyard. One John Chipman, bending over his cutting machine to make adjustments, was in some way caught by his coat and whirled head over heels a hundred and fifty times. His feet struck the ceiling so forcibly with each revolution that, before the machine could be stopped, the boards overhead were kicked through, his shoes torn off, and the bones in his feet broken. But if shattered nerves would not let him face the machine again, other work could be found.

When a carpenter, machinist, cutter, or blower became too weak for his own work, Mr. Jarves would provide another place more suited to his condition — perhaps as watchman to stroll about on the lookout for runaway fires from the furnaces or to tap on the glass panes of Jarvesville, rousing the workers in time for their shifts. There were the Newcomb brothers of Sandwich who "without speech or hearing had learned to read and write and had become familiar with the usages of polite society through the Hartford Asylum for the Deaf and Dumb." They were "employed in some of the most difficult and delicate work in the glass factory." No one who wished to work was ever turned away because of old age or physical handicap.

Not that, according to Mr. Jarves's report, there was much need for concern about the blowers. "An impression is very prevalent that glass-making is an unhealthy occupation," he once wrote. "It may have been thus in former times, but as a matter of fact, no mechanical employment is more healthy. Dissipated as glass-makers have been in former days, and careless of their health as they are at present, no better evidence can be adduced to prove the *generally* healthy character of the employment than the fact that the Glass Manufacturing Company in Sandwich, averaging in their employment 300 hands, had not a man sick through the influence of the employment, or one die in their connection for the space of twenty years."

Mr. Jarves was probably stretching a point or two in favor of his own interest, for sixty years later, the president of the Glass-Blowers' Association of America was reporting that, due to the early age at which boys went to work in glass-houses, serving three or four years as tending-boys before their five years' apprenticeship, and to the heat, poor ventilation, and changes of temperature, insurance records showed that most deaths occurred between the ages of forty and fifty, and early in life the workers became victims of rheumatism, catarrh, throat troubles, and tuberculosis. Nevertheless — perhaps because Mr. Jarves was one of the first to construct a high-ceilinged, well-ventilated furnace room with adequate chimneys to carry off fumes and because the factory ran only four days a week — the Sandwich blowers seem to have been a remarkably leather-lunged, asbestos-skinned group with a habit of reaching the hale and hearty eighties and nineties.

However, it was a different story with the cutters, who were a wretched lot, victims of rheumatism, arthritis, and all manner of respiratory diseases because of their constant handling of wet sand and cold water. But if a cutter coughed his life away, his widow could count on her Christmas barrel of flour from Mr. Jarves and place for her little boys to earn their three dollars a week as soon as they could trot with a red-hot wineglass in a forked stick from gaffer's bench to annealing oven.

Nine was considered the proper age for most young men of the time to begin their life work which, from a moral as well as financial point of view, could hardly be commenced too soon. Industry, from Puritan days, had been deemed the prime virtue to be inculcated in the young. If it were cultivated energetically enough, there would be no need to worry about sprouting vices because there simply would not be room for any to grow. The Reverend Mr. Higginson, first pastor of the Bay Colony, had rejoiced over the plantation because "little children here by the setting of corn may earne more than their maintenance."

In weighing the advantages of the industrial development in the new nation, Alexander Hamilton in his *Report on Manufactures* had stated that "children are rendered more useful by manufacturing establishments than they otherwise would be." Child labor in general was considered a boon to free the world from the "vice and immorality to which children are exposed by a career of idleness," and the manufacturer became the moral benefactor of humanity.

Mr. Jarves's sharp wiry little gamins leaping like crickets to the glory-hole with a long fork holding some half-finished article to be reheated or with a rack of finished glasses for the annealing oven were as well off compared to lads in the cotton mills as Jarvesville folks were beside the people in the usual mill village. Instead of a meager two dollars a week at the cotton mills, the glasshouse boys received three dollars a week for a shorter day.

To be sure, they worked two hours a day longer than the men, because while the men worked two five-hour shifts, a boy was expected to stay in the factory after hours during the interval between shifts to bring in wood for the glory-holes and clear up after one shop and make ready for the next. Still, this made only a twelve-hour day compared with fourteen in the usual cotton mill, and the youngsters had such high jinks during the hours they were left in the glass-house alone that little Billy Kern whose father hired another boy to take his place for the odd jobs after shifts always felt that he had been deprived of one of childhood's pleasures.

It was not like Mr. Jarves to leave the education of his Jarvesville boys to chance contact with a company library. Each boy was obliged to go to school for part of a session, either morning or afternoon according to his off shift. This left just six hours a day for recreation and sleep, and if this seems a rather rugged schedule for a nine-year-old, it lasted only four days a week. There was always the long weekend for sleeping and growing and learning, too, as the schools kept open all day Saturday as well as Friday for the benefit of the boys who worked in the factory.

In a sense, too, the employment itself was education, and glasshouse boys, unlike other factory children, were midway between the old order wherein a child's work was a preparation for life, whether in learning the care of soil and creatures or the skill of a craft, and the time at hand when child labor was an exploitation of animal energy as brutish as that of mule on treadmill. Seventy-five years hence, boys in glass factories would be in a class with pit boys in mines and bobbin boys in mills, but in Jarvesville, days were not a mere opening and closing of glass-blowers' molds and running from gaffer to glory-hole or lier or annealing oven. Often in intervals between two "moves" — as a lier full of articles to be annealed was called, the boys were allowed to try hands and lungs at blowing. A boy with no aptitude or serious inclination was quickly put in his place, but if a result was passable, there was always praise, and in the rare case of something brilliant, the article was sent to the cutters for decoration, and there was a keepsake for a lifetime.

When a boy grew so large that his feet began to get in his own way and that of the glass blowers, he could begin to work into a man's place as a duly signed apprentice. First, he set his name to an impressive document whereby he was bound to learn "the art, trade, or mystery" of flint glass:

> The said Apprentice his said Master well and faithfully shall serve, his secrets keep, and his lawful commands duly obey. He shall do no damage to his said Master, nor suffer it to be done by others without giving reasonable notice thereof. He shall not waste the goods of his said Master nor lend them unlawfully to any. He shall not contract matrimony within the said term; nor shall he commit any act of

vice or immorality which are forbidden by the Laws of the Commonwealth, but in all ways and at all times, he shall carry and behave himself toward his said Master and all others as a good and faithful apprentice should.

In return for all this sworn devotion, Mr. Jarves or "Said Master" with cautious restraint did "hereby covenant and promise to teach and instruct or cause the said apprentice to be instructed in the art, trade, or calling by the best way that he may or can (if said Apprentice be capable to learn) and during said term to find and provide unto said Apprentice" emoluments ranging, during various periods of the company's history from $2.50 a week to "good and wholesome food and clothing."

If, once in a while, an apprentice rebelled and sought escape from the rigorous schedule of instruction and moral rectitude, advertisements would promptly be broadcast in all the near-by weeklies :

ONE CENT REWARD

Absconded from the employ of the Boston & Sandwich Glass Company, Samuel Harper, an indented apprentice. All persons are hereby cautioned against harboring or employing said apprentice. The above reward will be paid, together with all reasonable charges, to any persons who shall apprehend said Harper and lodge him in any jail in the Commonwealth.

Aug. 6, 1833   Boston & Sandwich Glass Company by
                                            Deming Jarves

(Who received the one-cent reward and under what circumstances said Harper was apprehended is not known, but five years later the name of Samuel Harper appeared on the roster of the glass-factory employes.)

At the end of his term, the apprentice was rewarded with a more lavishly emblazoned document "granted by the President and Directors in Testimony of their appreciation of

his behavior during his Apprenticeship" and stating that he
had served "with fidelity to the Company and correct deportment to the Superintendent of the Manufactory." This certificate, signed by the President of the Boston and Sandwich
Glass Company, together with William Stutson, Superintendent, and Deming Jarves, Agent, was diploma for a completed education for a life's work.

If the "art, trade, or mystery" did not tempt a boy to give
up his three dollars a week for "good and wholesome food
and clothing," he could go into cutting or pressing or become a *tiseur,* or teaser, the furnace tender who kept the
fires burning evenly at the desired temperature by tossing in
the kiln-dried sticks at just the right intervals, his steady
jogging pace around the furnace almost like a ritual dance.
Wherever he worked from the first day to the last, there
would never be a dull one.

Here was no mechanical repetition of identical operations
— here was drama in everyday doings. The fascinating con-
glomerate of white sand and red lead, saltpeter, pearlash and
cullet (the handful of broken glass, needed, it was said, to
make the batch simmer into the proper consistency) mag-
ically became with ten thousand or twelve thousand degrees
of heat a liquid, seething brew. If there was a frothy scum
of bubbles on top, you had only to toss into the cauldron a
raw potato which would disappear with a hiss, and with it
all the surface impurities.

Even so, on some days the glass would be "ambitty" — the
workers' own word for thready, unmanageable stuff which
sometimes could not be worked, but had to be ladled out of
the pots. Furnace tender or fire may have been at fault, or
perhaps just the atmosphere. It was like bread which did not
come out well because the oven was not right. But on other
days, when the batch had been cooled off to the consistency
of very cold molasses, just right for gathering, it would be
"sweet," as the gaffers put it — sweet as honey, crystal clear,

and almost ready to flow into shape at the workers' will. Then in the wait between moves, the old gaffers sometimes showed what they really could do if they were not tied down by Mr. Jarves's orders and the stodgy needs of mankind. Their sleight-of-hand performance would produce toothpick holders like tall hats, little glass pipes and walking sticks and rolling pins and, if there was colored glass cooking in the little monkey pot, witch balls of red or blue, said to ward off evil spirits.

Boys always secretly hoped for the excitement of a broken pot — event dreaded alike by Mr. Jarves because of the forty to one hundred dollars expense involved and by the men because of the dirt, heat, and danger of the most disagreeable job to come their way. In fact, to insure their presence at the ceremony, the company had to establish a rule that "all hands must be present and absentees, except from illness, are severely fined." Of course, under the terrific heat, no pot would last much longer than three months before the clay walls became thin and dangerously weakened so that at any time it was likely to burst and spill its fiery fluid.

If there was only a crack near the top, the pot could be used half full and replaced over the week-end when the fires were low and the pots empty anyway. But in midweek, the fires could not be lowered because of the other pots in the furnace filled with molten glass which would be ruined if the temperatures were altered. So, from the boys' point of view, the fun would begin. The melt had to be ladled out and the casement of brick and clay around the pot at the furnace wall broken down. In the pot room, a new pot was being slowly fired in a great kiln where it was brought somewhere near the heat of the furnace. Still red-hot, the pot was trundled over to the furnace on an iron barrow approximately the height of the bed of silica sand upon which it would rest.

The transferring of the pot from barrow to furnace was

the real climax of the drama. In the ancient days of glass-makers' story, workers changing the pots had dressed in bearskins with masks and goggles to protect them from the heat and afterwards paraded through the village to frighten old women and little children. Now they tried to use protective screens made of barrel staves held together by barrel hoops and soaked in cold water, but these soon became flaming torches. Small wonder a pot-changing, whatever it meant to Mr. Jarves and the men, was a small boys' holiday!

Once the pot was safely in place, the men could share in the holiday spirit. From immemorial custom, a company always served drinks following a pot-setting. There were certain other situations when refreshment was provided for the thirsty, as shown by the account marked "Factory" in the company store book. "Drink — pot-setting — $2.00," "Drink — pot-scraping — 20¢." (Apparently only a small number of workmen involved.) Also "Lading-out pot drink," "arch drink," "mason's drink," and "weekly drink." This would seem a distressing state of affairs for the Reverend Joseph Mash and his "Cold Water Men" until, at last, the treat stands itemized as "2 gals. Beer and gingerbread." Beer, of course, was considered only a remote relative of King Alcohol and the Demon Rum.

Besides the traditional treats which made for good fellowship, Mr. Jarves had his own generous rewards for glassmakers who could discover ways of improving the color or consistency of the glass. The rewards, most frequently won by one of the Kerns or the Reverend Joseph Mash, led to purchases of antimony, magnesium, and other chemicals at the company store and to home experiments which made the lot of a glassmaker's wife something less than serene. But as a result, Sandwich flint acquired a reputation for silvery sheen and a musical ring which has become almost legendary.

Mr. Jarves knew how to use men as well as materials. The ablest were truly his own — men whose capabilities he had developed by giving them opportunity and responsibility. Even young Captain Roland Gibbs of the packet *Polly* had been a Jarves man from the days when, a lad in his teens, he had sailed as mate to old "Grandpa" Fisher.

Except in emergencies, such as the bringing of the Catholic Bishop to town, the packet sailed only in favorable weather. Grandpa Fisher had managed to combine seafaring with his farm seven miles back of Sandwich. One cloudy morning, Grandpa Fisher decided the day more fit for hoeing potatoes than sailing a sloop. Seven miles away in Sandwich town, the skies looked brighter, the wind was fair, and Mr. Jarves stamping and pacing in his impatience to send the already loaded *Polly* on her way., At last, the young mate murmured that if he had the papers, he could sail the packet to Boston as well as anyone. Mr. Jarves promptly gave him clearance, the trip was successfully made, and Grandpa Fisher's career ended with the old *Polly*.

Although factory business controlled the coming and going of her successor, the larger *Henry Clay*, Mr. Jarves more and more felt that the chief means of communication between Boston and Sandwich should be wholly owned by the company and not in shares by people of the town. Accordingly, Captain Gibbs was one day in command of the *Sandwich*, built beside the glassworks as a very model for sloops in the packet trade. She not only traveled to Boston, but made an occasional trip to Philadelphia as well.

At the factory, Mr. Jarves's chief aid and ally was his friend, Mr. Waterman, to whom alone he could confide his troubles.

Now about the matter of sand, the two men put their heads together — For long it had irked Mr. Jarves that he was dependent on outside ownership for such a bulky ingredient. He had been having most of it sent from Morris River, New Jersey, but he had tried one cargo from Pensacola and another from France. None quite satisfied him.

Berkshire sand was said to be pure quartz sand, but a load sent from near the window-glass factory in Lanesboro proved to have little flecks of clay which spoiled it for the making of diamond-clear flint glass.

However, a rumor came to Mr. Jarves, whose business it was to know all, that a certain Mr. Smith of New York was buying up every sand bed in Berkshire from Cheshire to Milford, Connecticut, and farmers were being paid fifty dollars for the right to dig sand on their land. Accordingly, Mr. Waterman of somewhere around Boston mysteriously appeared in Cheshire after dusk. Yes, he had driven all day up the mountainous wagon road, but he was not too tired to talk to folks at the hotel or the general store.

A moment's shrewd questioning by Waterman planted the notion that Mr. Smith was not giving them fair treatment. With a lantern, the townsmen took Mr. Waterman, too eager to wait until morning, to the site of a ghostly glass factory gone up in smoke a generation ago. The springs of a lake back of Hoosac Mountain scoured the sand, assayed in Boston as ninety-seven per cent pure quartz, and in this particular spot, it was without the clay found at Lanesboro or the iron ore of Dalton. Careful not to overextend himself, as Mr. Dame had done on Sandwich woodland, Waterman bought a meager ten acres which later was expanded to a larger tract. And there was another triumph for Mr. Jarves.

From Mr. Waterman to the newest apprentice, each one felt that the Jarves attention was focused on him personally. Workmen had signed their charter with the board of directors — Munroe, Rice, Hall, *et al.* — fixing rates of pay, terms of apprenticeship, and providing that "should the fires go out in ALL ITS FURNACES at any time, this charter will expire." Still, to them "the company" was Mr. Jarves, and he had a way of making them consider themselves partners in production.

If he shared his problems with Mr. Waterman, he turned

over to the little glasshouse boys the joint jubilation on the Fourth of July to celebrate the founding of the factory and the nation. By Mr. Jarves's order, each boy coming off shift would receive a shiny half-dollar for firecrackers, nothing but firecrackers, and, of course, Mr. Jarves's word was law. Amid the squeals of joy and the scamper to the store which sold an incredible amount of sparkling and crackling for fifty cents, Mr. Jarves seemed far greater to them than President Jackson, friend of the common man, whose person and benefits were so much more remote.

In 1836, Mr. Jarves celebrated his own satisfaction by sending an article to the *Patriot* which extolled his accomplishment in a very paean of facts and figures. The factory — capital stock, $300,000 — was confined to the manufacture of flint glass in all its varieties and tin, brass, and other trimmings for lamps. The aid of machinery to reduce the cost of articles of use or luxury was surprisingly manifest in this establishment, for a rich dish could be made in one minute, and of the smaller sizes, three in a minute. Among the numerous articles, the price of which had been reduced one half in the past seven years by improvements in machinery, were deck lights and hand lanthorns. Of the latter, over fifty thousand were made yearly, and large quantities of hall lamps and chandeliers for churches, many richly ornamented. The lamp trimmings, which passed through seventy different processes in their manufacture, were turned out at a price which one would suppose scarcely sufficient to pay for the stock.

Many hands were given constant employment in the manufacture of rich doorknobs and doorplates. The increasing use of these, according to Mr. Jarves, was the result of the fact that they made a material saving in labor to families and endured much longer than those of metal. More than nine hundred dozen glass knobs for furniture were made weekly. Moreover, in this establishment, the richest cut glass was also made. In fact, there was no article of flint glass made in any part of the world that could not be made of equal quality as to material and cutting in Sandwich. A set of rich (Mr. Jarves's favorite adjective in describing his product) cut glass was even then in the making for the King of Muscat.

The manufacture of packages for all this glass also kept at work many hands. The number of large casks used exceeded 6000 yearly. Over 200 tons of packing straw was used per year. Two packets were constantly employed between the factory and Boston transporting over 12,000 packages yearly to that city from thence to be reshipped, many of them. In 1835, more than 7000 packages were shipped from Boston, 2200 of which were shipped to New York. A great amount, particularly of pressed glass, found sale in foreign countries. The company paid $7000 annually for freight alone.

During the coming year, five or six vessels could find constant employ bringing Richmond coal to the works. The consumption of fuel at the factory per year was 1500 cords of pine and 500 cords of oak, 50 tons of hard coal and 40,000 bushels of sea coal. The average consumption of iron was 50 tons per year, and that of more costly articles, such as borax, ziffre, manganese, and cobalt, amounted to many thousand dollars a year. The weekly consumption of materials was:

Pig lead	10,500 pounds
(first manufactured into oxide of lead)	
Pearlash	8500 pounds
Saltpeter	1400 pounds
Silex	10 tons

The company had commenced their present works in 1825 with seventy workmen and in ten years had been gradually extending their operations and erecting new works until they now gave steady employment to 321 men and boys. Nearly all of the men now had families and, independent of their ability as workmen, were of good repute as citizens. It was estimated that the consumption of flour by the families attached to the factory exceeded 1800 barrels and that of corn from 5000 to 7000 bushels. It might justly surprise many to learn that for the last ten years, more than 3000 bushels of potatoes had been annually imported, notwithstanding that the surrounding country was abundantly fertile to supply them.

Like the Lord upon the seventh day, Mr. Jarves looked upon all that he had made and found it good. And notwithstanding their fondness for the occasional spice of revolt, workers and townspeople alike were, in the snugness of prosperity, inclined to agree with him.

Panic

IN THE EARLY DUSK of a chill late fall day in 1836, quite a crowd of men had gathered in front of the Sandwich Hotel — still familiarly called Fessenden's — to wait for the daily coach from Plymouth. This was much more than the usual little handful of glass workers off duty and small boys coming for the mail as an excuse to swap news and watch the prancing grays. Farmers ordinarily came for their mail, if any, only on their weekly trips to town to sell and shop. But tonight, as for several nights past, the street was lined with farm wagons. Here was no mere gathering of men of Sandwich; here were assembled the ranks of Whigs and Democrats awaiting word of the fate of the nation.

After two terms of Jackson, Whig hopes were stirring. Old Hickory might, as his enemies claimed, have perverted the American system of government by making himself a sort of tribune to foster the interests of a certain class (and that not the select "wise and good," but the more numerous newly enfranchised) and by pushing his way between Congress

114

and the people as a sort of patriarchal ruler. Still, he did not dare challenge the two-term limit set by the example of the Father of his Country. His chosen successor, dapper little Martin Van Buren, could, they felt, hardly hold a candle to the great Daniel Webster who was carrying the Whig banner for Massachusetts.

The Democratic *Patriot* might sneer at the Webster rallies at Faneuil Hall, thronged by "lawyers' clerks and bankers' boys," with "much speechifying over 'our broken country, our ruined country' if the policy of the present administration was pursued." Sandwich still lay under the spell of the Websterian presence. Though the great man now seldom came to hunt or fish, he did occasionally pass through to the Barnstable Courthouse. Only recently he had appeared as defense attorney for a Mrs. Derrick accused of stealing cranberries from the Sandwich town bog at Sandy Neck. It took some time for the glow of his personality to fade from the scene. And he had the enthusiastic support of Mr. Jarves, characteristically expressed in glass. "The Webster Vase is still on show," reported the newspaper. "The rare privilege of seeing this thing may be enjoyed a few days longer. We wonder how many votes its exhibition has gained Mr. Webster for the Presidency."

Now it was already rumored that Dan'l had swept his home state. The election had taken place some days in the past. But with the nation beginning to sprawl back into the woods and prairies, it took time for the count to be carried by coach and rider from the outposts and the results to trickle back to every corner of the country. Tension mounted with each day's delay. Each night the watch for packet or coach was larger and louder-voiced. At that time of year, fall gales made the coming and going of the packet very uncertain. But come wind or stormy weather, Mr. Boyden made the sandy, hilly drive each day to Plymouth and back with the mail coach. If a stubborn farmer blocked his way

on the narrow rutted road and refused to heed bellowed
threats, woe to the farmer!

The dauntless Mr. Boyden was the younger son of a Wal-
pole farmer who, like many farmers' sons, instead of taking
up new land farther west, found a new way of living in the
old settlements. With the sudden expansion of Sandwich,
he had moved in to fill the need of a daily mail with passenger service to Plymouth instead of the thrice-a-week post
rider. True, no one in his right mind would bump and
creak his way to Plymouth on the first leg of the backbreak-
ing trip of two days and two coach changes to Boston, if
packet weather was right. In fact, there were many Sandwich citizens who lived and died without going to Boston by
land. All the same, Mr. Boyden was secretly convinced that,
though the packet might carry the freight and most of the
passengers, his coach was the more important service.

In spite of periodic exposure to the "glowing anthracite"
of the Webster eyes, Mr. Boyden was an ardent Democrat.
In Jackson's victorious fight with King Biddle and the "monster of Chestnut St.," the United States Bank, Mr. Boyden
was Old Hickory's most enthusiastic and vocal champion
and could cause some inward squirming even among those
who leaned on the superior wisdom of Messrs. Jarves and
Webster. Perhaps — since Mr. Webster was supporting the
Bank — they did not go so far as to believe that the Bank
bought elections and bribed congressmen for the benefit of
the rich. But banking was a new and mysterious power
which, both farm and factory men felt, could easily be
twisted to some evil hocus-pocus.

To be sure, a few sea captains banked in Boston, and Mr.
Jarves with his Boston and Sandwich Company notes was
practically a bank in himself. Banks were even beginning to
creep into the pages of the schoolbooks. Where problems in
arithmetic once had concerned three men mowing a field,
seamen throwing overboard thirty tons of cargo to lighten

ship in a storm, or a thrifty Yankee storekeeper figuring how much water he must add to a hogshead of rum in order to make the desired profit, they now sometimes included exercises involving merchants and banks. However, most Sandwich folk, whether in factory or on farm, could keep their little fistful of surplus cash in an old sock tucked between husk mattress and feather bed. The town was not to have a bank of its own for about two decades.

The convention in front of Fessenden's began to slap and stamp the cold away from fingers and toes as the dusk deepened. Tall talk died while men peered along the street where lamplighted windows made golden patches in the gray twilight. As if by agreement, there were sudden silences when every ear strained for the first faraway rumble of coach wheels and faint clatter of hoofs. Usually, Sandwich could set its clocks by Mr. Boyden's arrival. It was a matter of pride with him. But if this were the night when he really carried the news, excitement might cause him to whip up his horses to greater speed — a thought which had caused the crowd to gather early. Or he might have delayed his departure from Plymouth to await the arrival of a post rider, expected but overdue.

Then there it was — the distant unmistakable sounds of coach and horses right on the appointed time. Nearer and nearer it came — the clatter and creak, the thud of hoofs rising — dying — rising with the gusts of the wind and the turns of the way, swelling to a thunder at the bend by the Unitarian church. Now there came a new sound — the sing and swish of the whip threatening the grays into a final triumphant prance.

"No good news for us," said the Whigs, turning away.

Van Buren had won. Old Hickory would head the government in spirit, if not in substance. The country was still safe for the common man. After the Whigs had recovered from the sting of Mr. Boyden's gloating, they were not too disturbed — especially as Webster's rival candidate, the unknown westerner Harrison, had carried off every Whig state except old Dan'l's own Massachusetts. After all, parties and presidents might come and go without silencing the voice of Webster. Besides, though the majority of Sandwichers thought the party of Mr. Webster and Mr. Jarves good enough for them, even the Whig in the street was willing to grant that there might have been wisdom in Jackson's last acts concerning the public lands to the west.

Everyone knew that the choicest tracts were being scouted out and snapped up by rich speculators with pockets rustling with bank notes. If they could not find a bank to issue notes to them, they made one. The poor homesteaders clutching their sweaty bills and coins, had to pay the gamblers double the government price of a dollar twenty-five an acre for the gobbled land — or else be dispossessed of the homes they had built and the fields they had tilled. Old Hickory had put a stop to that by the Specie Circular of 1836 which provided that all public lands must be paid for in silver and gold, except by actual settlers.

To Sandwich, of course, this was merely abstract ideal. What came nearer home was the law of 1836 providing for the distribution among the states of all the surplus in the treasury on January 1, 1837, above $5,000,000 from the sale of public lands. This luscious plum of $37,000,000 to be "poured into improvements or loaned to the needy" was enough to soften the hardest-headed Whig. The town promptly "voted to receive portion of the surplus revenue of the National Government, the interest to be used for the support of schools, for the maintenance of which $2000 was appropriated." Everything Old Hickory did seemed to make good sound sense to men in the fields and mills, regardless of results.

Results were not long in following Van Buren into office. With gold and silver flowing west to the opening of new public lands, and across the sea to British creditors distrustful of Jackson's money policies, banks began to stop specie payments from New Orleans to Augusta. Sandwich folk could read of a dozen bank failures a week, but the Democratic *Patriot* determinedly discounted this evidence. If "alarm and panic" had been raised about the "hard times and harder times yet," all was due to a wicked plot of the Monster of Chestnut Street to rule or ruin — a plot sure to be foiled by the followers of Old Hickory.

All cause for distress still seemed far away from Sandwich. If Mr. Jarves was not perturbed, the town felt that the foundations of the universe were still firm. Far from showing concern, Mr. Jarves had finally succeeded in launching his oldest son into the world with a bit of a flourish. Young George's glassworks still functioned under the active supervision of a partner while the boy was growing up. But the father had almost given up hope of settling James into anything useful, and it was a moral as well as an economic problem.

"In the United States, a wealthy man thinks that he owes it to public opinion to devote his leisure to some kind of industrial or commercial pursuit or public business. He would think himself in bad repute if he employed his life solely in living," said Count Alexis de Tocqueville, the young French lawyer who came to America to examine penal institutions, but made a far more penetrating study of the institutions of democracy.

Every year, the prospect of making James into a good American business man had become more remote.

At fifteen, James had been "seized with a temporary blindness and a rush of blood at the head which completely destroyed not only all hopes of literary distinction, but even of education — books tabooed, studies at an end, possible blindness even, lotions, bleedings, and bandages, dark rooms and spare diets." For once, he could not lay a disagreeable

condition to an unsympathetic father, but was just enough
to blame "my ambition which led me to the closest applica-
tion and most varied studies" and "the love of my mother
who had encouraged me more zealously than wisely for my
health."

There could be no Harvard now, and without Harvard,
how become a historian! By the time he had partially recovered his sight, he suffered a fresh blow in seeing "my own
ambitions frustrated" by the publication of Prescott's brilliant histories in the field in which he had done much boyish studying and dreaming. For awhile, he shifted his aims
to medicine, but when it came to dissection and surgery,
though he had, as he said, the appetite of a worm for a dead
body, he could not stand the *craunch* of the knife through
living flesh. Then quite suddenly he "arrived at the picturesque age of life which must as naturally be sentimental
and discover angels as fifteen years earlier catch the measles
and drive hoops."

The family had no objection to his choice of angels —
lovely dark Elizabeth of the Swain family of New Bedford
which had turned from seafaring to merchandise — boots
and shoes, to be exact. But here was no case of a young man
with his own land prepared to wrest a living for wife and
children in age-old ways. James was as dependent as a child
himself, and in Mr. Jarves's mind, marriage was not to be
considered. Altogether, James was a weightier paternal problem than the docile little George.

"I was myself imbued with so much of my father's spirit
as to chafe exceedingly at my enforced idleness," James reported later. "I longed for action, but the pursuits he had
suggested to me were so repugnant."

"How would you like to go and seek your fortune in the
South Seas?" the desperate father had finally asked, and must
have been relieved at the answer, "I should be delighted to
go."

Those were the days when, if one had the means, a trip
to Europe or the Orient was the favored remedy for all ail-
ments from tuberculosis to a broken heart. The flight from
reality was supposed to kill or cure, and there were an astonishing number of cures. So James was shipped out with what
was then called an "adventure" — money and merchandise,
including needles and jews-harps, to be turned to account
in trade with the natives. His father settled back with some
skepticism to await results.

James arrived in Honolulu only a little more than fifty
years after Captain Cook had been killed by the cannibals
at Kealakekua Bay and scarcely more than a quarter century after the arrival of the first missionaries. Honolulu, in
spite of being already considered by captains and capitalists
as the halfway house between America and the Orient, a
mart of trade for goods for the Mexican, Russian, Chinese,
and Californian markets, appeared to him "much like a collection of hay-ricks."

Coming from a land and period in which perhaps never
had people so swaddled themselves in clothing, he had a few
New England inhibitions to shed. "I shall not soon forget
my sensation of awkwardness on my first arrival in Honolulu.
While escorting a lady-resident through the streets, a fellow,
naked as Apollo de Belvidere, met us. He was the first I had
seen. I did as anyone would have done just arrived green
from a land of clothing — gazed very intently in another
direction while he passed by," he related, but concluded,
"There is something vulgar in an exposed white skin, but a
red one is so much like many other hues in trees and rocks
or walls about one that a perfect indifference to the common exposure of the person as seen in all warm climates is
soon acquired."

He was not quite so successful in acquiring a fortune, to
judge from the letter quoted in "Why and What Am I?" by
which he claimed that his father acknowledged the first results of his trading.

Dear son: —

The cases, with your letter, have come duly to hand. Your mother insisted upon opening them at the house. The stench from the box of shells, owing to their being packed before they were sufficiently cleaned, caused her a faint turn. So far from their being worth a great sum (the orange cowries you quote at $50 each, and chitons, murexes, volutes, helices, and other shells which, as you have not labelled them, I can not tell apart, at corresponding prices) there is no demand in our market for such articles, except as gifts for curiosity hunters. I sent them all, as a present in your name, to the Natural History Society. In return, they have enclosed to me for you a diploma as an honorable and corresponding member, and beg you to send them more, but to be very particular in packing and labelling their localities. I hope this return will be as satisfactory as your remittance was to me.

You say the natives call you "po kanaka" — the skull man — from your zeal in collecting human crania. I want no better proof of the want of brains in your own skull in sending me twenty of them invoiced as costing you $3.00 apiece in barter. Why, at that rate, you will tempt the savages to kill each other to sell you their filthy heads. I cannot recommend you to repeat the shipment. There is a charge of $43.61 freight which I have passed to your debit. Hoping something more satisfactory from the balance of the invoice in your hand, I am

Your affectionate father

With a letter of quite different tone he represented his mother's reaction.

My dearest son: —

I was delighted to hear of your returning health and all the interesting excursions you had made. The shells you sent were beautiful. I selected a few for the mantel-piece of my little library where everyone admires them. It delights me to have my friends thus reminded of you and to

hear their kind inquiries and predictions that you will one
day distinguish yourself.

Perhaps a particular Sandwich friend of Mr. Jarves, like
Mr. Waterman, heard of James's honorary membership in
some scientific society or other; when George Jarves's business failed, the news ran through the whole town.

There was no surprise at the failure, nor any great alarm.
Everyone knew that young George had played no personal
part in the business. Mr. Jarves, in his preoccupation with
the Sandwich works, had probably depended too much on
an unworthy partner. As yet the wave of panic hardly
rippled on Sandwich shores. Mr. Jarves's little world still
seemed to revolve steadily around him with all men buzzing
about like bees in the life of daily toil which, it was felt, God
had ordained for humankind. It was as unthinkable that
Mr. Jarves should not have work for men in the factory as
that the Lord should not provide food for men from the
earth.

There had, to be sure, been premonitory symptoms. Mr.
Jarves's article of 1835 had numbered the factory workers as
321. A business survey of 1837 gave the count as 231. No
more did Saint Peter's little choir with flute and viols make
the air of Jarvesville sweet with music. No longer was old
Sandwich scandalized by a black-vested priest strolling along
its cozy Calvinistic street — except on the rare occasions
when a missionary came down by packet to say Mass to the
dwindling faithful. Only thirty-two of the seventy original
founders of the church were left, and they could not afford
a resident priest. But no one saw here a warning of general
calamity to come.

"All the men worked in the glass-house," the Catholics reported of themselves, "and they told the Bishop it was a very
bigoted place, and the officers of the Company were much
opposed to Catholics."

This did not apply to Deming Jarves who had no red-hot convictions on religion and cared only about the efficiency with which his work was done. But it was a different matter with some of the resident bosses and some of the workmen themselves, including the Reverend Joseph Mash, Methodist minister, who was advertising for public sale at his home *The Awful Disclosures of Maria Monk.*

Then, too, whenever word of factories closed and men out of work penetrated Sandwich, folk here as elsewhere were apt to blame these foreigners who were swarming in to take away the jobs of good Americans. Thus, every once in so often, some Irish journeyman would go back to the friendlier clime of South Boston, and no one would be brought in to fill his place. No one seemed to notice that the vacant places were not entirely those of sons of Rome, but that in general the less efficient were being weeded out. The trend was at first regarded as a victory for Protestantism rather than a sign of the times.

Then one March morning, the Sandwich farmers looked out upon the cold, pale sky, and there was no pillar of smoke over Jarvesville. Sometimes during a summer heat wave, the fires were drawn, but here was crisp, cold glass-makers' weather, and there was not so much as a smudge on the horizon. Soon the woods were full of the shots of glass-makers a-hunting and the shouts of glassmakers in holiday mood. For surely the shut-down was only a holiday, and within a few days, Mr. Jarves would appear on the packet with a sheaf of new orders. After all, banks might come and banks might go, but people still would eat butter and sugar from glass dishes, drink tea and grog from glass cups and tumblers, lighten their darkness by glass lamp or candlestick.

In those days, there were no salesmen on the road and no printed advertising to create a demand — merely small news-paper notices of where demands already in existence might be fulfilled. Ordinarily, the glass was turned out steadily

through the year, packaged, and stored for shipment spring
and fall to Boston, New York, and Philadelphia where it was
sold to jobbers. There were agents in all three cities to take
care of orders for such staples as apothecaries' ware and
pomade jars — the little dark bears turned out by the hundred to hold the bear grease which added luster to gentlemen's locks and set ladies to crocheting antimacassars all
over the land. But with no money to pay for new demands,
there were no new orders. The unsold glass jammed up the
warehouses. Empty day followed empty day at Sandwich,
while rumors spread and grew.

The daily hunting and fishing soon changed from a pleasure to a chore, especially when a missed shot or unnibbled
bait meant a skimpy meal. Folk took to watching the bay
for the packet or grouping aimlessly in front of the closed
factory door. Sun-scorched land or pest-consumed crops hold
sure promise of better times with a new season, but a closed
door is blank of hope.

The wildest tales became black-and-white certainty with a
legal statement in the paper — a statement which had to be
read a half-dozen times to be believed:

> Notice is hereby given that the Boston and Sandwich
> Glass Company has assigned its estates and effects to us for
> the benefit of its creditors, according to an act entitled "An
> Act to Regulate the Assignment and Distribution of the
> Property of Insolvent Debtors"; and that the Indentures
> may be seen and executed by creditors at the Counting
> Room of the Company, Nos. 101 and 103 Milk St., Boston.
>
> David Dudley
Deming Jarves
Richard S. Fay
>
> April 15, 1837

This was followed in due season by the sales notices of the
company packets:

For sale: — the sloop, Sandwich, 50 tons burthen, a first
rate vessel built under the immediate inspection of the
present owner; carries a large cargo for her tonnage; is now
fit to run through the season with but a trifling expense.

For sale: — the schooner Cabinet, 50 tons burthen, an excellent vessel for shallow water, having a centerboard; will
be sold at a bargain.

                              Apply to Wm. Stutson, Sandwich.

Of course, the advertisement "for sale" did not necessarily
mean that anyone would buy. As a matter of fact, the *Sandwich* was not sold. But the sight of the two packets idling
at the wharf while they waited for someone to sail them off
forever struck chills of apprehension.

2

Men were bewildered from factory to farm. Two kinds of
hard times they had seen and understood — that resulting
from some blight on land or crop and that caused by war
which tore men from the soil and brought floods of worth-
less paper money. Both types the town remembered. In
1830, crops had failed in Sandwich, and schooners were sent
South for food and fodder. The oldsters, particularly the
captains with their broader experience, recalled that back in
1819 there had been a wave of business failures and some
hardship, but that was considered an aftermath of 1812 and
a backwash of the turmoils of Europe.

Here was a paper-money panic and there had been no
war. The soil had given forth its normal increase. The factories stood. Men's hands were willing to work, and men's
mouths still had to be fed and their bodies clothed. Yet
there was a general paralysis as mystifying as an act of God.
Six thousand idle masons, carpenters, and builders pacing
the sidewalks of New York! Two hundred females and forty
males thrown out of a closed mill in Dover, Massachusetts!

Sailors thronging the New Bedford streets from forty whalers tied up at the wharves! Furnaces cold in the big Boston and Sandwich Glass Factory! Others puzzled their heads besides the farmer and factory folk of Sandwich and the simple citizens of New York who conveniently ascribed the catastrophe to a spectacular fire which had destroyed millions of dollars worth of property.

Count de Tocqueville expressed the opinion that the commercial panic was an endemic disease of democratic nations. It was true enough that the common man, in a country and era generally conceded to be his, was finding that his newly granted freedom to outvote the propertied class did not necessarily bring him freedom from want. Yet pre-Victorian England, then hardly a democracy, was in the midst of a depression of its own and was singing its own song.

> Soon a panic came over the town
> And the small men were done most excessively brown
> And a heigh-ho, says Reilly.[1]

In England, speculation had come with the astonishing new steam railroad as in America with the limitless expanses of public lands, but in the hocus-pocus of both countries, it was the little people who were done the brownest.

With a man's hands earning only the tiniest fraction of his own consumption and all lives interlocked, any disturbance in production or distribution left not a soul untouched. Farmers, of course, fared best, except those like the Southern cotton planters who followed the new industrial way of specialization. But even the comparatively self-sufficient farmers of Sandwich felt the pinch. By feeding the factory workers, they had been able to buy their clothing and free their wives from the loom, leaving the weaving to the mills. Now, though they could be sure of keeping from starvation through the longest depression, they found their coats get-

[1] W. S. Kennedy, *Wonders and Curiosities of the Railway.*

ting threadbare and patched and their diet of pork, beans, and corn wearisome without flour and molasses from the store.

Meanwhile, Sandwich storekeepers sat with stiff smiles behind their empty tills and wondered how soon they would be reduced to eating their bars of soap. Soon the paper was carrying the telltale notices of the sheriff's sale of the store of Elisha Pope, the assignment of Gibbs & Burpee "for the benefit of their creditors," the "dissolving" of Ellis & Company, the failure of Joel Powers of the so-called company store, the meeting at the inn of the creditors of one William Thompson, merchant, insolvent debtor. Tailors silently faded from the scene. Glassworkers now had no thoughts of broadcloth suits. Mortgages on mechanics' homes were foreclosed. Houses and lots were "sold at auction in the Glass Factory Village — terms liberal, would rent for $150 a year" — if anyone had the money to pay. It was the thrifty who suffered most as those in company houses were not being evicted.

Everyone was hit, high and low.

"The factory stopped entirely, and had not Providence provided for us by opening the way for Josiah to go to the Legislature, we should have been entirely without support," said Auntie Bacon.

Josiah, once prominent as an anti-Masonic Republican, was now carried to victory behind the triumphant Democratic banner, aided perhaps by the staunch support of former Sabbath school pupils. Eventually, he and Auntie Bacon passed permanently from the Sandwich scene when he became superintendent of the Chelsea Marine Hospital.

Since human flesh is heir to ills, panic or no, the Widow Thayer, another sister of Mrs. Jarves, tried to eke out a living by becoming Sandwich agent for Doctor Bendroth's Universal Vegetable Pills "recommended by thousands of persons whom they have cured of Consumption, Influenza,

Colds, Indigestion, Dyspepsia, Headache, Apoplexy, Jaun-
dice, Fever and Ague, Typhus, Asthma, Gout, Rheumatism,
Liver Complaints, Pleurisy, Ruptures, Sore Eyes, Fits, Palsy,
Dropsy, Smallpox, Measles, Croup, Cholera Morbus, Whooping Cough, Quinzy, Cholic, Worms, Dysentery, Deafness,
King's Evil [Scrofula], Erysipelas or St. Anthony's Fire,
Ulcers, Cancer, Tumors, Piles, Swelled Feet and Legs, Erup-
tion of the Skin, Ringing Noises in the Head, Depression of
the Spirits, and Frightful Dreams." "Also recommended for
blasting rock in the western mining country," reported the
Patriot Editor who had apparently experienced the effect.

Michael Doyle, the Irish gaffer, put his savings into a
tavern on the main road, apparently believing that Sandwich would revert to a sportman's paradise once more, but
he soon failed. Mere sportsmen had even less chance in competition with hungry hordes to whom a successful shot meant
the difference between a full or empty stomach than they
had had during the days of the factory's prosperity.

Some workmen were said to be trying to squeeze out a
penny by melting their pewter buttons and making salt, but
this rumor was indignantly denied.

> Mr. Editor:
> Please publish the following quere [sic!] in your paper.
> When did the Workmen in the Glass House ever melt the
> pewter buttons on their coats? How long since they made
> ten bushels of salt per day at the Glass House? The com-
> munication ought to have been signed Munchausen. They
> have not made five bushels of salt in three months.
>
> Sandwich

But it is certain that they walked the streets and worried
and once in a while drifted off to the city, lured away by the
common human delusion that conditions must be better
elsewhere.

All at once, men rubbed their eyes and saw in the midst of

their social structure a permanent and steadily increasing class which did not derive a living from the land or special skills, but existed as a mere adjunct of the machine, to be thrown into idleness and want with every stoppage of the money-motive power which turned the wheels.

Reforms took voice and shape everywhere. The Jacksonians clamored for a complete separation of the money power from the government, an Independent Treasury. Wasn't credit — a gambling on the future with unreal money — the cause of the crash? A cash-and-carry government for cash-and-carry people, and the world would be firm again!

There was some reason for popular distrust of banks in general, for records of one year — 1839 — show "fiscal rascality and depredation" of bank officials on the public as amounting to $42,262,000. The roster ran from end to end of the country — from "Bank of Louisiana — by the cashier — $60,000" to "six Maine banks — $800,000."

An even more radical branch of the Democratic party, the Locofocos, made its voice heard in the land, a party of "mechanics and laborers, believing in free trade, equal rights for all men, opposition to all bank notes and paper money as circulating medium and to all forms of exclusive privilege in a crusade against banks and monopolies."

All points of view were heard in Sandwich. The constant clashes were highlighted by a scene in the stagecoach between the redoubtable Mr. Boyden and the Whig Representative in Congress which, after making the rounds of the town, reached the columns of the *Patriot*.

> When Boyden reined up his team at that most capital of halfway houses, Mr. Cornish's, and prepared to collect the fare, 'twas pleasant to notice the nonchalance with which that intelligent and gentlemanly contractor and driver (who is an independent democrat and whole-soul'd citizen) received the joke of his honorable and *witty* customer who

threw down a "yellow boy," alias a half eagle, to pay his
fare, accompanying his sleight-of-hand with the remark,
sneeringly and sarcastically to Boyden whose politics he appeared to be acquainted with, "There's the stuff you folks
like so well. I've been trying to get rid of mine."

"Well," says Boyden, "I'm your customer. I'll give you
suet-skins for all the *mint drops* you've got."

"Done," says the honorable, and suiting the action to the
words pulled out a little bag containing some half dozen
eagles.

Evidently beginning to relent as Boyden handled his big
pocketbook for the shin-plasters, "But stop — I must have
Barnstable Bank bills," hoping probably to find Boyden
wanting.

"Very well," says the latter, "I can accommodate you,"
and gathered up the glisteners with one hand, shuffled off
to the gentleman his own better currency with the other —
which was pocketed with a shrug of the shoulders and a
twist of the jaws while a thunder cloud seemed to pass over
the countenance which told emphatically that he enjoyed
the joke less than the rest of us. But his fellow passengers
enjoyed it and could not but admire the tenacity with which
those who ridicule a metallic currency cling to the precious
solids after all.

Of course, Biddle of the bankers had his answer to the
challenge of the times:

> The best friends of the laboring classes are the banks;
> what laboring people want is labor, work, constant employ-
> ment. How can they get it? In building ships and building
> houses, in coal mines, in making roads and canals, and how
> are these carried on except by credit in the shape of loans
> from banks. If there was nothing but gold and silver in the
> country, the banks would be limited to what could be paid
> by gold and silver, and the owners of gold and silver would
> be the only persons who could employ workmen so that all
> the men who had nothing but their industry to depend on

could have no chance of getting up in the world. The greatest misfortune to the laboring classes would be to banish
the system of credit. In fact, the present troubles are mainly
owing to the absurd attempt to force gold and silver into
circulation. Gold and silver are for the rich — bank notes
are the democracy of currency. The laboring classes ought
therefore to stand by the banks as their best friends.[2]

The more thoughtful who saw in the growth of capitalistic
power and the new insecurity of the worker a revolutionary
threat to good old ways were dreaming schemes which would
have a brief struggle for existence when once the numbness
of the shock of the panic had given way to the lusty reaction
of the forties. The efforts to make the new machine-age
power co-operative instead of tyrannical ranged from the
purely idealistic to the wholly fantastic.

Gentle George Ripley was devising his "Institute for Agriculture and Education" whereby head and hand could labor
together with equal reward and honor, an ideal which was
brought to flower in Brook Farm. Energetic Albert Brisbane
imported from Europe the socialism contrived by Charles
Fourier as a backfire to the utterly anarchistic red revolution
of France which, it was feared, would bring about a class war
destructive of all cultural achievement of the past. Its so-
called Phalanx or co-operative community aimed at making
industry attractive to the laboring classes and treating capital, labor, and talent as partners entitled to share the profits
in the proportions of five twelfths to labor, four twelfths to
capital, and three twelfths to talent. Eventually, Brisbane's
newspaper, *The Phalanx,* of the panic years, was to multiply
into forty others of the same views and bring into being no
less than thirty-four experimental Fourieristic communities.
But without the support of capitalists, who were more intent
on saving their own skins than making industry attractive
to the worker, these dream worlds soon faded into thin air.

2 R. C. McGrane, *The Panic of 1837.*

Besides, the feebly sprouting local associations of workers could see even less in Fourierism than the capitalists.

"All that Fourierism will agree to," said the Land Reformers, "is that a capitalistic class, having its origin in injustice, shall to all eternity live on the toil of the industrious." [3]

The Land Reformers offered their western "Rural Republican Townships" as cure-all — a complete, self-sustaining economic unit with its own farms, traders, small mechanics, and shops with no need for national or international trade or centralized industrial production. This was sponsored by George Henry Evans, an English immigrant, who advocated free public land to actual settlers, exemption of homesteads from seizure for debt, limitation of the land any one person might acquire: "Place the surplus mechanics on their own land in Rural Republican Townships, leaving full employment to those who remain in the cities — and all will be well."

Two Sandwich men, old William Fessenden, one-time innkeeper, and a younger partner, Charles Freeman, sought to profit by the surge toward western lands, advertising:

> Lots for sale in the town of Northampton, Illinois, known as Indian Tramping Ground. Extensive view of the Illinois River and Laselle River. Flouring and Saw Mills within one mile. Stone and coal is abundant. The cold and severe winds of winter are held back by a range of elevated woods. Pure water is obtained by digging 15 feet. First rate tavern house and stable where travellers can be comfortably accommodated. The subscribers erected a store in the village last summer. Terms — one half cash and the remainder in one year. Bills on broken banks or on some that call themselves sound, but are whited sepulchres, will not be received.

But the factory unemployed did not have even the cur-

[3] Norman J. Ware, *The Industrial Worker 1840–1860.*

rent purchase price of a dollar twenty-five an acre for public lands, and it would have made little difference anyway. Men of the mills were developing a herd psychology which made the lonely freedom of the farm fearful to contemplate. "We have always been used to live in a town where we could get what little things we want if we have money," they said, "and it is only those who have lived in the wilderness who know what the horrors of wilderness life are." [4]

They could more accurately have remarked that only those who have *not* lived in the wilderness can feel for it the utter terror of the unknown. But results were the same. Men of the factories and tenements preferred to huddle in companionable wretchedness. A Rural Republican Township was not an opportunity, but an exile. So in the bitter winter of 1838, people of the cities starved and froze to death or became disease-ridden by the thousand. Folk who had always earned their bread begged up and down the streets. Poorhouses were stuffed to overflowing and "the number of unemployed increased to such a degree that the ordinary means (private charity and municipal almshouses) were inadequate to relieve even those who were destitute of every one of the necessities of life."

In New York, a flour warehouse was stormed by a hungry mob. In Sandwich, the paper offered helpful recipes for arrageen or Irish moss to be gathered on the shore and combined with a two-cent lemon or "savories" which might be found in the woodland. But where wood could be had for the cutting, fish and game for the taking, no one froze or starved to death. However, the lean, leathery cheeks of the Democratic Coachman Boyden, who was also church deacon, were wet with tears in listening to the plaints of the poor applying for aid, and he was known to pass out help from his own pocket as well as the church treasury. As far as the glassworkers were concerned, their problems were solved

4 Norman J. Ware, *op. cit.*

without any violent acts, inflammatory words, or airy experiments.

One day — one more day when men made their mechanical round of dreary inspection of the closed factory door,
tense hours with rod and gun, hopeless watching for the
packet, there was the packet indeed, low-laden in the water.
New orders? None, but a goodly supply of flour and
molasses, corn, beans, beef, and basic food-stuffs, and once
more a company store and storekeeper; not to sell, but to
dispense free food to the needy. There was also posted a
notice that when the factory was closed, no rent would be
charged for the factory houses. Mr. Jarves had not entered
fully into the spirit of the new capitalism whereby the people were used in good times and cast off in bad. This was his
factory — in his own mind, at least. This was his Jarvesville
and these were his people. It was his duty to care for them
as the feudal lords of old cared for the peasants on their
lands.

Mr. Jarves also had the undying faith in the future which
has been the country's greatest asset. Hard times could not
last forever, and when they ended, here would be his skilled
workers at hand and not scattered to the cities for other
glasshouses to recruit. Besides, Anna had given him fresh
hope in the form of yet another son — "the ninth child and
the sixth son," as the youngest scion himself liked to express
it. Besides James, George, John, and little Billy of the croup
express, there had been a boy babe still-born. This was not
counting the three young daughters, Anna Maria, Mary, and
Isabella. The new son was, Mr. Jarves realized, a last hope
and with his unfailing optimism, he named the baby Deming, Jr.

In the midst of the turmoil, the eldest, James Jackson,
arrived back at 64 Boylston Street — last and most impressive
of the successive Boston residences of the Jarves family.
Ever playing out his chosen part as romantic wanderer, he

had not taken the conventional voyage around the Horn, but had journeyed by horseback across the Isthmus from sea to sea — a trip which few white men had taken from the days of Balboa. Though as devoid of fortune or business prospects as when he had departed, he married his Elizabeth and they soon set out together. California was their goal — land of promise, flowing with milk and honey, taken over from Spain by Mexico after she had won her own freedom. There had been glowing accounts from Elizabeth's brother, one of the many adventurers of English, French, and American blood who had flocked in, seeking personal gain and *de facto* possession for their respective countries after the Spanish mission fathers had been ousted from their rich holdings.

Here was a spirit of enterprise of which Mr. Jarves would thoroughly approve. Neither he nor even the doting Anna were quite so approving when accounts began to come back of the leisurely and luxurious voyage along the coast of South America. The bridegroom was, in spite of his early ill health, of a stalwart build with burning eyes which held a challenge for all women. The bride was dark and glowing as the loveliest señorita, and adored the babble and bustle of society. Every time the ship stopped in a South American port, the rich young Yanquis were greeted with a royal welcome and in Valparaiso, they gave a glittering ball which made local history — while Mr. Jarves was supplying the bare necessities to his idle workers. James found in California too crass a grabbing for gain and passed on to the lush indolence of Hawaii where trade could be at a minimum and love-making a business in itself. Settling down, he gave only perfunctory service to commerce and became the owner and editor of *Polynesia*, the first newspaper in the islands.

Back at the factory, conditions teetered from bad to slightly better. Mr. Jarves had effected some sort of settlement of the bankruptcy proceedings. Once in a while orders dribbled in. The coronation of England's young Queen helped the situation with a vogue for Victoria cup plates for export trade. The glasshouse began to run by fits and starts, to the great disgust of John Trout who alone had gloated over the smokeless chimneys.

A sportsman visiting Sandwich in 1838 reported meeting

> old John Trout in the fresh of the morning with the same basket and landing net he carried when Webster was a boy and took his first lesson in killing a monarch with ground bait. John only throws a fly now and then. The old veteran is as keen at the sport as ever, and somehow neither cold water outside nor fire water in has used him up. There is not an old root or eddy or covert in all the brooks 20 miles around that old John has not dropped his hooks into. In all but sentimentality, he is a very Walton. John shakes his head at your glass-houses, factories, and modern improvements with the sovereign contempt of leather stockings for clearings. They have played the mischief with the streams and, as John said, subdued nearly all the brooks. The old fellow will talk over the deeds of former days, shoulder his rod, and show the marks of the fish he used to land, and then sigh that things are not what they were. One of the glass houses has stopped in Sandwich for the present which is a great comfort to John.

The traveler also reported that, compared to the rest of the country, there was little sign of the hard times to be seen in Sandwich. But "the people have seen and felt just enough of the mischief of banks to despise them, and if there is one universal sentiment in the country, it is opposition to banks."

Besides the banks, the chief sensation of the times was the presence of a wolf in the woodlands, the last to appear in Sandwich in many a year. This beast — which no one had seen — assumed legendary proportions. The longer it prowled, the larger grew the stories — and the reward for the slayer.

It surely sucked the blood of many an old shéep, but it was said to crunch up little lambs, skin and bones. Now it was no longer a wolf, but a tiger escaped from a shipwrecked schooner bound for Boston. Its footsteps were so broad and sunken that a "man's meager foot was literally buried in their depths." The last and most daring of its exploits was "said to have been the devouring of a black woman by the name of Follow who left Sandwich to walk through the woods to Mashpee plantation, a distance of nine miles, and has not been seen or heard from."

Children were kept away from lonely places. Every man who entered the woods with his gun had hopes of winning the reward of $100 and fear of ignominy if the creature, sighted, should get away.

Finally, however, the *Patriot* headlined "TIGER DEAD PROVES TO BE WOLF. It was shot dead by Mr. George A. Braley, teamster in the employ of the Boston and Sandwich Glass Co. who will now become richer by $100, a very pretty present in these hard times."

For awhile, the pelt was nailed to the front of the town hall. Then, with the family initiative which would lead in a later generation to the founding of the famous Chicago packing firm, William Swift, the horse trader and cattle farmer of North Sandwich, bought it to exhibit for admission up and down the Cape. The excitement was over. Once more the chief topic of talk was the panic.

In the middle of 1838, with the repeal of Jackson's Specie Circular and the defeat of Van Buren's Sub-treasury, the banks all resumed specie payment again, and it looked as if hard times might be over. But Biddle and his big United States Bank of Pennsylvania, as the "Monster of Chestnut St." had become, had been speculating in cotton. The bank crashed, carrying with it the banks of most of the cotton states.

New York and New England banks still held firm, but

new panic spread, and in a panic, even a "pet" bank with U.S. Treasury deposits was far from immune. Van Buren once more pressed for his Independent Treasury. "To place our foreign and domestic policy under the control of a foreign moneyed interest has impaired the independence of our banks," declared his message of 1839.

The great Clay and Webster once more came to the aid of banking powers. Clay cried alarm at an act which would unite the power "of the sword and the purse." Webster shrewdly pointed out that the sole concern of the Independent Treasury Act was relief for the government — not a thought had been given to relief for the people.

"Is government," he trumpeted, "to care for nothing but itself? I think not! I think the government exists not for its own ends, but for the public utilities."

Mr. Jarves, as always, staunchly supported Webster and the Websterian views. The Democratic *Barnstable Patriot* printed the carefully spread rumor that "workingmen who vote contrary to the wishes of their employer need not expect further employment after election."

Such attempted control of the workers' votes was common practice among many mill owners of the period. In some cases, operatives were herded into vans and delivered at the polls. But such was not the way of Mr. Jarves. Promptly after the published insinuations of threats to the workers by "missionaries from the city" came a positive denial, signed by seventy-five glassworkers:

> It is being insinuated around that it [this reported coercion] is intended to apply to the Boston & Sandwich Glass Co. We do declare that we have been employed in this establishment for varying periods — some for ten or twelve years — and that we have during this time suffered no molestation on account of our political principles, and though of different political opinions, no attempt has been made by our employers to move or control us in the manner charged

in the above article. It is also known to us that when the
reduction took place in the number of hands, men of both
parties were discharged and in the same way have men of all
parties been employed since the increase of business. In regard to "missionaries from the city," we have seen no person
but Mr. Jarves, the General Agent of the Boston Glass Co.
who has been in the habit of visiting the works in the Spring
and Fall of each year and returned recently from his accustomed visit (which business might seem to require) of
about 10 days. In justice to the gentleman [who is probably referred to in the above article] we do not hesitate to
express ourselves that he never entertained or expressed any
such intention or design as imputed to him, and we believe
the article to be wholly false.

Among the signatories were old town names — Hallett,
Fish, Chipman, Nye, Freeman, Swift, the aristocracy of glassmakers — Samuel Lloyd, the Kern, Haines, Lapham, and
Mash brothers, and the sons of Saint Peter's — Daniel Fogarty, Thomas McCarthy, John Murphy. There were also
Ebenezer Chamberlain, the ex-convict, Samuel Harper, one-
time runaway apprentice, and the deaf and dumb Newcomb
brothers.

3

Amid the thunder of Websterian oratory and waves of
economic uncertainty, Sandwich reached the two hundredth
anniversary of its founding.

Two hundred years before, in 1639, the first settlers had
stopped on Sandwich shores because here God had provided
all that man needed to live in abundance by the labor of his
hands. Now though there were men for whom there was no
sure labor and no sure living, to the folk of the old town
tilling the land their forefathers had cleared, the two centuries of continuity made cause for celebration, regardless of

present or future. They began to ransack their attics that Edmund Freeman and his founding band and Doctor Nathaniel Freeman's Revolutionary Crusaders to Barnstable Courthouse might ride the streets once more. To their surprise, a delegation of glassworkers came forward and offered to add a "float" to the parade.

An ancient gaffer had remembered how, in the processions of the guilds in old London, the glass blowers had carried off all the honors, and they promised a show for Sandwich no less spectacular. Here was a chance for them, too, to feel their connection with a worthy past and display pride in honorable traditions of their own. They made a miniature furnace of clay and firebricks about twenty-seven inches in diameter with three tiny clay pots, each containing about two pounds of glass. This was set up in a large wagon, the floor of which had been covered with clay and then with iron. The furnace and its iron chimney were braced firmly in position by stout iron guys to the sides of the wagon. The workers who manned it were spangled with gaudy glass baubles and flashed sashes of bent glass rods slung over the right shoulder and under the left arm. Flaunting its banner of smoke and drawn by prancing and apprehensively wild-eyed grays, the rolling show held the eyes of the crowd and attracted a cavalcade of small boys who ran after it along the street.

With the jouncing of the wagon over the sandy road and the breezy unevenness of draft, the little glass furnace was not wholly a success, but the bystanders could not realize it in the midst of the sleight-of-hand performance that was taking place. Even if the melted glass which had been ladled into the little pots at the factory could not be worked as wished, the men had brought some glass tubes, and by heating them over the little pots, they made small glass balls — some blue, some red, as well as crystal — which they airily tossed out to the throng. They also had slender glass rods which they heated and bent and twisted into fanciful shapes with their tools. Holding them in their pincers, they reached them out over the side of the wagon to the eager boys who would grab them red-hot, and then tuck them suddenly under their arms to ease their scorched fingers while the glassmakers would roar with laughter at their grimaces.

It was a dazzling show of skill, and Sandwich vaguely felt there was something wrong with a world where there was no steady market for the labor of such craftsmen. However, Congress was still arguing over setting it to rights. Henry Clay had a few last words to say in favor of banks and against the increased concentration of power in a central government. "For long years we have been warring against the alarming growth of executive power . . . under all the usual false and hypocritical pretence and disguises of love of the people and desire for reform . . . but I again thank God that our deliverance is at hand, and that on March 4, 1841, a great and glorious revolution without blood and without convulsion will be achieved."

For catching the popular vote, Old Hickory had shown that there was nothing like a general. Though with General William Henry Harrison of the Indian campaigns and War of 1812, the Whigs had lost the last presidential election to Van Buren as Jackson's heir, they dusted off old Tippecanoe once more. And to their good fortune the opposition, in attempting to belittle Harrison's presidential qualifications, unwittingly supplied some very effective campaign slogans. Wrote the Democratic *Baltimore American*:

"Give him a barrel of hard cider and settle a pension of two thousand a year on him, and my word for it, he will sit the remainder of his days in a log cabin."

Here was the man for the masses! He did not crave the presidential palace, but would be satisfied with the log cabin of the humblest. He drank the common man's hard cider, and not champagne like Van Buren who, they had heard, ate from gold and silver plate.

The West came forward with a song:

> Ole Tip he wears a homespun suit.
> He has no ruffled shirt.

New York concocted another:

> What has caused this great commotion, motion,
>   Our country through?
> It is the ball a-rolling on
>   For Tippecanoe and Tyler, too,
>   Tippecanoe and Tyler, too.

Having sung of a commotion, the Whigs proceeded to whip one up. They brought forth large log cabins to dispense hard cider to the crowds, little log cabins to be paraded on wheels, festoons of coonskins, and months of frolic and song in a rollicking, rabble-rousing campaign without equal before or since. The Boston and Sandwich Company hurried to swing into the prosperity parade. The designers of pressed ware rushed out a new mold in time to catch the trade — the "Industry" pattern — log cabin bordered by two toiling plowmen, ship in full sail and factory in full smoke. It was supposed to typify the bustling, prosperous world to be brought in by Tippecanoe, and though the factory had its prominent and recognized place, the log cabin here, as in the minds of most people, still held the center of the stage.

This time Mr. Boyden bore the news of the election returns to Sandwich with no flourish of whip. Old Tippecanoe swept in on a landslide and promptly died, leaving his place to the not too thoroughly converted Democrat, "Tyler, too" which was rather more than the Whigs had bargained for. But the panic, like a fire, had just about burned itself out, and business was beginning to show signs of life again.

What with continued breakage over the years and a surge of new styles, agents in Boston, New York, and Philadelphia reported that once more there would be a good market for glass in the spring and fall sales. And if any glass sold, it would be that of the Sandwich factory which had supplied even the White House in Washington with gleaming flint tableware and a great sparkling chandelier.

Orders increased in 1840:

> 50 casks of "Buttres" in Roseleaf, Clod, and Mica designs, 50 barrels and 90 small boxes of salts in Cape Cod and other patterns referred to by number, 30 boxes and 95 barrels of Nappies in Cape Cod, Comet, Vine, Washington, and numbered patterns — of the "Fire Polished Shank Articles," 50 casks of goblets, 30 casks of champagnes, and 30 barrels of Wines in Utica, Huber, and Raised Diamond patterns; — in the famous Opal Ware — one move — or lier full — of match boxes and covers, 10 small packages of Bird Founts, 5 small packages of Bird Baths, and casks, barrels and boxes by the tens and the dozens of Square Butters, Opal Sets, Niol Jugs, 7 in. Nappies on feet, and salvers; and 100 barrels of Flint sets of sugar, creamer, and spoon-holder together with miscellany such as bowls, cake covers, celleries, light peppers, and fish globes.[5]

Once more the *Patriot* carried one of its panegyrics of the plant: "There is no establishment in the United States for the manufacture of glass so extensive and well-arranged as the one at Sandwich, nor is there one on this or the other side of the Atlantic which manufactures the great variety of glassware in such perfection as at that place."

A Mr. Keer of a reputedly "famous China Hall in Boston" added his endorsement in the form of an anecdote:

> Some two or three years ago, Mr. Webster had been at a dinner party in Philadelphia. A few days after, he was in Mr. Keer's store making certain purchases, and mentioned to Mr. K. the splendid set of imported glass that adorned his friend's table. To his astonishment, Mr. K. informed him that every article of the admired set had been manufac-

5 Frank W. Chipman, *The Romance of Sandwich Glass.*

tured within 20 miles of his own residence, and in confirma·
tion of the fact exhibited his books to him, containing the
original entries of debt and credit. Mr. K. declares that no
foreign glass can be compared in clearness and beauty with
that made at the Boston and Sandwich works.

To celebrate the return of better times, or perhaps for
advertising purposes, Deming Jarves presented a set of flint·
glass tableware to his hero, Daniel Webster. Webster, who
as Secretary of State was the only member left of the Harri·
son cabinet, acknowledged the gift in the usual vein of
urbane courtesy and calm:

Washington, July 10, 1841.

My dear Sir: —
    I have to thank you for your very handsome present of
glass which arrived yesterday. All the pieces came safe and
are exceedingly elegant.
    They have substance as well as beauty, and I shall have
much pleasure in exhibiting them as specimens of the skill
and industry of Massachusetts.

Again a market was rising for "the skill and industry of
Massachusetts." The factory stacks now smoked steadily,
though there were still a fifth fewer hands employed than in
the peak of 1836. Stores reopened in town. Two new
tailoring shops appeared on the scene, for glass blowers
could buy broadcloth suits again. All was well with the
world — until the next time.

Full Steam Ahead!

GLASSWORKER on the sloop *Sandwich* and farmer on the
sloop *Sarah,* homeward bound from a Boston holiday,
strained at the rail as the rivals, for all the creak and roar
of a billowing breeze in a full head of sail, seemed to inch
past well-known landmarks. Little boy and loafer on the
home wharf bragged and bet their last pennies as they waited
to cheer the winner into the channel of the creek. There
was nothing that stirred the blood like a good packet race
down the blue bay from Boston. On the question of the
relative fleetness of town and company sloops — and the sea-
manship of the various captains, Atkins, Gibbs, and Fessenden — hung the possession of the spare change and control
of the stray tempers of Sandwich and Jarvesville.

Though Mr. Jarves had named the packet sloop built for
the glassworks by courtesy in honor of the town, Sandwich
would have none of her. In spite of the expansion and material benefits the coming of the factory had brought, townspeople unconsciously resented a feeling that they were com-

146

ing to be considered thralls of the company — and Mr. Jarves. It would feel good to outwit Mr. Jarves — and the company — in so small a matter even as the speed of a packet. Accordingly, the loyalties of the townspeople were all with the *Sarah,* successor to the *Henry Clay* which ran to and from Boston with passengers and wood.

Once the native Sandwichers accepted the fact that Mr. Jarves's boat so outclassed the *Sarah* that there was no fun in bragging or betting, they appeared from Boston one fine day with a schooner, the *Nancy Finlay.* Here was cause for gloating, for what was a sloop beside a schooner? Exultation was short-lived, however, for the Boston and Sandwich Company had soon purchased a schooner of their own, another *Sarah,* which made the old *Nancy Finlay* look like a wallowing tub. Townsfolk tried again and again. Town and company competed not only for speed, but for passengers in the good old free-for-all American way. Fares dropped by degrees from one dollar to twenty-five cents, and many a villager found to his indignation that it cost just twice as much to ride by hack from wharf to hotel in Boston as for the whole trip up by packet from Sandwich.

Sandwich soon found in tests day in and day out that Mr. Jarves generally had shrewdly seen that he had the best. They then gave up the struggle on equal terms. After all, why did they need a heavy freighter when most of the freight was for the company and carried by the *Sarah?* So they bought the lean, lovely racing sloop *Osceola,* for speed alone, and now with a favoring breeze, enough bets were won by devoted townsmen to make life worth living once more.

Of course, the master and owners of the *Osceola* did not spurn such company freight as overflowed the *Sarah's* hold. They might beat the company packet once in a while, but they could never stand up against company power. They could only as "most respectfully your verrey obedient servants" express to the Directors of the Boston and Sandwich

Glass Company "their earnest desire that a mutual understanding shall exist that neither their own or the Company's
Packet shall be expected to leave port on the Sabbath Day." [1]

The petitioners could well be very respectful and obedient. The pendulum swing back from panic to prosperity
had left the increasing numbers who could not live on their
own land more firmly in the clutch of those who controlled
the new machinery of living. Wages shrunken by the depression did not improve with the times. Worse still in the eyes
of most of the workers, was the loss of self-respect and social
standing which had accompanied their change of status from
that of craftsmen to mere hired "hands" supplementing the
monotonous operations of a machine.

They began to protest "a state of servitude less enviable
than that of the vassals of the feudal lords and princes — because they may hold the name, but lose the right of freeman.
They [the capitalists] seem to think that the workers are designed for no other purpose than to be their subjects. They
seem to think — that the laborer is not as good as other
people."

The end of the depression, moreover, had not calmed the
fear of the intellectuals of social revolution caused by the
"new commercial feudalism and subjection of the producing
classes to the absolute control and tyranny of capital." Horace
Greeley was advising the discontented worker to "go west
where independence and plenty may be found" — in other
words, to flee the problems of the present into the security
of the way of past generations.

Workingmen began to develop ideas of their own, and in
1845 a laborers' union of South Boston resolved "that as
practical laborers who have not the means or the inclination
to withdraw from society, we deem it incumbent on us to
use all the means in our power to remove existing evils
from the present state of society." The workers' own ideas

1 Ruth Webb Lee, *Sandwich Glass.*

ran mostly to producers' and consumers' unions. They covered a wide range. There was a plan, never more than pure vision, for a "unitary edifice" with community store on the ground floor, hall for concerts, library, art gallery, and school in the second story, and manufacturing operations, such as printing and shoemaking shops in the third. But there was also a consumers' co-operative in practical operation with "enough in the union to charter a small vessel to the West Indies for sugar and molasses." [2]

Because of the foresight of Mr. Jarves in selecting his site, Sandwich workers were well insulated by distance from the ferment working in the cities. Sailors of the packet *Sarah,* squirming in a fear that souls as well as bodies were in the control of the company, could only add a protest to that of townsmen and crew of the *Osceola* and

> hereby represent that ofttimes we have been constrained to leave port on the Sabbath day from the consideration lest we should not give satisfaction to our employers. We have feared that if the wind and tide were favorable and we did not improve them, even though it were on the Sabbath, we might be charged with negligence of duty. We have labored, some of us at least, under the painful apprehension — that in our course we were not giving satisfaction to our Creator. We have proportionately to our frequent violation of the law and rest of the Holy Sabbath been debard and shut out from the privileges of The Sanctuary and we are fully persuaded neither to our own or the pecuniary benefit of the Company whose servants we are.[3]

It is doubtful whether this plea impressed the directors of the Boston and Sandwich Company with the pecuniary advantage of one idle day in the week. Moving out the company freight on a good Sabbath tide might be compared with the Biblical rescue of the ass from the pit. Whenever work-

2 Norman J. Ware, *The Industrial Worker 1840–1860.*
3 Ruth Webb Lee, *Sandwich Glass.*

ers anywhere ventured to protest their hours, they were promptly met with the arguments that "the human system was peculiarly adapted to long hours of labor" and that shorter hours would only "encourage idleness and vice to divide the land." Besides, it was pointed out that capitalists, too, worked long hours — a fact which was true enough in a land which had as yet no leisure class.

Meanwhile, flouting the honored American tradition of a life of industry for rich and poor alike, James Jackson Jarves had arrived lightheartedly home from Hawaii with his wife, two babies burdened with the names Chevelita and Horatio, and the material for two books. His years as editor of the newspaper *Polynesia* had netted him little more than a libel suit, and he was still as financially dependent as a child.

The publication of the two books, *History of the Hawaiian or Sandwich Islands, embracing their Antiquities, Mythology, Legends, Discovery by Europeans in the Sixteenth Century, Rediscovery by Cook, with their Civil, Religious, and Political History* and *Scenes and Scenery in the Sandwich Islands and a Trip through Central America: Being Observations from my Note-Book during the years 1837-1842* fulfilled to some extent the boyish ambition to be author and historian. His style ran a bit lushly to fairy-jewel dewdrops and misty-bosomed mountains. Before "Dear Reader" could fall into a stupor, however, he would be jolted wide-eyed by a surprising appreciation of the manner in which the missionaries had augmented the income of native kings by adding to the profit from copra the "fines of women caught in fornication"; or some such rare anecdote as that of the wife of the lone white missionary who, "sent for to assist at the accouchement of the young and pretty wife of the chief who ruled the island" was dismayed at "the extraordinary whiteness of the infant which the mother somewhat naïvely accounted for by her having eaten for some time before much *white* bread."

Though young Jarves could not fulfill his father's last hope of a respectable life for him by harnessing his restless mind to some learned profession, he soon found his literary fame too limited for any prolonged basking. There was not much profit or romance in the career of author and world traveler at a time when New England was full of sea captains who had touched the uttermost islands and most exotic lands in the common course of trade. Besides, in those days, travel to odd corners of the earth did not hold the same sense of hardship and adventure that has given it an aura of romance in a later age of swift and comfortable transportation on the world's highways. After all, whether in Sandwich or the Sandwich Islands, modes of conveyance by sail and horse power were essentially the same.

With the help of James Jackson Jarves and the money made by glass in Sandwich, Massachusetts, the Sandwich Islands had preceded the New England village by some years in one of the appurtenances of civilization. In 1845, years after *Polynesia* had flourished and faded, a certain enterprising Mr. Phinney set up the first newspaper in Sandwich. With one eye on Sandwich and the other on Jarvesville, Mr. Phinney steered a non-partisan course and kept clear of the fiery politics of his Cape contemporaries. His little twenty-four-column folio, *The Sandwich Observer,* was devoted to "general and local news and miscellany" which included an occasional essay by Mr. Deming Jarves on the history and manufacture of glass.

Of "general news" there was aplenty. The country was in the midst of that period of a nation's development, always so painful to its weaker neighbors, when its "manifest destiny" was expansion. This destiny Mr. Keith reflected by adding the making of Conestoga wagons to his line of vehicles. These schooners of the plain and prairie were carrying the vanguard of the army of westward seekers for freedom from the growing complications of the machine age, mostly old-stock folk who could not be herded into factories like the waves of immigrants fleeing the various tyrannies and deprivations of Europe. American arms had wrested Texas free from Mexico. American eyes were on Mexican California and British-claimed Oregon.

Sandwich, of course, cut its views of "manifest destiny" to the words of its idol, Daniel Webster, opposing annexation of the independent republic of Texas with its resulting Mexican War, and hailing the Oregon Compromise as averting needless hostilities with England. Webster was still clinging stubbornly to the ideal that the American nation should be an example and shining light to the world, and this ideal did not include indiscriminate land-grabbing. So Sandwich in general nodded approval of Webster's attempts to avert war and discussed in voices low with sympathy the fate of his hot-headed son who, in defiance of his father's course, had joined Caleb Cushing's regiment of volunteers and got himself killed. Since it was largely a volunteer war, Sandwich, which did not choose to fight, was untouched except by sympathy and news stories.

2

Through war, peace, or politics, no news which the *Sandwich Observer* carried in those stirring times moved the people like the word that the railroad was coming. Of course, a road of rails in itself was no novelty to a town which for years had watched the horse-drawn bogy sliding across the marsh to the deep-water wharf, and elsewhere coaches on rails had been hauled by horse or even blown along by sail. But come travel by air or travel by atom, nevermore would there be such a complete break with the past as that brought about by steam locomotion. Later inventions might bring swifter, smoother, and less expensive forms of mechanical transportation. Not again would come the almost incredible miracle which was about to supplant the God-given power of wind and brute, and it was a miracle which would change the face of the world.

Hitherto, kiths and cultures had clustered along waterways and had been walled off into alien entities by the barriers of mountains and waste lands. Perhaps if mankind had been blessed from the beginning with the secret of rapid and easy transit, humanity would not have had its endless bloody wrestling with the apparently never-to-be-solved problems of the Old World. America was in danger of going the same way when Peter Cooper's puffing little "Tom Thumb" blew a band and lost its tortoise-and-hare race to the stout gray coach horse on the Baltimore Line. There was the industrial and commercial Northeast with its seaboard and river system, the rapidly growing West with its only outlets the Mississippi and the St. Lawrence, and the cotton South, already so long isolated in its separate culture that it could be kept in union with the rest only by a bitter civil war.

Of course, canals — manmade extensions of nature's waterways — had formed the earliest attempt at solution of the problem of transportation.

The arrival of the railroad naturally brought calamity cries from canal promoters, substantiated by lurid tales from the experimental South. The little "Best Friend" had blown itself and crew to kingdom come when the Negro fireman, not liking the hiss, had put his thumb over the safety valve. Now passengers rode insulated from the engine by a car of cotton bales. Jeremiahs always had dire predictions to circulate. Smoke from the engine would kill all birds and game. Sparks would set fire to fields and houses and ruin the farmers. Passengers would not be able to breathe while traveling at such speed. The shock of such a fearsome sight would cause premature birth pangs in woman and beast. A few towns, like Dorchester in 1842, resolved in town meet-

ing "that our representatives be instructed to use their utmost endeavor to prevent, if possible, so great a calamity to
our town as must be the location of any railroad through it."

On the other hand, sentimentalists argued the humane
consideration of supplanting a means of transportation in
which yearly more than thirty thousand coach horses were
whipped on until they burst a heart or broke a leg in the
effort to keep up the speed of ten miles an hour in carrying
the mail on schedule. Moreover, the shrewd pointed out
that when the Middlesex Canal had opened the upper
reaches of New Hampshire, lands on either side of the canal
had increased one third in price and woodlands rose from
two to six, eight, or even ten dollars an acre. Might not the
railroad have the same effect?

Fortunately for Boston, most towns did not feel as Dorchester did. A railroad came to be considered a mark of community importance. Boston became the hub in railway connections with the busiest centers of commerce — Boston and
Lowell, Boston and Portland, Boston and Providence, Boston and Worcester, culminating in the Boston and Albany
in 1841. With the opening of the Boston and Worcester line,
the locomotive reduced to a mere three hours the weeks'
journey of a baggage wagon over the road. With the Boston
and Albany, New York real-estate values dropped abruptly,
and Boston and New England could join with New York,
Philadelphia, and Baltimore in the rush for western trade.
From the so-called trunk line, branches began to sprout in
every direction. There was very early a Taunton Branch of
the Boston and Providence line. In 1838, a company called
the "Old Colony Railroad Corporation" constructed an extension to the whale oil of New Bedford. Now, in 1846, the
Old Colony proposed a Cape Cod Branch to run from Middleboro to the glass of Sandwich.

Cape opinions were changing with the times. Fifteen
years before, the *Patriot* had cried down the building of rail-

roads anywhere as a "tax upon us and our children to fill
the coffers of metropolitan capitalists." Now both the Sandwich and Barnstable papers were declaring that it was im-
mensely important that the work should be prosecuted with
vigor.

The need for the railroad was urgent, it was said. On a
recent Saturday, Mr. Boyden had carried seventy passengers
in stages over the road to Plymouth. And what a road!

> It is intolerable to be near 4 hours travelling the short
> distance of 20 miles and yet feel that the horses are unduly
> driven. We learn from Mr. Boyden that he has lost quite
> a number of horses this summer, even travelling over it at
> the slow pace already spoken of. It is a disgrace to a town
> to let roads remain in such a shape.

Another later traveler found it

> in worse state than ever before, though there has been no
> breaking-up of winter and melting of snow bands and delug-
> ing rains to gully and upturn the side hills and suddenly
> demolish the little patching the road has received hereto-
> fore. We witnessed the extreme suffering and agony of a
> lady passenger in the stage from Plymouth occasioned by
> the intolerable jolting of the carriage with the holes and
> gullies between Plymouth village and Cornish's tavern. She
> was unable to proceed further than the latter place, and a
> carrier was dispatched thence to Sandwich for a physician.

Auntie Bacon always traveled by stage because she was
seasick on the packet. While she never complained of danger to life or limb, she did bewail the constant clouds of dust
and the meager summer fare of weak tea and blueberries to
be had in Plymouth taverns if it happened to be packet day.

The packets were famous for their sea-food dinners which,
when waves were gentle, all aboard tackled with ravenous
appetites. If the weather was fine, nothing was jollier than

a sail across the bay. Passengers were not all glassworkers or country folk. There was always some sea captain who, leaving his ship in Boston, was home for a spell to build a new house or beget a new child, and he would be full of tales of the world from Calais to Calcutta. And there might even be the thrill of a race.

But even a trip by packet could have its news-making inconvenience.

> Two of the crew of the packet schooner, Sarah, got caught in a risky affair on a recent trip. It seems they took a bottle from the pocket of a passenger who had retired to his berth and appointed themselves a "smelling committee" to ascertain the contents. In full confidence that the stuff was gin and nothing else, one of the men took a deep swig and before he could say there was a mistake, his comrade had snatched the bottle and taken a pull himself. Evidently there was something wrong about the spirits, and pains which soon seized the men strengthened the suspicion. They roused the passenger who confirmed their worst fears by the information that the bottle contained a powerful medicinal preparation of which a safe dose was only a few drops. The Sarah was then as far as "The Rocks" on her way hither, but she put back to Boston that the men might obtain relief. They escaped with their lives, but were dreadful sick.

However entertaining the episode seems in print, the delay must have been very annoying to an official of the Boston and Sandwich Glass Company on a business trip. And if the weather was too bad, the packet did not sail at all. It was a great talking point for the railroad that perhaps by Thanksgiving anyone might eat turkey in Boston and be back again the same day.

So "where are the capitalists? We hope that those of our Cape Cod friends in Boston who have the means will put their shoulders to the work. Walk up, capitalist, for a good investment!"

The dull stage lines and the protracted trips by packet have taken up days and hours that could be better employed in other respects. Nowadays, no man thinks he is in the current of business until he is within sound of a railroad whistle. If any considerable manufactory got into existence in any secluded part of the country, the enterprise which reared it rests not the sole of its foot till a railroad is in full operation connecting it with the metropolis.

These words were aimed at the Boston and Sandwich Glass Company in general and Mr. Jarves in particular. The response was as desired. Mr. Jarves made a twofold investment since, by a happy coincidence, he owned the land favored for the location of the Sandwich depot which was "secured at a liberal price to the seller."

The first board of directors for the new venture included Deming Jarves and Captain Stutson and a Tobey, a Hoxie, and a Perry of the old Cape names as well as a few men of substance from Boston and Middleboro. There were small as well as large fry among the stockholders. Sea captains and merchants scraped up their surplus, and the most prosperous farmers dug into their sack of savings, lured by the six per cent dividends of the Old Colony and the promises of seven per cent by the new enterprise. There seemed nothing at all risky or revolutionary about the purchase of railroad stocks. For years, the well-to-do of Sandwich had invested in a "piece" of a packet or cargo schooner. Why not a "piece" of a railroad? And anyone who could scrape up one hundred dollars could feel himself a capitalist just like Mr. Jarves.

With the ownership of stock scattered among the population, the railroad seemed Cape Cod's own project and took shape amid fanfare from the *Observer* and *Patriot* every step of the way. Surveyors were engaged to locate the road. Then it was announced that a large portion of the road was under contract — and to a native Mr. Hoxie. Most of the grades were easy with but little earth to be removed. Some grading would be done that winter (1846–47). It should be finished by the first of August and have time to settle before the laying of the rails. The rails and sleepers had already been purchased and a large part landed at Wareham. Without doubt, it would be a cheap road and one that would pay good dividends to the stockholders. "Subscribe! Subscribe, capitalists! There is yet a large balance of stock to be taken up."

As unforeseen delays occurred and expenses mounted, the newspapers continued to "cheer for the Cape Cod Branch," every inch of the way, while the air resounded with the ringing pick and mallet blows of the shouting shanty Irish imported by Mr. Hoxie, the contractor.

> When the railroad is completed, mechanics and artisans will find it to their advantage to reside in Cape towns rather than in cities where rents are higher. Facts show that every railroad built in Massachusetts has had a tendency to create business for its support. To Sandwich, the completion of this road is of vast importance, especially to owners of real estate, and we are surprised at the apathy. Work is progressing and nothing is wanting but funds to complete it by November 1.

There was at this date no hostility to the railroad, and the lag in the sale of stock was mostly due to the fact that the region had been quite thoroughly drained of surplus capital. By this time, almost the only bitter opposition to the railroad anywhere came from stagecoach proprietors and innkeepers who might suffer from technological unemployment, a state of affairs which certainly would not take place in Sandwich. As Sandwich was a railroad terminal and a junction with coach lines down Cape, inns here could look for more rather than less patronage.

Still, the railroad was furnishing incidents to bolster the ideas of those who distrusted new-fangled mechanism or methods of finance. There was an accident on the Old Colony near the junction with the Cape Cod Branch. It was caused by a "misarrangement of the switch." The locomotive was considerably damaged, and a man was badly scalded. An Irish laborer was killed on the Cape Cod Branch, but no blame was attached to anyone connected with the trains. He fell between the cars and was crushed to death by the wheels. Moreover, railroad stock proved not all income, for due to over-optimistic estimates and unforeseen expenses, "the third assessment of $10 per share of the Capital stock of the Cape Cod Branch has been ordered."

Finally, even the paper admitted that "great anxiety existed among stock-holders and others to know how the work progressed." There had been some delay due to the sinking of the road a short distance in the marsh. It was now a question of whether to use piles or an embankment, but the embankment was more permanent and so was considered more economical in the long run. Bridges over the Monument River and Cohasset Narrows were to be finished in October. A general superintendent of work was to be appointed. In three weeks "at the fartherest," laying of rails could be commenced. And at the end, the Editor states with somewhat false cheer that the enterprise was gaining favor even among those skeptical from the beginning.

Though delay followed delay, the skeptics finally had to grant the day to the enthusiasts when, on May 10, 1848, a train of cars loaded with railroad iron passed over the bridge at Cohasset Narrows and down to Herring River in Sandwich. On the train were the president and engineer of the corporation and other gentlemen and twenty or thirty laborers, drawn by the engine "Mayflower," an auspicious name for the first locomotive passing over Cape Cod soil. There were only three and a half miles left to connect Boston and the world beyond with the Sandwich depot, and the materials were at hand. A few days would complete the work.

Next came the announcement of a welcoming committee for the grand opening of the railroad. The twenty names included Captain Stutson and his son, William Stutson, Jr., Mr. Waterman, and Theodore Kern of the glass factory, Doctor Leonard, Isaac Keith, the carriage manufacturer, and the more prosperous of the Fishes, Wings, Nyes, and Ellises. The first duty of this committee seems to have been to take "steps to provide a suitable collation."

Not even the beginning of the glass factory had brought such excitement to town. On the great day, everyone from miles around with his children and grandchildren and cousins and aunts flocked by the wagonload to the high places where long stretches of track lay open to view. Rumor had predicted that the contraption would fly by so fast that you would have to look quickly in order to see it. Some left their horses a good way behind, out of sight and sound of the terrors of the modern age. Others, with horses of sounder nerves, stood by their heads at a safe distance from the tracks, figuring that if steam had come to stay, both man and beast might as well become used to it. The scheduled hour drew near. Eyes ached along the shining rails so as surely not to miss the comet flash of speed.

Then someone's ear caught a strange rattle along the rails. Soon everyone could hear the rhythmic wheeze. As all necks craned, the noble "Cape Cod" dressed in holiday suit with flags, evergreens, and bouquets, came puffing over the sand hills. If there was not the speed of lightning, there was no less cause for wonder, for behind the little locomotive trailed more coaches than two dozen horses could have drawn, fourteen in all. Without sail, without steed or God-given aid, the small black iron beetle was pulling its burden on the way to the future. None of the onlookers had thought left for the realization that this train to the world-to-come was cutting through and by the old town of Sandwich. The so-called Sandwich station lay beyond the older settlement, not far from the glassworks in Jarvesville, and the railroad, marking out an American social pattern which was to become typical all over the land, had placed most of Jarvesville definitely on the other side of the tracks.

3

A crowd of between seven and eight hundred had flocked around the depot, which like the noble "Cape Cod," was bedecked with bunting and greenery. As the train came to a stop, one long shout arose from the massed spectators. About this time it began to rain, so that the fourteen carloads of dignitaries and substantial stockholders, including Mr. Jarves and the mayor of Boston, were hustled inside. Small boys nosing the new panes could see the festoons of "overarching evergreens with merry singing birds interspersed, brilliant tables glittering with rich cut and colored glassware from the rooms of the Boston and Sandwich Glass Co. intermingled with beautiful flowers." On each plate lay a symbolic sandwich.

"The 'Welcome' of the citizens on the wall was as neatly inscribed as if by a fairy wand," reported *Observer*, adding that the scene seemed fairyland indeed "especially in the morning before the ladies had left the hall."

"The company proceeded to partake of the bounties spread before them" while all but overwhelmed with oratory. Then after the speeches came the masterpiece of the poet laureate of the Cape Cod Branch:

> Hurrah for Cape Cod, for we're coming along
> To open a railroad and sing you a song.
> And though to us all very strange it may seem
> 'Tis true we can visit the Cape now by steam.
>
> We've done altogether with packet and stage
> For Railroads and Engines are now all the rage.

There's Otis of Yarmouth and Borden and Jarves
And Seaver and Hunnewell quite at your sarvice.

When the assembly must surely, after twelve verses, have
feared that he would proceed from the directors to the stockholders, it was suddenly discovered that "the time had nearly
expired." A procession was now formed and hurried up to
Main Street behind a band. After all, these Bostonians could
not be left with the impression that Jarvesville was Sandwich. They returned to the cars shortly before 4 P.M., and
the train started for Boston, arriving at the depot in Boston
at nine and — apparently to the surprise of everyone — "without any accident."

From this day, the railroad was the darling of the town.
Here, as everywhere else, it received the devotion with which
men were to worship the gadgets of their own creation
whereby, with increasing speed, they could give themselves
the illusion that they were whizzing along to some desirable
destination. The wheezy little "Mayflower" and "Cape Cod"
enjoyed the status of town characters, and their every virtue
and idiosyncracy were affectionately discussed on the station
platform before each train time. The engineer was the envy
of all the small boys. Even the gaffer with his magic skill had
to retire to second place.

Stockholder's Day in November became the event of the
year with half the town, on their own or borrowed certifi-
cates, taking the free ride to Boston for the shopping spree
which led Boston stores, so the paper hinted, to mark up
prices for the occasion. The railroad paid its first dividend
in January and, all things considered, had done remarkably
well. The running expenses were light, as far as could be
judged, and the superintendent had managed with great prudence. The paper had "no inclination to retract success of
the enterprise or value of the stock."

Captain Atkins of the town packet had become station
agent. Mr. Boyden found that, as he had anticipated, busi-

ness down Cape became brisk enough to compensate for the loss of patronage to Plymouth. The *Patriot* reported that six heavily loaded stages passed Barnstable to and from Sandwich each day, and with this heavy travel, Mr. Boyden should see fit to reduce fare from the exorbitant fifty cents for the ten-mile ride between the two towns.

The progressive Reverend Joseph Mash added still another line to his glass-blowing, preaching, and dissemination of anti-Catholic literature. After repeated solicitations by the friends of temperance, he "opened his commodious house for the entertainment of the temperance public." The house was opposite the front of the depot on the corner of Liberty and Factory Streets. Stages passed the door each day. Good stabling for horses. The name of the new hostelry was appropriately enough "The Temperance Traveller's Home."

Less than ever was community life centered near the vicinity of the old town tavern, the new town hall, and church spires. Now townsfolk had to make the pilgrimage to Jarvesville if they wanted to get out of the rut of the past. With the depot and principal stage stop, in addition to the factory, Jarvesville was the focus of the town. This was fitting enough. The paper gave credit where credit was due, stating that the Cape should be grateful for all this new life not only to her native sons, but to one who had been "active and efficient in securing her so many facilities for improving her commercial, agricultural, and social condition — Deming Jarves of Boston."

Consequently, there was consternation among stockholders and townsfolk at the newspaper announcement May 22, 1849, that

> our friend, Deming Jarves, has resigned his place as Director of the Cape Cod Branch Railroad. Why is this? Mr. Jarves has been supposed to have a large interest in this road, and he is known as one of the most judicious and efficient of

directors of any business he engages in. Much blame has, within the last few weeks, been thrown upon several prominent gentlemen in whose ability and integrity the public had much confidence, who were directors of the Norfolk County Railroad when it failed. We have more than once heard the inquiry made in a very significant and suggestive manner since Mr. Jarves's resignation. Why does he resign now? We hope all is right.

It was not reassuring to read immediately afterward of the launching of the schooner *Cohasset* of one hundred and eighty tons burthen, "one of the most substantial vessels of her class ever built in the county, to be employed by the Sandwich Glass Company." Next it was announced that "repairs have been commenced on the road to the packet for the purpose of carrying freight by water. For some months past, the freight of the Sandwich Glass Company has been carried over the Cape Cod Branch Railroad."

This looked like war between Mr. Jarves and the railroad, and the small stockholders could only speculate on reasons and anxiously eye results. One anguished stockholder wrote to the *Sandwich Observer* that Mr. Jarves had not resigned. He and Messrs. Hoxie, Perry, and Tobey — the Sandwich men most interested in the success of the railroad, "the mainspring of prosperity to whom the whole community was indebted — all four had been 'kicked out.' " How? Proxy voting, whereby through some hocus-pocus the votes of a hundred were subject to one man, had done it. A few prominent proxy getters had rounded up the votes of those who could not attend. Had all been there, matters would have been different.

Soon another version circulated. It was said that there had been an attempt to sell a ten-thousand dollar block of stock to a certain wealthy individual by guaranteeing him a goodly dividend regardless of what the other stockholders might receive. "It is understood that Deming Jarves is the ex-director who, while director last year, was applied to, to sanction the assumption of this guaranty. He refused to be party to this trickery and for that was kicked out. He was too honorable a man to be let into this trick in the first place. He proved too faithful to his trust to be part of it after it was consummated."

People with pride in their railway were bewildered by all this talk. They felt that they owned a very model of a railroad. The initial cost of the road and equipment had been less than the cost per mile of any other railroad in the state, less than half the average for the railroads of Massachusetts. The railroad had reduced the time to Boston to only three hours at a fare of little more than three cents a mile. There were almost no accidents, although the first year alone the passenger fares reached the astonishing number of 66,825.

Of course, there was a large floating debt incurred at the beginning. In an effort to get the stock on a firm footing, it was voted to sell one third of the unsold stock at fifty cents on the dollar to old stockholders. The directors of the Sandwich Glass Company, very large stockholders, by unanimous vote decided not to take the new stock offered at $50 a share. Mr. Jarves advertised his stock for sale at "a scandalously low price."

Panic was started among the other stockholders. Ten shares were sold at $42.50, originally bought at $100, together with some recently offered at $50. Then stock was reported to be selling at $38, and finally in May, 1850, "21 shares of Cape Cod Branch Railroad stock was offered at auction, and not a bid could be obtained for this futile, miserably managed, unprofitable railroad."

Example followed example of the "rottenness" of the present board of directors, although all conceded the efficiency of the managing superintendent. A bad situation was not made better by throwing out a new branch line and adding a few more stations every now and then — thirty-four in thirty-seven miles — at every four corners where there was a stockholder. Certainly, no one cared to face the fact that the line ran through a country too poor in industry to support a railroad, except for the terminal in Sandwich. The figures told the story. In contrast to the receipt of $35,430.47 for passengers in the first year, $14,972.79 was taken in on freight.

The wildest rumors went the rounds. The "ornaments" of the Sandwich station alone had cost ten thousand dollars. No, it could be proved that the whole station had cost only nine thousand dollars. Why, asked a stockholder, had a certain Captain H. S. B. watched vessels of rubble for the road-bed when more were paid for than he checked? As a climax came the affair of Mr. Keith's railroad cars.

Though the Boston and Sandwich Glass Company now sent all of its long-haul freight by packet, it was still business economy to use the hated railroad for the short haul of coal and iron landed on the south side of the Cape, thus saving the long sail around the end of the Cape. A news item stated that a vessel with cargo for the Sandwich Glass Company had been held up at Cohasset Narrows on the south side because the railroad could not furnish freight cars.

This was not the first instance, commented the editor. The Glass Company's freight paid better profit to the road than any other, and the Sandwich Glass and other manufacturers had been obliged to ship large quantities of their materials and wares by packets at a loss because there were not sufficient cars on the road to transport wares over it. The loss of the freight which would have been paid in this one case would have bought one costly car. No wonder the bonds of the railroad, so fraudulently put off on Cape people at par, were now selling for eighty-two dollars on the hundred.

The president of the railroad countered with the news that he was even then awaiting delivery of four freight cars from Worcester. Then the hue and cry was on. Mr. Keith,

Sandwich's enterprising blacksmith and carriage builder, who had followed the trend of the times with stagecoaches and Conestoga wagons, was now building railway cars — first-class freight cars. He had them on display right beside the tracks of the Cape Cod Branch. The price was plainly marked, and that price was fifty dollars less than that of the Worcester cars which had been purchased. A statement by the president of the road that the Worcester cars were really worth seventy-five dollars more than the Sandwich cars had an opposite effect from the one intended. Here was an attempt by mean insinuation to injure the standing of the mechanics of Sandwich.

"The mechanics of Sandwich feel that they can match any other mechanics in quality and faithfulness of work."

Now stockholders and townspeople were united against the management. Mr. Jarves no longer seemed a benevolent despot to be bested in friendly rivalry. He was a champion of the cause.

"Enough of twaddling and tinkering! Enough of dickering with stage contractors, quarrelling with best customers, and spiting home manufacturers! What a feeling of gratification if old and able and faithful friends would take hold again!" In any increase or change of directors, interest demanded that one should be Deming Jarves, possibly the largest stockholder, whose "superior abilities, long experience as a businessman, good judgment and clear foresight" would do more than anything else to "relieve the concern of its present embarrassment." "It was strange to see several of the board, having taken occasion to belabor Mr. Jarves's name and character with indecent and ungentlemanly epithets now looking for a plausible pretext for adding that gentleman to the same board." Mr. Jarves had resigned because he did not receive "decent, gentlemanly conduct." Though he would be invaluable in the direction of affairs, there was some doubt that he could be prevailed upon to accept.

Mr. Jarves did not accept because Mr. Jarves was never invited. At last, the paper gave up conjecture and admitted that though there was "considerable veiled reference to difficulties with the Sandwich Glass Company," there was "no information whatsoever on the subject." There was, however, advice and prophecy!

> If the road ever wants the good will and profitable patronage of the glass company, which now pays it more than $10,000 and with proper treatment would pay double that at least, it must change management. Anything short of this will, in our opinion, secure a now-contemplated permanent opposition to your freighting business of a more important and formidable nature than anything yet encountered. We mean the running of a powerful propeller steam vessel between Boston, Sandwich, and Plymouth. That such a vessel is now being built, designed for that business, we are reliably assured. That she will be put on that track unless a change is made in the management of your road acceptable to the glass company, we know. Let such rapid and certain water communication be once established and that company enlisted in it, and the $10,000 now paid by the company to the road instead of being swelled to $25,000 will be dwindled to $500.

The facts behind the furore were that, with packets sailing off into the past, the directors of the Cape Cod Branch felt that they had on the Boston and Sandwich Company the strangle-hold with which railroads were to squeeze mines, factories, and farms everywhere until the embattled Patrons of Husbandry fought through railway legislation to curb the monopolistic power. At any post mortem over financial difficulties, the most promising course of action seemed to be to hoist Mr. Jarves's freight rates. Mr. Jarves might own considerable stock, but he could easily be outvoted.

He had always advocated independence of outside sources in ownership of raw materials and means of transportation.

Now, to his chagrin, he found himself considered in a position of helplessness. In the face of smug smiles, he angrily announced that he was through with common carriers. He would build a steamer and take all the freight away from the railroad. After all, a steamer would make the trip to Boston in nearly the same time as the railroad, and its hold would be more capacious than a train of little baggage wagons. Then exorbitant freight rates would be gone forever.

The board of directors of the Cape Cod Branch of the old Colony Railroad was not impressed.

"The acorn is not yet planted," scoffed Mr. Bourne, the superintendent of the line, "to grow the timber for such a vessel."

"Wait and see," said Mr. Jarves, marching out.

Sandwich was waiting, and in the end Sandwich saw. First came the rumor that Mr. Jarves was having a steamer built in Philadelphia especially for him. Next it was known as a definite fact that the steamer had reached Boston. Naturally, the town turned out to a meeting called by Mr. Jarves whose man-to-man manner could soften the most crusty antipathies. He enlarged upon the advantages of steamer transportation and the importance of Sandwich with both railroad and steamer service. The steamer was ready, and he was ready. But during the years, the channel from the bay had filled in with sand. It would need deepening and a new canal would have to be cut through the marsh to the company wharf. After the company had gone to the expense of a steamer — and Mr. Jarves could make even railroad stockholders almost believe that the steamer was a company present to Sandwich — he was asking of the citizens only the contribution of two days' labor toward cutting the new canal — an investment of their time for the greater growth and glory of Sandwich.

Once more men of Sandwich succumbed to the Jarves spellbinding. Those too poor for the importance of being railroad stockholders felt that they could work out a stake in the steamer. On the appointed day, great numbers turned out with picks and shovels and sea boots for a sort of lusty work-picnic.

However much the directors of the Boston and Sandwich Company may have approved of Mr. Jarves's ability to exact free labor from the town, they found the project hardly without expense. By the time Mr. Jarves's powers of invention had played out, the total cost, irrespective of the steamer, was twelve thousand dollars. In addition to the canal, he constructed a lock so that after boats and lighters had come in to the wharf on the high tide, the closed gates would hold the water at wharf level while vessels loaded and unloaded through the ebb — an engineering feat which eliminated the need for the bogy road or scows poled painfully along the creek.

At last one fine day Sandwich saw a smoke smudge on the Bay where only sails had been seen before. Soon a trim little craft plowed toward the shore with no heed to the way of the wind. The name neatly painted on prow and stern was — the *Acorn*.

Thereafter, the steam engine on the shore and the steamboat on the bay shrilled their whistled daily defiance. Mr. Jarves, in high glee, celebrated his victory with glassware in an Acorn pattern. Townsfolk and railway directors admitted with varying degrees of rue or admiration that you couldn't get the better of Mr. Jarves — at least, not for long. But what no one sensed — and least of all that gentleman himself — was that the world had begun to steam ahead too fast for even Mr. Jarves.

Heyday and Hope

BY CONQUEST and by compromise, the nation had spread
from sea to sea. The railroad had already reached St. Louis
when the first grain of gold gleamed in Colonel Sutter's mill-
race. The trickle of adventurers to California swelled to a
torrent while wealth flowed East. The United States had
won its war with Mexico in the nick of time.

Now working men banded together, stopped worrying
about their loss of social standing, and began to fight for a
share in the material prosperity. There were strikes for the
ten-hour day, for $1.75 a day for carpenters. "It is useless
for us to disguise the fact," said the National Typographical
Society, "that under the present arrangement of things, there
exists perpetual antagonism between capital and labor."

Greeley, seeing the attitude of the workingman changing
from defensive philosophy to aggressive demand, took alarm,
declaring the workers "fatally misled if they suppose the employers can pay good wages whenever they please. Just now

171

they can. California is drawing away our labor and pouring in gold."

This seething state of affairs did not reach Sandwich, even by rail. After all, gaffers worked no more than ten hours a day, and gaffers made more than $1.75 a day.

When the glassmakers of Sandwich finally came together, it was not to consider wrongs of their own, but of their fellow workers in England, Ireland, and Scotland who were facing locked factories and starvation for having dared unite "against the oppressive acts of rich masters." The Reverend Joseph Marsh, as he now signed himself, was elected president of the assembly. Resolutions were passed to the effect that the glassworkers of Sandwich considered it a duty and privilege to aid in the struggle and would "subscribe to their ability to relieve suffering and would continue to do so as long as there was need."

In Sandwich, there was no visible oppression. Glassmakers could meet freely, as long as they were orderly, for any purpose they desired. Somewhat later, the glassmakers in the employ of the Boston and Sandwich Company at Sandwich unanimously

> Resolved: that we have good reason to be glad that our fellow workman, Joseph Marsh, is named as a fit person for a seat in the Congress of the nation. Resolved: that there is no man within our knowledge in the 1st Congressional District more deserving or better qualified to defend the manufacturing interest of the North and to plead the cause of free well-paid labor than the above-named gentleman. Resolved: that it concerns the interest of every mechanic and laboring man that a well-qualified workingman shall go to Congress, and Mr. Marsh is the man. Resolved: that we will use every honorable effort to secure his election, desiring as we do to see an industrious workingman qualified in every other respect in the Councils of the Country.

Unfortunately for the Sandwich glassmakers' hopes of

political action, the name of Joseph Marsh was no more than mentioned and did not even survive the caucus. Still, there was always a chance that where workingmen could vote, a workingman might one day sit in "the Councils of the Country." Seen from Sandwich, America was decidedly a land of opportunity, even for the mechanic.

Mr. Jarves, as ever, was ready to venture with the times. On February 7, 1849, the *Sandwich Observer* advertised that "a company is forming for California under the auspices of Deming Jarves." Who fared forth from Sandwich and with what results is not known. On April 4, 1849, before any Sandwich company could even have reached its destination, a listing of amounts of gold dust from California entered at the Boston Customs House by fifteen different individuals and firms credited Deming Jarves with $9094. The amounts ranged from $25,000 to $200, and Mr. Jarves stood fourth from the top of the list.

In 1849, also, a schooner load of tableware in the Ashburton pattern set out from Sandwich to California, and in 1849, Deming Jarves enlarged his plant with a new and more imposing glasshouse — a so-called "Lower House" of brick beside and connecting with the original wooden "Upper House," as it now came to be called. In this new Lower House, as in the Upper, there were two ten-pot furnaces so that the capacity of the factory was doubled. Soon there was a thrice-weekly private packet coming for loads of glass tableware to fill the ships for California.

New workers came in to the enlarged factory, and Yankee folk of Sandwich now heard on their streets not only outlandish twists of their native speech, but the mumbo-jumbo of unknown tongues. Added to the usual Dublin and Waterford blowers escaping the perennial Irish hunger, there were gaffers from France and Alsace and an occasional feudal servant fled from the glassworks of the Duke of Brunswick. Europe was at one violent end of its periodic seesaw from revolution to reaction, and the New World offered shelter and opportunity for the harried and helpless.

While America was seeking to bind together its wide reaches by the railroad, Europe was even more desperately trying to nullify the railroad's conquest of natural barriers and to cherish its old rooted fears and jealousies by changing the gauge of the rails at nearly every border. James Jackson Jarves was now flitting his butterfly way over "the lands of old Europe — to the young American, fields of storied interest, of high and noble deeds, of dark and sanguinary passions." Arriving in Paris just in time for the excitement of street barricades, stray shots, and bloodstained pavements which marked the coup establishing the power of Louis Napoleon, he saw railroad tracks torn up to keep the inflamed provinces from rushing on the capital.

Yet the purely local effect of the railroad track in Sandwich, as in many other American towns, was to make even more distinct the already existing social divisions. The distinction between Sandwich and Jarvesville was now narrowed to "above and below the crossing." Plenty of glassworkers had built neat cottages on Pleasant and other streets between the county road and the old factory village "above the crossing." Thus the track did not mark any dividing line between factory and non-factory families. There now could be no such boundary as nearly every family in town by this time had at least one member working in the factory. There was rather, in spite of the presence of the Reverend Joseph Marsh and some of the Catholic leaders, an implication that the less thrifty, the more foreign lived below the crossing in the vicinity of the company houses.

"If downtown young men went above the crossing or uptown young men went downtown after dark, it was a signal for a good fight," relates a glass-factory granddaughter.

The tension between uptown and downtown folk was heightened by the fact that the forces of temperance had never had more than a temporary victory and were now hopelessly outnumbered. On each side of the tracks were those ready to serve customers from over the crossing. In any fracas which came before the law, victory was invariably with the uptowners.

One Christmas night, a James McKune went to the house of William Swift. Apparently he was not a welcome guest, because "after some difficulty" he left for reinforcements. He returned with friends, and, in the restrained wording of the court record, "a serious disturbance took place," with resulting "wood and brick brought into the courtroom said to have been thrown through the window by persons outside." In the heat of the brawl, one of McKune's companions, young Daniel Fogarty, was shot and killed by a guest in the Swift house.

Murders were rare in Barnstable County and at the trial "many ladies were present in the audience, attracted by the celebrity of the case." The defendant pleaded self-defense. He had witnesses to testify to "character of gun and precautions used by defendant." The fact that the defendant bore the old Sandwich name of Perry was also in his favor. "After three quarters of an hour, the jury found him not guilty." Then they proceeded to press a case against James McKune, charging him with responsibility in the fracas in which Daniel Fogarty was killed. He was held in $300 bail, and eventually pleaded guilty and was sentenced. A friend killed and himself jailed — here was a lesson to downtown lads who might itch for a rousing uptown brawl.

However, the day was at hand when minor offenses "downtown" would not be handled by an unsympathetic Nye as justice of the peace. In 1851 appeared the first "downtown" name among the town officials for the year — "special constable for the Jarvesville district — P. McGirr." Downtown Sandwich or Jarvesville about this time also acquired a doughty champion in the Reverend Father William

Moran, six feet of fighting Irishman sniffing battle from afar, who arrived in Sandwich to challenge what he considered the Yankee bigotry of Cape Cod.

He had begun his career, in the tradition of American Catholicism, as missionary to the Indians in Maine where he had gained fame in being able to outrun death and the fastest messenger in the grim race to snatch souls from the devil in the wigwams of the dying. He came physically and spiritually prepared to handle with equal effectiveness Know-Nothing hecklers and obstructionists within his own parish. He found both. On a missionary visit to Wareham, he was accosted by a band of young hoodlums. They were about to haul him out of his carriage when prevented by the chance passing of a more tolerant Yankee farmer carrying a shotgun.

He faced a congregation at home divided into two loudly argumentative factions on the matter of a new church. There was no question of the need for expansion as the congregation overflowed the little wooden box brought down by packet. Many were for an enlargement of the old church on the old site, but not so Father Moran! With the Protestants now split six ways into Congregationalist, Calvinistic Congregationalist, Universalist, Unitarian, Methodist, and Quaker, Saint Peter's had by far the largest congregation in town. It should have a fitting church.

The plans which called for an expenditure of twenty-five thousand dollars made the more frugal gasp. Before they could catch their breath, Father Moran had dazzled them with the vision of a building of brick — not lumped out from a local clay pit like the factory, but Philadelphia pressed brick brought in by ship and rail along with brownstone trimmings. It would have beautiful stained glass windows, of course, three altars, and the luxury of padded pews and kneeling benches. But most impressive would be the tower one hundred and sixty feet tall with clock and bell and, near

the top, a great gleaming ball of ruby glass to reflect the sun
and cheer the sailors miles out at sea.

With force and fury, Father Moran prepared to fight his
dream through to reality — a reality which rather bore out
James Jackson Jarves's observation that while Protestant
churches in America were being derived more and more
from the mediaeval Catholic Gothic, American Catholic
churches seemed inspired by the architecture of the factory
or penitentiary.

As far as customs and manners went, it was the newcomers
who fell in with the old ways. To raise money for a church
bell, the parishioners of Saint Peter's turned to that old
Sandwich standby, the Social Pick-nick with the usual tables,
laden with meat, pastry, and fruit, floral embellishments,
"and the addition of a Cornet Band." "Although the first
occasion of its kind carried into effect by the Catholics of
Sandwich," the newspaper reported in apparent surprise
that "harmony and good order prevailed."

While old Sandwich was adjusting itself to a peaceful and
not unpleasant relationship with the alien in its midst, it
was applauding Daniel Webster who, wearing his famous
buff and blue with gleaming buttons like a soldier, was
throwing away his future, almost his life, in a thundering
battle against the rocky wall of sectionalism which swift
communication and transportation had come too late to bat-
ter down.

In this growing tug-of-war, Webster was fighting with all
the power of his mighty voice for his country, his country
united:

> What am I to be? An American no longer? Where is the
> flag of the republic to remain? Where is the eagle still to
> tower? or is he to cower and fall to the ground? To break
> up this great government? To dismember this glorious coun-
> try? No, Sir! No, Sir! There will be no talk of secession.
> Gentlemen are not serious when they talk of secession. —

> Sir, I see as plainly as I see the sun in heaven what that disruption itself must produce. I see that it must produce war, and such a war as I will not describe ——

Driven on by his zeal for what he considered the major issue — the union — he was willing to back Clay's compromise with its support of the Fugitive Slave Law. Although he found many Abolitionists to be "honest and good men, perfectly well-meaning men" who "think they must do something for the cause of liberty," he deplored Abolition Societies. "I do not think them useful. I think their operation for the last twenty years has produced nothing good or valuable." He added some sound psychology as to their effect on the South. "There is no public man who requires information more than I do or desires it more heartily, but I do not like to have it in too imperative a shape. — I cannot but see what mischiefs their interference with the South has produced." And he cited that where once the Virginia legislature had freely discussed some possible long-term plan for ending slavery, now any mention of the subject was taboo.

However, the primitive American missionary spirit was in full sway, and the famous Seventh of March speech was cried down by even former supporters as treason to the cause of liberty, even as a calculated bid for Southern votes for the presidency. Bitterly angry and frustrated, Webster stuck to his course. To a protest from a Cape Cod village, he returned the answer, "My friends of West Dennis, discourage fanciful ideas, abstract notions, and all inconsiderate attempts to reach ends which, however desirable in themselves, are not placed within the compass of your abilities or duties. Hold on, my friends, to the Constitution of your Country and the Government established under it. Leave evils which exist in some parts of the country, but which are beyond your control to the all-wise direction of an overruling Providence."

Sandwich alone did not turn to reproach its onetime hero.
There was anti-slavery sentiment, to be sure. An Abolition
Society for the last fourteen or fifteen years had quarreled
halfheartedly as to ways and means. The once vociferously
Democratic Joseph Marsh showed up surprisingly as an anti-
Taylor Whig at a gathering in Town Hall in 1848 to which
"in view of the existing state of political parties, all the true
lovers of Freedom, the haters of Despotism and oppression"
had been invited "to consult pertaining to the duty of American freemen."

Mr. Marsh was in company with the Bournes, Fishes, and
Swifts from the old families, a Haines, a Lapham, and a Kern
from the factory together with Mr. Hiram Dilloway, the
master mold designer, who usually kept a quite aristocratic
aloofness from town affairs. They were strange associates,
but with the Democrats representing the slaveholding South
and one of the leading Whig candidates, General Taylor, a
plantation and slaveowner in Louisiana, the opponents of
slavery were in a difficult position.

However, in these days before *Uncle Tom* appeared on
the literary scene, Sandwich had read only vague general-
ities about slavery, and Sandwich had memories of a former
pastor, the Reverend Abraham Williams, who had brought
to town among his belongings a gentle black man. This
Titus, who had slept like a dog in a special cubby-hole under
his master's front stairs, had lived an apparently contented
life of sanctified slavery. Set free at the death of Mr. Williams, he had spent the rest of his days, in a tiny house on,
appropriately, Liberty Street, and left his accumulated
hoardings to buy a church bell. In the sweet sound of its
ringing, more than one staunch churchgoer must have considered this well-ordered Christian servitude a worthier way
than the free savagery of Africa.

Mr. Jarves's opinion, too, carried some weight, and to him,
as to most of the Boston business men, the Websterian mid-

dle-of-the-road way was the right one. As usual, he gave his moral support the tangible form of a present of glass — quite the most elaborate piece of pressed glass ever undertaken. This was a bowl twenty-one inches high, twenty-two inches in diameter at the top, and weighing sixty pounds. The newspaper editor was invited to witness the pressing of this bowl. He reported with awe that the machine for pressing weighed between two and three tons.

> It is worked with the accuracy of a steam engine. The glowing metal was taken from the furnace at its greatest fusion by the workmen, placed by hand in the machine which was set in motion. In a few minutes, a perfect bowl of rich design was turned out, spreading a most intense heat around which none but those accustomed to the business could stand. It was interesting to note the arrangement made in working the machine. Each workman had his allotted place, and it was surprising to see an article of this weight and size handled with so much judgment and skill that in one minute, it was taken from the press by the head workman and carried to a side furnace to receive a fire polish. As soon as that was done, it was taken to the annealing kiln and placed therein to cool which requires eight to ten days.

"It claims the merit of being much the largest piece of flint glass made by machinery in any part of the world," Mr. Jarves wrote in his letter of presentation to Daniel Webster. "Two machinists were employed six months in forming the mould. This bowl is the first made in it and is called the Union Bowl. The name will not render it less valuable."

Perhaps the Union Bowl was of some comfort to the statesman in those heartbreaking months when his stubborn stand brought only the downfall of the Whig party and a final disappointment of his lifelong ambition to be President. It brought Mr. Jarves a certain amount of renown. Apparently, Union Bowls were never pressed and sold in any quantities, however, for there seem to be none listed in the hands of collectors. And it is doubtful whether the board of directors of the Boston and Sandwich Company appreciated the six months' profitless labor of two men required to make the huge iron mold with its lovely lacy intricacy of design.

2

Directors, however, barely had time to shake their heads over the problematical value of any one of Mr. Jarves's inventions and innovations before being dazzled by the next one. Some of the less successful experiments, too, were carried out beyond the range of their vision. In his *Reminiscences,* Mr. Jarves wrote of the trial of a new furnace which burned unkilned wood and "saved one quarter in fuel, but used up pots so rapidly as to prove to be no economy in the end."

Since this test, as he said, took place in South Boston, it doubtless occurred at George's Mount Washington Glass Works, now revived with a new partner. After all, Mr. Jarves had to have some fun for his money. George had never developed the slightest interest in glass beyond what he considered a filial duty. While he mildly enjoyed the pleasant social rounds of the young Boston gentleman, his glassworks had been under the active management of one partner or another and would continue in that way even without George — a subsidiary source of income to Mr. Jarves and an occasional outlet for his experimental urge.

Except for the brief bright period after his early vision upon the sands, these years were the most hopeful and creative in Mr. Jarves's long life. To be sure, it was a somewhat Pyrrhic victory which the *Acorn* had won over the railroad. Freight rates had been forced down to a point where regular use of the steamer was no longer profitable. She now lay at the dock except for an occasional emergency cargo or holiday fishing trip of glassworkers.

But the new rates made it possible for the factory to use coal exclusively for fuel. Shipped to Buzzard's Bay on the south side of the Cape from the newly opened Virginia and Cumberland mines, it could be transported quite cheaply by spur track to the factory. This was a fortunate state of affairs, since the company woodlots were reaching the point of depletion, and it was essential to find a way of meeting the competition of the Pittsburgh glasshouses mushrooming in the neighborhood of the coal mines.

> Next to pots, furnaces are the most important for the success of a glass manufactory [he wrote]. Long ago it was seen that the old English plan was defective. They consumed coal at an extravagant rate, not a serious drawback in England because the furnaces were located near coal mines. English furnaces were constructed with reference to durability, usually 8 ft. in diameter at the interior base and 6 ft. near the crown. The writer, having occasion to build an extra furnace, adopted the novel plan of one 14 ft. in diameter at the base in the clear and only 5 ft. at the crown, braced by binders with cross-ties, which was a success. A furnace on the old plan consumed 2575 bu. of coal weekly and refined only 38,000 lbs. of raw material. The new refined 35,000 lbs. with a consumption of only 2000 bu. of coal.

There had been, as he pointed out, little change in the construction of furnaces or glassmaker's tools for four hundred years.

> It is no undue arrogance of claim to say that the very many improvements in furnaces, working machinery, tools, etc. (such as enable the manufacturer here to melt with the same fuel double the quantity of glass that can at present be done in European furnaces) are entirely owing to the progress of the art in this country.

He was too modest to dwell upon his own very considerable part in modernizing the ancient craft, though he was

forever fussing with fuels and drafts and improved designs.
Resin was tried out in the glory-holes. The factory was the
first in the country to use coke in the annealing ovens.

It is rather a question now as to whether gas was a by-
product of the coke or vice versa, since the use of both was
introduced by Mr. Jarves. The Boston and Sandwich Company was soon illuminated by gas on the night shift instead
of the primitive whale oil or camphene which gave a weaker,
more flickering light and kept one man busy tending the
lamps.

When asked by his expatriate son, James, why he had not
chosen to live in England rather than this crude new country, Mr. Jarves had answered that only the New World gave
him full scope for his inventions. One of the reasons that
he so loved glass was because of its endless opportunities for
experimentation in machinery, material, and methods. His
fascination with the history of glassmaking, his visions for its
future, he expressed in print for the benefit of his employees
and the townspeople of Sandwich.

After the *Sandwich Observer* and its successor, the *Sandwich Mechanic,* had passed out of existence, Deming Jarves
"because of the partiality of friends rather than his own
opinion of their value" was "induced to present to the public the articles upon the history and progréss of Glass Manufacture originally published in the columns of a village newspaper." The object of the little book, *Reminiscences of
Glass-Making* was, as Mr. Jarves himself put it:

> to present in a condensed and convenient form whatever
> of interesting information could be gained from authentic
> sources in regard to a branch of manufacture which has at-
> tained a position among the useful and elegant arts scarcely
> rivalled by any other of those which mark and distinguish
> the progressive character of our country. Aside from his-
> torical or mechanical facts, there is much of romantic in-
> terest attaching to the progress of this department of art.

Romance he offered aplenty — from Egyptian tombs and ruins of Nineveh and Babylon, through Tyre and Sidon to the first crystal-clear flint glass in the time of Nero. There was Pliny's legend of the shipwrecked sailors who first found the accident of glassmaking in the fusion of sand with the herb, kale, beneath their campfire; the swashbuckling scene of the sheriff of Kent drinking the health of James II in a flint wineglass three feet high; the story that Roger Bacon at sixty-four was imprisoned for ten years for experimenting with convex and concave glasses and burning glasses.

The artist usually lives upon a distillation of the past; the scientist on a foretaste of the future. While the oldest Jarves son was in the midst of his "embalmed monuments of proudest genius," seeking to bring the spiritual message of bygone centuries to the New World, his father was writing:

> Where would science find itself without the aid of glass? The astronomers' and chemists' vocations would be gone. The seaman would blunder his way on the ocean, lucky if he guessed aright and cursing his "stars" when he did not. Its loss would throw the world into antediluvian ignorance, not to mention the countless eyes it would deprive of sight, of their intellectual food, and freedom of way. That the art of glass manufacturing is destined to greater progress and higher triumphs cannot for a moment be denied.
>
> It is no undue stretch of the imagination to conceive that lenses shall be perfected whose purity will enable the astronomer to penetrate the remotest region of space; new worlds may perhaps be revealed, realizing all that the "moon hoax" promised —
>
> > The spacious firmament on high
> > With all the blue ethereal sky
> > And spangled heavens
>
> may be read as a book, and man perhaps recognize man in other worlds than his own.
>
> It may be that in its triumphs, it is destined to concentrate the rays of sunlight and make the eye pierce into the

secrets and deep places of the sea "Full many a fathom deep." Man may be enabled to read the wonders and hidden works of the Almighty; it may be that the power of the traditional lens of Archimedes upon the fleet of Marcellus shall be realized in the absorbing and igniting and perhaps useful power of some feature of its progress. It is no visionary speculation to believe that, by the aid of machinery, it may readily be rolled into sheets, as is iron and lead now in use. It will minister more and more to the necessities of mankind and contribute largely to the many and various manufacturing purposes of the age. Its applicability, in some form, for vessels of large size and certain shape and, strange as it may seem, for tesselated and ordinary flooring and pavements are among the results we think yet to be demonstrated in its progress.

Without peering too far into the future, Mr. Jarves could see his glass following every trend of the time. With gas came the making of gas globes. After the invention and widespread use of lucifer matches, the old-fashioned holders for spills or twisted paper lamplighters were made as toothpick holders, or in larger form, spoon holders. His product now ranged from the massive Union Bowl to little lacy doll dishes fit for a princess, from sets of elaborate cut ware for the individual order of kings, statesmen, and millionaires, to the ever increasing flood of plain pressed lamps and tumblers pouring out to the spreading settlements of this country and the far reaches of the world.

During this period, the expansion of market tempted a corresponding new spurt of American enterprise. If the Boston and Sandwich Company had more orders than it could fill, why was there not a chance for someone besides Mr. Jarves to profit? A group of Cape Codders — Swift, Dillingham, Jones, Nye, *et al.* — started the Falmouth Glass Company, luring Edward Haines away from Sandwich to act as superintendent of the glasshouse. Never in any sense a rival of the Sandwich Company, since it employed only twenty-seven men, it failed — in spite of local fanfare about the quality of the glass. After six months, it was reorganized as the United States Glass Company with the same eventual results.

In the glass business, failure seemingly was more common than success. In his *Reminiscences,* Mr. Jarves had reported that "prior to 1852, no less than 42 different attempts in the manufacture of flint glass had been made in the Atlantic States; 28 had failed entirely, 2 retired, 2 retired without loss, having been measurably prosperous; and 10 were still in operation. The manufactory in Sandwich," he ended a bit smugly, "has been eminently prosperous."

With the prosperity of this time, other new industries started in Sandwich. Besides Mr. Keith's manufactory making railway cars, there was a tack factory in Wing's old cotton mill by Wolf Trap River, axe and nail factories in the Bourne section where metal and coal could be shipped in from the South, and an ironworks, the Pocasset Iron Company, which had recently cast the first fancy top and bottom for an airtight stove. Sandwich had become a busy manufacturing town, with the population increased by 530 between 1840 and 1850.

From the factory, gas was piped to the line of stores and the more substantial dwellings where the roads up from the Factory Village joined Main Street. Sandwich with its gaslight district seemed quite metropolitan to the simple countryside round about.

There was now too much money around town to be kept in an old sock or under a loose board in the floor. In 1854, the Sandwich Savings Bank was established. Banking no longer seemed remote and somewhat sinister when one could deliver one's spare dollars into the care of leading citizens who certainly had been canny enough with their own. With Captain Stutson among the directors, the Sandwich Savings Bank was likely to be as solid as the Boston and Sandwich factory itself which had weathered even the now legendary panic of 1837.

In other ways, Sandwich was showing the effects of time and the influence of the outside world. Where once anti-Masonic Democrats, led by Auntie Bacon's Josiah, had cried down the "impious rites" of Freemasonry, there was now a DeWitt Clinton Lodge A.F and A.M. Neighboring Barnstable had its Odd Fellows. No fraternal organization could be launched without the blessing of Mr. Jarves in the form of a present of glass shades. Even more than twenty years before, Mr. Jarves was monarch of all he surveyed, a benevolent master, but one whose power could not be denied.

The principal street from town to factory — fittingly called Jarves Street — was the main artery of community life. Up Jarves Street toward town clanged the glossy red factory hand-pump with its glasshouse crew, drawing its enthusiastic flock of small boys like the Pied Piper. Mr. Jarves allowed its aid to Sandwich fires not too hopelessly far in the hinterland and few fires were considered too far away.

Down Jarves Street toward the factory, grim-faced mothers dragged their reluctant small fry, whooping their little heads off, for the daily hour of breathing the fumes of the gashouse tar room, said to be the best remedy for what ailed them. It was an experience to become a lifelong memory for all who lived through it.

The name of Mr. Jarves was one of the first on a child's lips and the factory influence was foremost in his life. As soon as he could toddle, his first toy was likely to be a little cart homemade from a box mounted on the worn and discarded brush wheels used in the cutting room for cleaning, smoothing, and polishing. When he could walk a little farther, he was sure to come to the factory door to earn his first three dollars a week.

The variety of work done by boys in the factory was surprising. Besides the "block boys" who held and removed the molds for the blowers and the "taker-in boys" who carried the smallware on forked sticks to the annealing oven, there were "spare" or general utility boys, "door boys," "push boys," "clay boys," and "rimmer boys." Such jobs as "hole filler," "pipe minder," "shovel holder," and "jigger holder" were also filled by child labor, to judge from the three dollars per week listed as pay.

The types of positions open to men were as varied. There were the blowers, pressers, cutters, potmakers, clay men, coal wheelers, coal loaders, a blowing furnace man, furnace keepers, and "teasers," or *tiseurs*.

This last was much more skilled labor than simply stoking, and Mr. Jarves paid tribute to the fact:

> Much responsibility rests upon the furnace tenders. Constant care on their part is required. A slight neglect affects the quality of the glass. A check upon the furnace in founding time will spoil every pot of metal for the best work. Overheat, too, will destroy the pots, and the entire weekly melt will be launched into the cave at a loss of several thousand dollars. Even with the utmost care, a rush of air will not uncommonly pass through the furnace and destroy one or more pots in a minute's space.

There were also a number of other jobs — blacksmith and blacksmith striker, machinists, carpenters, skimmers, splitters, coke cleaners, teamsters, hostlers, watchmen, and just plain "labor." This was in addition to the bookkeeping and accounting department which was considered more genteel and drew from Sandwich families like the Fessendens who looked upon themselves as rather above the common herd.

Fewer and fewer of the town young men were going to sea or the city. The expanding factory seemed to offer opportunity for all. Once in a while there was a reversal of the trend. William Kern, a departmental superintendent, who had been with the factory from its earliest days, saw one of

his four sons break away from the clan craft. Tyler Kern —
as much a freak to his father as James was to Mr. Jarves —
took to whaling at a time when sons of sea captains were
going into the cutting room at the Boston and Sandwich factory. Old folks might say there was judgment in store for
sons who forsook the ways of their fathers. While one son
of an old whaler was falling slow victim to the peculiar
paralysis of thumb and forefinger which sometimes afflicted
cutters, young Tyler Kern on distant seas had a leg sheared
off by a shark.

The other three young Kerns went into the glasshouse as
soon as possible and duly served out their apprenticeship.
Billy and Henry blew the clock around on alternate shifts.
Albert went into the cutting room, probably because other
blowers had sons and it was felt that two Kerns were enough
to accept from one family.

The number of apprentices accepted in glass-blowing was
strictly limited in order to keep wages high — a practice of
which Mr. Jarves often bitterly complained. However, with
cutting, etching, and engraving more and more prominent
in the company output, there was always a place in the cutting room. Cutting required a steady hand and skill of the
highest order to make diamond-clear facets of patterns
marked in red crayon on the heavy "blanks" or to engrave
cameo-like surfaces with a copper wheel. On piecework, an
expert cutter could make as much money as any except the
gaffers or master blowers, and though he had to work constantly with his fingers in wet grit, a cutter could sleep in
his bed at night.

If ever Mr. Jarves had an illusion concerning the perma-
nence, the continuing progress of his life work, it was now
when young Marshes and Kerns and Laphams were growing
up in his glasshouse. He watched over these glass-factory
youngsters as if they had been his own sons, as, in a way, he
considered them. Billy Kern developed an exceptional dex-

terity with the blowpipe and a knack of handling men. Deming Jarves soon had him marked for an eventual supervisory position. But his chief pride and joy among the youngsters was James Lloyd, the son of the jolly Welsh blower, Samuel, and his strong-willed Vermont wife.

Young James Lloyd developed a genius for the chemistry of color. Mr. Jarves still had a passion for color as intense as when he was a child splashing paint on paper. He loved the glass colors of glowing jewel and flower tones — golden ruby, pearl, jade, sapphire blue, emerald, amber, rose, iris, lemon, and also salmon and dove. Now young Lloyd seemed able to concoct even more colors than Mr. Jarves could dream.

So Mr. Jarves sent him on a tour of Europe to learn from the latest developments there. It was a tour which profited Mr. Jarves far more than any of his son James's peregrinations. Lloyd brought back to his patron a notebook stuffed with valuable information:

> Fluorspar you can buy in New York as well as in England. If you get it from England, the best house is Hall and Co., Marble Works, Derby. Their price is .75 for 112 pounds, but what is bought in France is as good. In Europe, the best man for felspar is Monsieur Jouket, Allier, France.
>
> Uranium you can get the best from Poulenc Wittman, rue Neuve, St. Mary, Paris. Price $5. It is better than the English. Sulphate of copper get anywhere in Boston. Pick out pieces which have no yellow stains in them.

One of the highlights of Lloyd's tour was a visit to the Belleek china factory in Ireland. He came home with some very lovely pieces of ware and a plan for copying them in glass, perhaps leading to the famous Sandwich alabaster which was developed specifically when a chemical and cosmetic firm sent an order for jars of a distinctive color never before used.

James's experiments in color were Mr. Jarves's special delight. Behind the locked doors where the mysterious "batch" was compounded which in due season would be wheeled in barrows out to the alchemy of the furnace, Mr. Jarves would watch Lloyd in endless fascination, almost regarding the young man's career as an extension of his own dreams. James Lloyd developed a recipe book which became his most valuable and secret possession. But with great gusto, Mr. Jarves recorded his own favorite recipes in his *Reminiscences* for all to read.

It was a fascinating conglomeration of chemicals which were fused into the richly glowing colors:

Alabaster: To 500 lbs. of flint batch add:
    30 lbs. phosphate of soda
    10 lbs. allmine — i.e., calcined alum
    3 lbs. calcined magnesia
Canary: To 100 lbs. of batch add:
    8 oz. best oxide of uranium
    1 dr. oxide of copper
Agate: To 150 lbs. batch add:
    10 lbs. phosphate of lime
    6 lbs. arsenic
Light Emerald Green: 200 lbs. flint batch
    $2\frac{1}{2}$ lbs. filings calcined
    $\frac{1}{2}$ lb. antimony
Oriental Green: 110 lbs. flint batch
    1 lb. oxide of uranium
    2 oz. carbonate of copper
Opal: 500 lbs. batch
    60 lbs. phosphate of lime
    4 lbs. arsenic
    20 lbs. nitrate of soda

The prize of the collection was, of course, the so-called Golden Ruby "which takes the lead both in cost and richness."

Take one ounce of pure gold. (Tradition says this took the form of $20 gold pieces, but development of the recipe shows that some difficulties would be presented by gold in this form.)

Dissolve in a glass vessel 2 oz. pure sal ammoniac acid and five oz. pure nitric acid which will take 6 to 7 days. Drop in at a time say 1/20 part of the gold. When the first piece is dissolved, drop in another 1/20 portion of the gold, and so on until the oz. of gold is all dissolved. This will require 24 hours. Evaporate the solution to dryness.

Then prepare in a glass vessel 6 oz. pure nitric acid, 2 oz. muriatic acid, and one oz. of highest proof alcohol. Mix them well together and drop in pure grained tin a bit at a time, but *beware of the fumes*. (Since no definite amount of tin was stated, apparently the mixture was simply concocted to the right consistency by trial, rather in the manner of old-fashioned cooks.) Stir it well with a glass rod. Dilute the solution with 80 times its bulk of distilled water. Then take the prepared gold, dissolved in a quart of distilled water and pour it steadily into the solution of tin as above prepared, stirring all the while.

Let it settle 24 to 30 hrs., pour off the water, leave the settlings, pour in 2/3 qt. of water. Stir it thoroughly and let it settle 30 hrs. Pour off as before and filter the precipitate through filtering paper. The result is the purple of Crassus [Cassius].

The oz. of gold thus prepared must be well incorporated with the following batch — say 32 lbs. fine silex, 26 lbs. oxide of lead, 16 lbs. refined nitre. Melt the same in a clean pot, one little used and smooth inside. When filled in, put the stopper to the pot loose, leaving it slightly open. Leave it 5 or 6 hours or time to settle. Then a back stopper can be put up. In the usual time, it should be ready to be worked out in solid egg-shaped balls and exposed to the air to be partially cooled. They are then to be placed in the lier under a strong fire which will in 2 or 3 hours turn them to a red color. Then the pans may be drawn slowly to anneal the balls. [These were probably the famous "witch balls," believed by mediaeval glass blowers to ward off evil spirits.]

There were those like Billy Kern who prized the crystal-clear flint more highly than colored glass as requiring greater skill. Color might cover up an inferiority in the "batch." Mr. Jarves, in his *Reminiscences* gave some credit to this point of view. There were, he stated, plenty of recipes for the composition of flint or crystal glass. Every gaffer, as a matter of fact, had his own favorite. Theodore Kern, Billy's uncle, was famous for the high-quality glass he could make from an economical "batch" which used the largest possible amount of cullet or old glass — either broken bits or pot scrapings.

"But no mixture that we know can secure a uniform shade in each pot," Mr. Jarves continued. "The component parts of glass are well-known, and the mixer's sure guide is to watch the effect of heat on each pot, for he soon finds that the mixture that gives good color in one pot will in another in the same furnace prove bad."

As the ultimate in crystal glass, Mr. Jarves gave a recipe for "Diamond Glass." "Four lbs. borax, one lb. fine sand, reduce both to a subtile powder and melt together in a closed crucible set in an air furnace under a strong fire till fusion is perfect. Let it cool in the crucible and a pure hard glass, capable of cutting common glass like a diamond, which it rivals in brilliancy, is produced."

Each recipe in Mr. Jarves's book represented patient hours of trial and error on the part of his skilled workmen. The Jarves rewards for successful experiments had gone on to the second generation. Glass blowers were continually stirring up all sorts of odds and ends of chemicals, sand, and glass in home cauldrons. Books have it that some constructed miniature glass furnaces in their cellars. Billy Kern's niece laughs at the idea and tells how he drove his wife nearly crazy with his "doll's kittles" set among the coals of the kitchen stove while pies and cakes were trying to get themselves baked.

But glassworkers' wives of the younger generation were uncommonly tolerant of glassmaking messes because they had mostly come from glass-factory families themselves. With the larger glass-factory population, there were more clannish intermarriages than in the early days when so many young bachelor blowers had been shipped into town. Kerns married Laphams. Pretty Irene Dilloway, daughter of the company's moldmaking genius, became the bride of James Lloyd.

In 1854, the ultimate in glass-factory romance was expressed in a piece of glass which might even have satisfied the aesthetic urge of James Jackson Jarves who was inclined to look down his nose at almost anything originating in his father's factory. All the skill and good will of the workmen, all the artistry of the designer went into the large tulip-shaped chalice, crystal-clear, etched on one side in a frosty pattern with an armored knight on horseback bearing on his shield the letters "J. W. J." and on the other in a wreath of dainty filigree, "Mary Waterman." John Jarves was engaged to little Mary Waterman, the seventeen-year-old daughter of Deming Jarves's old friend and assistant.

Mr. Jarves was delighted. It seemed that at last he might count on one glassmaking son to follow in his way. He had lost all hope of the others. In 1850, young George, always so docile, always so disinterested, had fallen prey to consumption like so many of his young cousins of Stutson blood.

"G —— second son of my sister J —— died in March. He was a young man of 25. Of course, death was to him unexpected and undesirable. But ere it came, he sought and (we trust) found the Savior," reported Auntie Bacon.

The father had long since accepted James philosophically as an act of God and could even display an offhand pride in seemingly casual reference to the latest book "from the pen of my son." When Deming, Jr., on reaching his teens, had declared a fierce and determined ambition to be a sailor,

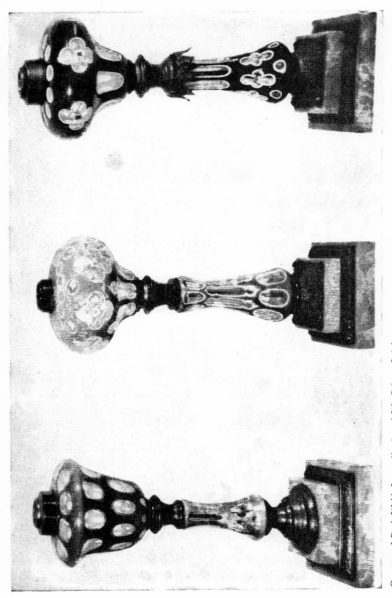

Courtesy of Ruth Webb Lee; collection of W. Colston Leigh

These rare overlay lamps were used for kerosene lighting at the height of the period of Victorian ornateness.

The wedding of Deming Jarves's son, John, and Superintendent Waterman's daughter, Mary, was the occasion for the creation of this etched crystal chalice.

Mr. Jarves with a sigh set him out on a trip around the world as lone passenger in one of Mackay's clipper ships.

It was a kill-or-cure proposition. After bucking wintery gales around the Cape of Good Hope, being hurled from here to heaven in a China Sea typhoon, and landing in the midst of the Calcutta Mutiny, Junior came home as tamely as could be in the Cunard paddle-wheeler "Niagara" to serve as clerk in his father's glass salesrooms at 51 Federal Street. But there was no interest in glass. It seemed rather as if the uncommonly lively young man were merely gathering fresh energy for some new and unpredictable venture.

That left only John. Part of Mr. Jarves's zest during these years had been attributable to the fact that John was so often by his side to share in his enthusiasms. John is supposed to have had a hand in the making of some very lovely ruby salts with silvered panels. John — grave and slender — had his picture taken in the midst of co-workers and bottles of chemicals. But if John ever had his moments of following other interests, the father must have felt cold fear lest he slip away like the others.

Now his heart would anchor him to Sandwich. Though Mary Waterman was nearer the age of young Deming, Jr., it was the older and rather serious John who had been charmed at the transformation of the lively pretty child into a lovely young woman with a warm vivacity, derived from her French mother, that made Bostonian damsels seem somewhat stodgy. The Watermans were not ready to give their blessing immediately. To them, Mary was still a child, and a child could be easily dazzled. She could not have helped knowing the small-town sensation that her courtship made in the eyes of Sandwich and Jarvesville, and she would not have been human if she had not enjoyed playing the heroine in the glasshouse romance. And she had nothing but a Sandwich background against which to evaluate the experience. Was she in love with John or merely with the idea of marrying a Jarves? She was sent away for a year to a girls' boarding school on the Hudson to acquire some outland graces and test her constancy of heart. She came back with heart unchanged to be married to her John in 1855.

Brother James sent his blessing in the form of a Murillo nativity painted on tile, the authenticity of which is somewhat doubtful. Mr. Jarves expressed his satisfaction and his hopes by building a house for the young couple on Main Street at the head of Jarves, next door to the rather ugly frame dwelling of Captain Stutson (of late years erroneously called the "Jarves House.") It was a rather charming Victorian villa with the newly stylish arched windows and brought a hint of Brookline and the fashionable Boston suburbs to the Cape sands. The imaginative could read into certain knobs of the decorative scrollwork Mr. Jarves's triumphant Acorn motif.

Mr. Jarves had the house built of brick with a wood shell inside and out to be snug and solid as possible against Cape Cod gales, since John was subject to colds perhaps aggravated by the change of temperature from the heat of the glasshouse to the raw sea air. In spite of Mr. Jarves's care, Sandwich callers found the paneled, high-ceilinged rooms, dim in the shade of elm boughs, a little chilly after the lowstudded houses of the preceding generation. But it was an appropriate setting in which the young bride might entertain in her most gracious New York finishing-school manner. Even as though on Boylston Street, she could receive old friends by gaslight before a massive marble fireplace. She began the custom of regaling with late lunches company directors down on the one o'clock train to witness a "pouring" from some new formula at the factory. And on entering the house all guests were confronted with a staircase quite as elegant as could be found anywhere. Describing a half-circle in its descent there was — as if Mr. Jarves had had a thought to the future — a wonderful curving banister for sliding grandchildren.

Root and Fruit

MR. JARVES'S DYNASTIC HOPES would depend largely on potential Sandwich grandchildren. His son James's Hawaiian-born Horatio was not likely to put his nose inside a glasshouse. There was a possibility that he and his sister might not even grow up as Americans.

James's European visit was no conventional grand tour. He clung to the continent tenaciously, settling in Paris with the excuse that it offered his children "superior advantages of education to what exist in the United States." What his father thought of the proposition mattered little. As long as factory dividends held high, whatever J. J. J.'s whims, his mother usually managed the wherewithal to satisfy them.

The booming years of the late forties and early fifties marked one of the country's most expansive periods of gain. Some cotton mills were making an annual profit of forty per cent — or more than was paid to all the "hands" of the corporation for labor.[1] Smoking furnaces and clattering looms

[1] Norman J. Ware, *The Industrial Worker 1840–1860.*

were turning out the reservoir of riches necessary to free some part of the population from the compulsion of daily toil if a culture is to grow from simple folkways. On family dividends, young men were sent on intellectual and artistic conquests of the Old World; they came home with a cargo of culture that made Boston known as the Athens of America. With experiments in living and learning taking shape on every hand, there was the urge for leadership in charity and enlightenment as well as liberty and culture.

James Jackson Jarves found "something degrading" in the thought that the progress of art, science, and even religion depended to a great extent on the time and means yielded by money. He never gave, however, any hint of a clear realization that the pattern of his own life was as direct a result of the despised industrial system as the cheap glass pressed out by mass production in the Sandwich factory.

In both the prosperity of the period and its cultural and ethical by-product, the Boston and Sandwich Glass Company had its part. Since the Boston and Sandwich Company averaged a six per cent dividend for its sixty-three years of operation, including in the reckoning periods of panic when no dividend was paid, this must have been a very fruitful period indeed in company history. And the fruits were not limited to the Jarves family.

Considerable money of the Howe family, gained in shipping and the manufacture of cordage, flowed into the Boston and Sandwich Company. And while Joseph N. Howe at one time was president of the company, his brother, Doctor Samuel Gridley Howe, became a pathfinder in the education and care of blind and idiot children, an undertaking no doubt supported in some measure by dividends from the Sandwich factory. Doctor Howe's wife was the already famous Julia Ward Howe. Her sister, Louisa Ward, had married the expatriate sculptor, Tom Crawford, creator of an Armed Liberty for the Capitol and a Beethoven for the

Boston Music Hall, which was said to be the first statue in the country raised to an artistic genius. A Sandwich glass dollar or two doubtless found its way to Rome to fatten a lean year when there were no commissions for what young Jarves contemptuously called "old clothes" statuary.

The surplus wealth of the country with its cultural ramifications had passed far beyond the tithes squeezed from hard-handed farmers who, while they might split hairs seven ways in their own beliefs, felt it a duty to thrust an orthodox God and tidy New England ways into the oddest corners of the earth. As theology was the first science and preaching the first art in America, so the missionary had been the earliest exportable object of culture — and the missionary spirit became a permanent American characteristic.

Subsidized by Sandwich glass, James Jackson Jarves had arrived in Hawaii with the mission in his own mind of bringing Bostonian culture to the Polynesians.

He found the church missionaries already in Hawaii "shrewd, intelligent, hard-working men" very successfully teaching the natives "how to handle a hoe, a broomstick, a plough or needle as well as to spell ab and ba, measure the revolution of the planets, and draw forth instruction from the well of living waters." In this last respect, they were least successful, achieving a state of grace for the Polynesians which the somewhat bewildered natives themselves described as "mikonaree here," pointing to the head — "ole mikonaree [no missionary] here," designating less exalted portions of the body.

James Jackson Jarves did not have much better luck with his mission of culture. "To demonstrate the capacity of the Polynesians for civilization was my pet youthful hobby," he wrote. "It was with pain that I perceived the actual truth."

When at last he resigned himself to the fact that the Polynesians had no particular urge for civilization as he saw it, he came home to turn his missionary zeal upon his father

and the Boston and Sandwich Company. He felt a burning
need for his efforts.

> While men have to contend with stern nature, winning
> civilization step by step from the wilderness [he preached],
> they have no desire for aught but the necessary. The useful
> is the next step. Then come the requirements of ease and
> luxury and their attendant train of degenerating influences.
> In the U.S. we have arrived at that period of our national
> career; or rather while on our frontiers, the strife of man
> with nature is in constant progress, on our sea-board, we
> have enslaved her to all our sensual comforts to a degree
> that no other nation has ever rivalled on so gigantic a scale.
> Mechanics racked to construct in quantities those things
> that tend to glitter or mislead, machinery multiplied for the
> fabrication of all objects, not only of use, but of ornament,
> art degraded to manufacture, all bespeak a people with their
> eyes yet unopened to a sense of their full capacity for great-
> ness and refinement.

This quantity fabrication of "things that tend to glitter"
could certainly apply to the imitation elegancies for
workingmen's wives which flowed forth from Sandwich. As
a boy, he had deplored the cheaper mass manufactures of the
Boston and Sandwich Company, the pressed glasses, the plain
lamps, the bitters and apothecary bottles which, contrary to
present belief, formed the bulk of the trade. The repug-
nance intensified as he saw how primitive peoples who fashioned their utensils with their own hands made things of
use, such as the Polynesian paddles and canoes, also things of
beauty. He found that in some objects to which heart as
well as head were devoted — the beloved gadgets of speed
and production, fire engines, locomotives, machinery, and
tools, Americans indeed had combined "that equilibrium of
lines, proportions, and masses which are among the fundamental causes of abstract beauty."

However, glass was a striking contrast. Once in a while,

he would approve some glowing new color or admire an intricate bit of cutting. He gave credit where he thought credit was due:

> Our cut, engraved, and colored glass excels in transparency, polish, outline, and lucidity of design — mere mechanical excellences; but we meet, as in all other ornament, a wearisome repetition of the same patterns and styles, each the exact counterpart of the other, to satisfy the modern desire to have sets of objects. In old times when brains guided hands in fashioning objects of art, the mind of the artist got into his work, and no two things were ever precisely alike. Our age holds to cheapening and multiplying articles rather than to their artistic worth. Hence, its productive energies tend to substitute mechanical for aesthetic excellence and to employ machinery in place of fingers. Everywhere we meet manufactured repetitions.

These observations were true enough. Though he might have approved of the artistry which went into the original iron molds for the lacy glass work, he shuddered to see pieces machine-pressed by the thousands. Besides, even lacy glass with the comparatively expensive molds was slowly giving way to the modern urge for cheapness and quantity. The fashion was no longer for elaborate cup plates, compotes, and nappies to supplement fine china, but for complete sets from sauce dish to goblet in cruder and cheaper patterns.

J. J. J.'s distaste for his father's glass in a way symbolized his feeling for his country as a whole, for Boston and Sandwich ware had expressed every phase of the country's growth to a greater extent than any other manufacture. This expression could be seen both in pattern and article.

The earliest patterns had been inspired by Old World tradition — Gothic Bar and Grecian Border, Acanthus, Lyre, Horn of Plenty. Now there was a decided New World trend — Blackberry, Blue Jay, Holly, Daisy, Grape, Morning Glory, Shell, Moss Rose. Then there were pictorial and commemorative patterns for every hero and event — Lafayette and the ship *Cadmus* which brought him to America; Henry Clay; the frigate *Constitution,* saved from destruction by Oliver Wendell Holmes's stirring "Old Ironsides." In later years would come the three feathers of the Prince of Wales to celebrate the visit to America, and the Cable design to mark the laying of the French cable to Cape Cod shores. In significance, designs ranged from Mr. Jarves's purely personal Acorn to old Tippecanoe's Industrial Pattern with its smoking factory already at hand to crowd the log cabin and plainsman from the scene.

The product was equally varied, ranging from costly cut glass for special orders to the endless flow of cheap articles for the convenience of Mr. Jarves's always carefully considered "humbler classes." Wares changed with the times. Beautiful candlesticks in color or in dolphin or Grecian designs were still being made, but crucifix candlesticks had come in for the Catholic trade. And now, even in the days before kerosene, there were increasing numbers of whale oil and spirit lamps. These followed the new Victorian ornateness of design with vari-colored globes and feet. Some clear flint globes had even received an outer coating of color through which patterns were cut to the underlying crystal base.

Mr. Jarves made certain that whatever way the world and the country took, glass — his glass — would play its part. To the manufacture of ship lanterns had been added ruby railroad lanterns. Gas brought in quantities of gas globes for the cities and larger towns. With the population growing, times changing so fast, workmen could hardly stop to putter with so much loving care over the old intricate molds.

This state of affairs was as satisfactory to Deming Jarves as it was deplorable to his son. It was the father who was the man of the future; he found it wholly desirable to bring cheaper goods to more people, to see glassmaking "tributary

to the comfort of man" and bring its comforts and elegances
within reach of "the poorest and humblest." The son considered only the individual, stifled in the fundamental human urge for creative expression. He set forth his ideas in
a way which might have held warning for a world in the
making:

> Machinery is an advantage to the artisan only to the de-
> gree that it saves him time for the enjoyment and cultiva-
> tion of his intellectual faculties. Modern civilization is
> treading a dangerous path in converting the working classes
> into mere automatons for the production of objects into
> which no thought of their own can by any possibility enter.
> Statesmen should ponder over the results of merely time-
> consuming, soul-deadening labor. To it may be traced the
> restlessness and misery of so many of the working classes
> throughout those nations in which Science is paramount to
> Art.

Granted virtues in both viewpoints, there was little
chance of reconciliation when they were held by different
members of the same family.

"That awful pressed stuff!" James finally remarked bluntly to his father. "I don't at all like the idea of your making
it."

"But you like to spend the money it makes, don't you?"
was the characteristically ironical reply.

James could not deny it. He was among the first to attempt the paradoxical escape from the machine age by means
of its profits.

2

Like all expatriates, the farther he wandered from home,
the greater his theoretical appreciation of his native land.
England at first enchanted him with its combination of art
consciousness and what passed in those days for adequate

sanitation. He became acquainted with John Ruskin, and
perhaps unwittingly began to pattern his career after that of
the already famous English art critic. Partly as a result of
Ruskin's aesthetic sermons, England was undergoing an
awakening of art interest. James Jarves wrote enthusiasti-
cally of eighty schools of design scattered through the land
for "the education of artisans and the benefit of manufacturing interests," and praised the "reform of ordinary utensils showing that even pots and kettles could be made as
comely as solid."

Yet he forsook England as soon as he had grasped the personal meaning of the immutable British caste system. He
found class consciousness even in art, commenting that in
gazing on British portraits "we are reminded more of position than of mind." If the United States was not without
social division, society was still in a highly fluid state in
which the domestic or laborer of one day might by a fluke
of luck or a spurt of genius find himself on top of the heap
the next. James Jackson Jarves, who had enjoyed himself as
"the rich squire's son" of Sandwich, was in England hopelessly immured in the mercantile middle class together with
his children and grandchildren after him. If classes were to
be rigid, it was not good unless one could choose one's own.
Education which could instill such slavish acceptance of a
status quo was not what he wanted for his children.

As France seemed to offer an ideal combination of republican virtues and Old World graces, he settled in Paris. He
treated the French with the same sharp impersonal scrutiny
he had borne upon the Polynesians, however. When seized
once more with writer's itch, he produced the two volumes,
*Parisian Sights and French Principles Seen Through Ameri-
can Spectacles.* Amid the glitter of French household decora-
tions — looking glasses, clocks, bronzes, candelabra, and
gilded furniture — he first came to an appreciation of the
"useful and unpretending mechanical arts of the United

States, the convenience of bath-rooms, good closets, economical fire-places, nice fitting doors or easy and ingenious locks
and door handles."

He showed his greatest critical acumen in an analysis of
the basic governmental differences in the two republics. In
the United States, he found the authorities

> so jealous of civil liberty that they leave much latitude to
> rogues and charlatans rather than intrust any power with
> the arbitrary control of individual acts, even though the
> general welfare may seem to warrant its exercise. It is only
> where a nuisance has become intolerable that society bestirs
> itself for a remedy. The result is that many lives are lost
> and much injury done by carelessness, quackery, imperfect
> construction of boilers, burning of boats, or collision of cars
> before the public becomes fully sensible that the right of
> public safety is paramount to the right of private gain.

The French government, on the other hand, based on the
theory that "no member of the community has the right to
do that which is hurtful to the public at large" left nothing
to chance in the protection of the populace. Long before
such matters had been considered in the United States,
Jarves found every steam engine tested before use, buildings
inspected for safety, meat for the city of Paris slaughtered in
authorized establishments "with the utmost regard to humanity compatible with the business and an economy of
material that leaves no waste." But he was soon irked by the
ridiculous red tape of the "all-meddling authority" which
prevented him from replacing a drain without a police per-
mit and even locked adult and presumably sane railroad
passengers in a compartment until time for a guard to herd
them aboard train, lest, left to their own devices, they might
stand talking on the platform and let the train go off without them.

There was one feature, however, of the paternalistic state
of which he approved with all his heart. From the Jardin des

Plantes with its specimens running into the hundreds of
thousands to the infinite and dazzling beauties of the Louvre,
the government fostered collections on a gargantuan scale.
To the born collector, France was a delirium of delight.

Slowly J. J. J.'s grand life mission was taking shape and he
began to preach, with what a British reviewer of his books
called the true "missionary zeal." ("Thanks for the word!"
was J. J. J.'s fervent amen), "the educational advantages of
galleries and museums and their conservative and refining
influence on society." "To stimulate the art feeling, our
public should have free access to museums or galleries in
which shall be exhibited in chronological series specimens
of art of all nations and schools including our own." Realizing the difficulty of converting his countrymen to any project
which did not appeal to "that Yankee thrift which judges of
the utility of an investment by its monied dividend," he
argued museums as shrewd national financial schemes because of the profits to be derived from fees for the checking
of canes, umbrellas, and parasols.

His life now became wholly dedicated to art, and he voiced
his creed in the words, "Art is universal. It unites mankind
in common brotherhood. As missionary of civilization, its
message is to both heart and mind."

Of course, in the end, art led to Italy. Once more, his children provided the immediate reason for the move. He had
caught French tutors bribing them to learn their lessons instead of teaching them to love knowledge for its own sake.
In Florence, he found tutors docile and cheap. Living quarters, servants, and food were equally inexpensive. There
were also "a laughing landscape, treasures of art, and a hos-
pitality which makes Florence Paradise for exiles in pursuit
of artistic ease or literary quiet."

Best of all, he had found that "society in which idleness is
still held in honor" which de Tocqueville had described as
the goal of American expatriates. To be sure, the small

group of other Americans already in Florence were for the most part not quite gentlemen, but sculptors busily purveying dying Indians to the European trade and turning out quantities of standard-brand statesmen and an occasional titillating pseudo-Greek nude for home consumption. But the tools of a writer are not so obtrusive. As long as the factory was smoking steadily away at Sandwich, he was able to achieve the appearance of utter indolence, the carriage and coachman, and box at the opera which, he reported, were the only requirements for being accepted into Florentine society.

He enjoyed heading his letters and footing his prefaces, "Casa Dauphinée, Piazza Maria Antonia." It was pleasant to interlard his writings with offhand references to his good friends, the Brownings of Casa Guidi, John Ruskin, George Eliot, Rossetti, "Monsieur Crescendo," as Rossini was called, or "the famous Mrs. Trollope who has done Americans a world of good by her abuse."

With Trollopian bluntness, James hammered away at American art "ordered as one orders a style of calico from a cotton factory," infected with "a virulent epidemic of sunsets." . . . "Our artists go in for *bigness, greatness, largeness* culminating in what one artist calls 'full length landscapes' — icebergs, tropical scenery, Niagaras painted mostly to display the painters' autographs."

Despairing of getting Americans to take any but a utilitarian view of art, he felt that perhaps the country would make its soundest artistic progress in architecture. He admired the spare, functional lines of New England farmhouses, and hoped for further development of native forms to match the growth of the country. Hence he decried servile copying or unfortunate scrambling of European styles — "bastard Greek temples for banks, colleges, and custom houses, ignoble and impoverished Gothic chapels converted into libraries — an ironical use since Gothic was evolved by and for a generation which could not read."

To be sure, he considered the classic trend at Washington well suited to what he called the city's "chess-board outline" (he preferred Boston's wandering ways), but the Capitol "beautiful before its enlargement," he declared "marred by the disproportionate height of the florid cast iron dome placed with crushing effect on the roof of an edifice complete without it." As for the projected plan for the Washington monument, he found the phallus a not inappropriate memorial to the Father of his Country, but objected to the "extraordinary portico of pillars. The nation will be in possession of the tallest shaft in existence rising from a forest of Lilliputian columns, much as a handle is stuck in the broom at its base. Our children will be glad, it is hoped, to pay a million of money to pitch the monstrosity into the ocean." Perhaps for once in his life, J. J. J.'s countrymen heeded his words, since the Washington monument eventually stood in the approved "stern nakedness" of Bunker Hill.

At the same time, James Jackson Jarves was no purblind idolater of the art of Europe. Italian art, for all its superlative virtues, he found remarkable for an absence of humor and domestic life. It had taken the French school two centuries to understand the value of nature and equally long to find out there was a people to paint for. Rubens's infant cherubs resembled "little boys just recovering from the excitement of a whipping or a dose of gin."

Neither was his mission confined to the abusive negative approach. On his periodic brief visits home, he would even spend a day or two with John and Mary in Sandwich where it was pleasant to be pointed out on the street as "the writer" even if no one there read what he had written. He now made one last attempt to convert his father and the factory to Old World artistry.

"Examine the fantastic glass of the Venetian Republic," he said. "So flexible, light, varied, and gleesome are its tinted or lucid forms that it seems like crystallized laughter of the immortals — frozen breath which the next warm breath will dissolve into new shapes of air-like matter."

Here was a direct challenge to Mr. Jarves who did not like to admit that anything in glassmaking was beyond his powers. But gleesome glass proved too much for Sandwich blowers. It had a way of popping off under their noses in a thousand splinters that soon killed any urge for further experimentation.

Their inventive talents and pride ran in such directions as the ware stamped:

> MARSH'S NEW
> PATTERN BLOWN BITTER
> BOTTLE WITH SCREW CAP
> MADE BY HIMSELF
> J. MARSH
> 1 LIBERTY ST.   SANDWICH

And bitter bottles, apothecary ware, commercial lanterns, and cheap glasses would continue their uninterrupted flow while J. J. J. retreated across the sea for fresh perspective.

Then, after an interval, he could again appreciate the New England town like Sandwich, "desperately utilitarian and homely" though he might consider it, where the Yankee had "secured his personal and political independence, made an orderly and comfortable home, built his school and his meeting house, connected his village by railway and telegraph and put steam to his hardest labor." In comparison with the Italian hamlet's "stone hovels huddled together, few or no panes of glass, rooms small, dark, bat-like — reeking filth of an unwashed population where water is often far-fetched and hard-to-get," even the presence of "goats beloved of Pan, donkeys of Bacchus, grape-laden peasants and lithe maidens in scant draperies" could not prevent his asking, "May not the picturesque cost humanity too much?"

Art, however, had a meaning which transcended the mere

question of the utilitarian versus the picturesque. Over and over again in his great series, *Art Hints, Art Studies, The Art Idea, Art Thoughts,* he hammered on his two tenets of artistic faith. Art must grow naturally from physical and spiritual needs. Its only valid foundation was in the hearts of the people. He found something debased in all art which owed its existence wholly to the patronage of wealth and nobility. Surely, the freedom, the initiative, the bursting vitality of his own people, so much admired when he was at a safe distance from the stir, should produce a worthy art.

Accordingly, he devoted a great deal of effort toward "stimulating the art-feelings" of "the vast multitude who are the bone, muscle, acting and thinking brains of the nation, deciding our destinies for good or evil." He foresaw New York's Central Park in the future as a "University of the People" with opportunities for

> glorious music, invigorating games, the humanizing sight of merry childhood, the zoological and horticultural gardens, and lastly, galleries of art, science, and history enshrined in beautiful temples, open to all without cost.
>
> If art be kept a rare and tabooed thing, a specialty for the rich and powerful, it excites in the vulgar mind envy and hate. First, therefore, educate the people in the principle of art and then scatter among them with lavish hand, free as water, its richest treasures.

But where were these treasures to scatter? He could only express the hope that, with the rapid accumulation of riches in the new republic, some day great private collections would be formed by "individual exertion." "The city of America which first possesses a fine gallery of art will become the Florence of the continent."

Then one fine day the thought came to him that his might be the exertion which would make his Boston the Florence as well as the Athens of America.

After hours, or during a lull in business, glassmakers often made some of their finest pieces for themselves; this table set of silvered glass is from the original collection of Gaffer Edward Haines.

One reward of present-day Sandwich-glass collectors is a dining room like this in the Yarmouthport home of Ruth A. and Leslie Pfeiffer.

Threaded glass, of which this window in the Sandwich Historical Society Building is made, was one of the latest developments of the Sandwich glassmaker's art.

3

When inspiration came to him, he was at work on what he considered his greatest book, *Art Studies*. This was a treatment of his favorite period in the history of all art — early Italian religious painting, the development of Christian art from the stiff stylized symbolism of the Byzantine to the glorious climax of Raphael before the debasement of the Renaissance. These works were created before the invention of printing when art was the sole medium of expression of ideas for the people. Therefore, J. J. J. felt that they held the deepest significance for his countrymen as art not artificially cultivated, but springing naturally from spiritual soil. "Confessions of faith," he called them, by men "not artists only, but prophets who foretold the joy of heaven and the woe of hell."

He had begun to collect a few for his book to illustrate "by well-chosen examples the historic development and progress of Italian art." Now this handful was to be expanded to "the project of an historical series of Old Masters," a Jarves collection, "the nucleus of a public gallery in Boston."

It was an ambitious, but not an impossible goal. He knew exactly what he wanted to do. A few good pictures, as he said, were far more effective than a myriad collected solely in reference to number.

For ten years, he haunted auction rooms and stirred up the dust of attics and the filth of peasant hovels in his quest. With a gusto of self-appreciation, he advertised what a not so ardent admirer called "the immense labor without regard to cost, the hairbreadth escape from dirt, knavery, and superstition, the self sacrifice and intense enthusiasm of said Jarves in his search for said canvases."

"The funds were in part my own earnings," he said, although his income from his books and random buying and selling of pictures would hardly have covered household expenses, "and partly loans from a relative who, in consenting to render substantial aid, warned me I was half a century too soon."

The cost of his collection before he had finished amounted to $66,000. In 1857, the flow of money was stopped at the source.

"The Sandwich Glass Company, like numerous other corporations, has recently been made the subject of rumor in respect to their solvency," Sandwich folk were reading in their paper. "We need only say that such rumors are entirely destitute of foundation as the company was never freer from embarrassment."

The reassurance was a bit of unwarranted optimism. All-pervading panic was gripping the land once more. The company stopped paying dividends.

Naturally, there was no surplus for Old Masters. But if no physical hardship daunted J. J. J., he was equally undismayed by financial hazard. When funds from home were not so readily forthcoming, he simply mortgaged the pictures already purchased and kept on his course.

In the end, by one means or another, he had acquired works by nearly one hundred and fifty Old Masters. In addition to names which at that time had meaning only to the student of art in Italy were those becoming familiar to all fairly literate people — Botticelli, Leonardo, Raphael. European critics and Italian curators warmed his heart with praise. He was given credit for originating "the idea of a chronological series representing the progress of art during five centuries from the triptychs of the mediaeval epoch down to Raphael and Andrea del Sarto."

"Italy will lament the loss of so many treasures of art designed for the nucleus of a gallery in Boston, the Athens, or more properly speaking, the Florence of America," declaimed one. "If these pictures had ears to hear me, I should say from the depths of my heart, 'Go to the New World, become missionaries of culture to a great people.' "

Boston proved as unready as Honolulu to receive J. J. J.'s mission of culture. He had seemed to imagine a city and countryside panting for the uplifting influence of Italian primitives. But Boston people and the folk who flocked from the rural towns like Sandwich thought that they had access to art enough in the "upwards of 1000 Costly Paintings and Rare and Valuable Engravings among which are Sully's great picture of Washington Crossing the Delaware and Portraits of the Governors of Massachusetts and all the Presidents" to be found in the great Boston Museum. There they could also see "Sterling and Witty Comedies, Thrilling and Ingenious Dramas, Soul-Inspiring Operas, Mirth-Moving Farces, or Gorgeous Spectacles." Additional attractions ranged from fossils to "living novelties such as giants, dwarfs, and Orang Outangs." The advertisement appearing in the newspaper in Sandwich, as in other towns served by railroad, was topped by a little woodcut of the choicest curiosity of all — the Remarkable Feejee Mermaid, flicking her tail and admiring herself in a hand glass. Since all this "splendid, chaste, and amusing entertainment" was only twenty-five cents, children half price, who could be expected to care a penny for a gallery of dingy-seeming, second-hand pictures from Florence, Italy?

If J. J. J. could have given his pictures outright, perhaps the Florence of America would have deigned to offer a shelter. But when Charles Eliot Norton and Francis Parker, as a committee of the Boston Athenaeum, made a gesture of mild interest, he had to reply that, though he would have been glad to give the collection to his native city, he could, because of the mortgage, only donate a portion of the cost if friends of art would contribute the rest. A halfhearted attempt to raise the price of purchase failed, and the effort precipitated an embittering controversy.

Mrs. Harriet Beecher Stowe, it is true, pronounced the collection "incredibly good — a very fine one even for Italy. What then would it be for Boston?"

There were other points of view. One day, a certain Athenaeum member touring Italy sneaked a preview of the private gallery in the Casa Dauphinée in Jarves's absence. Old Masters, particularly primitives, have varying effects upon the beholder. Two lions licking their teeth as they stood over the infant Saint Mark frightened J. J. J.'s small Florentine-born daughter, Firenze, into docile behavior and convinced her even in infancy that she had had art enough for a long lifetime. A single glance at the gallery brought Mr. Wales of Boston to the same conclusion. He saw only "uncouth faces and awkward forms" without the transfiguring "religious fervor and saintly glow." He carried home "false impressions to persons who might otherwise have favored the enterprise."

J. J. J. was soon complaining bitterly that "besides the expense and toil incurred in getting valuable old paintings, the owner in America is virtually called upon to show that he is not a rascal in having them while not a few individuals are inclined to treat him as if he were trying to bring a pest into the country."

In the midst of financial harassment and personal pique, he relieved himself with the autobiographical novel, *Why and What Am I?* Lamenting a lack of appreciation on the part of the whole world, his mother excepted, the "Inquirer" posed as the romantic victim of an unhappy marriage: he loved books and his wife loved balls; he rose early and she slept late; he drank red wine and she drank white. There was also a *soupçon* of adultery, and he concluded with the aphorism: "Marriage can be made self-corrective by viewing it in its true sense as a school in which to train the virtues for heaven. If its trials are sore, so are its years few."

He might later insist as much as he wished that the book was wholly fictional. More than one "Dear Reader" must have drawn his own conclusions from the fact that the "Inquirer" had called his recalcitrant angel Constantia Russell while J. J. J.'s own wife had been Elizabeth Russell Swain.

J. J. J.'s "affectionate friend," Elizabeth Barrett Browning, wrote, "My sympathies have gone with you and glowed as they went."

His daughter declared, "He gave my poor mother trouble enough to hasten her days on earth."

When, at last, in 1860, he received a lukewarm invitation to exhibit his pictures in New York, gay lovely Elizabeth lay forever still in a foreign grave. Along with the Old Masters for New York, he brought back his three children to deposit with his parents in Boston. In his chagrin at lack of American appreciation of the "missionaries of culture," he felt only a petty personal annoyance at the storm brewing in the nation and failed utterly to heed the American tragedy working itself out at 64 Boylston Street, Boston, and Jarves Street, Sandwich.

End of an Era

ONE DAY, the president of the Boston and Sandwich Glass Company arrived in Sandwich for a formal tour of inspection. As, cigar in mouth, he approached the door, he was halted by a watchman who pointed to a "No Smoking" sign.

"Don't you know who I am? I am the president of the Company," announced the visiting dignitary.

"I don't care who you are," answered the watchman, who had seen presidents come and go, but Mr. Jarves remain, "you can't go into that factory with that cigar."

The president turned back to finish his cigar outside. Within the factory, Mr. Jarves's will was law. With his knowledge of the number of glasshouses gone up in flames, he did not depend overmuch on the little red hand-engine. He had made the most rigid regulations against smoking on the premises although a "no smoking" rule might seem a bit finicky in the midst of flying sparks and the falling of molten glass. Disapproval of the directors bothered Mr. Jarves not in the least. After these many years of running the factory according to his will, he had come to think it his own as much as if it had remained in fact a personal enterprise instead of expanding into a corporation.

Mr. Jarves had found that if ever the directors dared object to any highhanded action or seemingly extravagant course, he had only to threaten to resign. At once and in high alarm would come a unanimous refusal to accept his resignation. What would the company be without Mr. Jarves? And so Mr. Jarves would go serenely on his charted way, not noticing that the refusals may have become a little halfhearted with time and custom.

It is true that the directors did not object when Mr. Jarves supported the company through the worst days of the depression of the late fifties on his personal fortune.

> How he carried the Boston and Sandwich Glass Company through the panic of 1857-1858, few of those who benefited by his sacrifices will ever know [was the feeling comment in the local paper]. How he sustained the credit of the company and upheld the integrity of its stock and at what loss he did it, they may not exactly see. The fact that Mr. Jarves advanced in cash to the company more than $73,000 in the great panic of 1857-1858 and kept a cash balance at his bank averaging $20,000 for over three months of the hardest times, daily subject to check, and he not the treasurer of the company, indicates what kind of assistance he afforded.

But the directors were becoming less enthusiastic about Mr. Jarves's endless experimentation. If the experiments made money, well and good, but fussing with fuels and monkeying with chimneys and drafts could be costly. Why not let well enough alone as long as the dividends rolled in? The experiments that failed were always the best remembered. The directors could keep in mind the futile hours spent on mock Venetian glass and the *Acorn* idling at the dock more easily than the abstractly progressive policy which had kept the Boston and Sandwich Company in the lead of the glass manufactories of the country.

If Mr. Jarves spoke of feeding and sheltering the workers through the panic as before, that was rank extravagance. If, with a surge of optimism in his country's future, he ran the plant night and day not only upon such random orders as the tall blown-glass vase "presented to the First Church, Sandwich, by the Female Benevolent Society, 1857" but on regular ware to be stored for a better day, it was pure folly.

No one has ever found out exactly what went on behind the closed doors of the directors' meeting of 1858. It has been believed that, in the middle of a stormy session, Mr. Jarves uttered his favorite threat once too often and this time, by previous agreement, the directors voted to accept the resignation. At any rate, when Mr. Jarves emerged, tight-lipped and stony-faced, he was, at sixty-seven, frozen out of the enterprise which he had created and to which he had given the thirty-three best years of his life.[1]

This phoenix brushing the ashes of defeat from his wings, gave the town no chance to gloat or pity. There was an immediate rumor that Mr. Jarves was to build a new glass factory in North Sandwich. Mr. Jarves understood the business of glassmaking as well as any man in the United States and had energy of character and ample means to prosecute the work. The citizens of North Sandwich were to be congratulated. No — a month later — a firm was to erect a woolen factory on the site where Mr. Deming Jarves a short time ago planned his glassworks — a mythical New York firm and a fabulous factory employing five hundred hands.

Now Mr. Jarves was to erect his factory just west of the new Catholic Church, directly on the line of the railroad with which he had entered a contract on the same terms made with the Boston and Sandwich Company. The business would be carried on under the "style and firm" of J. W.

[1] Sterling Lanier, *A Cloth of Glass.*

Jarves and Company. J. W. was, of course, his son John who
would play the part of Captain Stutson in the old company
and be general superintendent in Sandwich. The "and Company" was Henry Higginson, Mary Jarves's husband, who
would handle the Boston end of the business. But everyone
knew that the new factory would be "built and owned by
Deming Jarves, Esq. of Boston, a gentleman noted for enterprise and benevolence and who rightfully has been called,
'The Father of Glass-Works in the United States.' "

Here was fact. There was an immediate planting of about
fifty shade trees which would make the site "an ornament of
the town." The main building — one hundred and eighty
by fifty feet — was started September 1. The cone — eighty
feet high — was built in twelve days during the severest
weather of the season, "it having been built under the shelter of a tent and with a furnace inside." On December 14,
1858, to celebrate the laying of the last brick on the cone,
the Reverend Joseph Marsh stood on a staging erected at the
very top and offered a prayer and blessing. Afterwards a
"repast" (temperance, no doubt) was partaken of on this
lofty perch.

The first glass was melted on January 26, 1859, and the
newspaper editor was "assured by the enterprising proprietor that he would be prepared to execute orders in April."
The only reason that the plant was not in full operation was
a delay in the arrival from Scotland of a crown for the furnace. Here was the answer to "the enemies" of the new company who had "gone so far as to say that glass would never
be melted there."

Thus the Reverend Frederick Freeman, Cape Cod's first
historian, stated:

> 1859 — Another large establishment at Sandwich for the
> manufacture of glass, "The Cape Cod Glass Factory" has
> been reared by Deming Jarves, Esquire, the intelligent and
> enterprising proprietor of the Boston and Sandwich Com-

pany, and its superintendent until last year. It stands forth
a worthy, but not unfriendly rival of the older establishment.[2]

Here was both inaccuracy and euphemism: this was no
friendly rivalry, nor even an impersonal business war, but
almost a family feud.

More than a hint of the bitterness of feeling spilled over
into the newspapers in the announcement that the payroll
and similar duties in the new company would be in charge
of C. C. P. Waterman, Mr. Jarves's old friend and John's
father-in-law, who had performed like services for the Boston and Sandwich Company.

> Having heard at times of slight innuendos respecting the
> dismissal of this tried servant of the Boston and Sandwich
> Company [commented the *Patriot*], we take pleasure to do
> him the justice to publish some facts. Mr. Waterman was in
> the company from the start. In June 1858, a new order of
> things commenced, but on June 11, Mr. Waterman received
> a copy of a vote by the company that all present employes
> of the company be notified and requested to continue their
> present duties under the direction of the president and treas-
> urer. The president added that the board of directors hoped
> that Mr. Waterman would continue his efforts to serve the
> company with fidelity and energy. Thus assured, Mr. Water-
> man kept on his station. Before the end of the month, how-
> ever, he received notice of the following vote in a communi-
> cation dated June 29. "Voted — that the duties now per-
> formed by Mr. Waterman be transferred to one of the
> clerks now in the counting-room and that the services of
> Mr. Waterman be dispensed with on or after July 1." A
> man employed for 32 years is thus dismissed with only one
> day's notice.

---

2 Sandwich's favorite misconception. Since the first year, Mr. Jarves had
not been proprietor or superintendent but company agent in charge of pro-
curement of materials, production, and sales.

The account seemed to imply that equally shabby treatment had been given Mr. Jarves

> whose consummate ability in glass manufacturing not even his enemies can deny. The County of Barnstable and Town of Sandwich owe a debt of gratitude to Mr. Jarves that can never be repaid. How much he has done to give employment to laborers and mechanics, how much money he has disbursed in our county in times past, it would be hard to calculate. Now he has done another noble work in erecting the new manufactory and opening a new field for labor and source of employment.

Mr. Jarves had set his new factory under the noses of the Boston and Sandwich directors for a purpose. Because of his foresight, for these many years the Boston and Sandwich factory had escaped one of the most annoying troubles of glasshouses — the "seduction" of the workmen by offers of higher wages by rival firms. Now, by establishing a competitive wage scale, Mr. Jarves determined to do a little seducing on his own account.

Though he kept a contact with the Boston and Sandwich Company which still used formulae developed while he was in their employ, James Lloyd, the young color wizard, had some financial interest in the new firm and gave it his chief loyalty. His father-in-law, Hiram Dilloway, had followed a similar policy with both the Boston and Sandwich and the New England companies, and now, of course, Dilloway molds were at the service of the Cape Cod Glass Company as well.

When the Reverend Joseph Marsh was made superintendent of the glasshouse, the *Patriot* editorialized:.

> His influence with the workmen cannot fail to be salutatory and potent. We shall hope to hear that profanity, intemperance, and all unmanly conduct shall gain no foothold in the Cape Cod Glass Company. If at the outset, the right ground is taken and persisted in, how much influence

for good may emanate from the employes of the factory. It speaks well for the arrangements and appointments of the new works that they have more applications from competent workmen than they have places to fill.

Plainly, a glass blower would have to be an ardent "Cold Water Man" to seek work under the supervision of the Reverend Joseph Marsh. Perhaps for that reason, some of the more prominent of the glassmaking families stayed with the older concern. The younger-generation Kerns would, of course, prefer to work under "Uncle Theodore," who was still superintendent of the glasshouse in the other factory. Others had a pride in the very size of the old company. Charles Lapham, who had blown the first piece of glass, often boasted, "If it's glass, we make it."

Mr. Jarves was no longer aiming at size. He was not going to repeat the mistake of his earlier enterprise. This factory was to be kept within his control — small, but superlatively good.

In 1860, a New Bedford paper published a comparative description which gives the best picture of the rival plants. The Boston and Sandwich Company had four ten-pot furnaces and employed five hundred hands. The Cape Cod Glass Works had one ten-pot furnace and one hundred and twenty men and boys. The Boston and Sandwich factory was powered by two steam engines of eighteen and twenty horsepower. Besides one steam engine, the Cape Cod Company had four caloric engines of five horsepower each.

With the Boston and Sandwich Company, emphasis was always on size and number. Each article passed through thirty-two hands before completion. Seven hundred tons of Berkshire sand at seven dollars or eight dollars a ton were used yearly. The molds and presses cost seventy-five thousand to one hundred thousand dollars. They were cast at Herring River, North Sandwich, shipped to the factory in separate pieces and there assembled. There were over a thousand of them and a large force of hands was employed just in cleaning them. Articles, after being molded, were passed by a railroad (almost the equivalent of the modern assembly line) to the cutting, burnishing, gilding, and packing rooms. The building was heated with a steam pipe three quarters of a mile long. The hands were paid every fortnight, the payroll amounting to five thousand dollars.

Concerning the Cape Cod Glass Works, enough was said about size so that no one would mistake it for a dinky little twenty-man glasshouse, like the one which had risen and failed in Falmouth. Over five hundred tons of stone, aside from brick, was used in the building and it was all taken from one rock about a mile from the works. Rafters made of strips of board nailed firmly together formed a rounded roof. It would have its own cutting shop one hundred by forty feet. There was a machine shop and blacksmith shop connected and a large pot room seventy by forty feet where pots for the furnace would be made. A cooper's shop turned out casks for packing. There was a room for fitting cappings to lamps and another for the making of glass bottle stoppers. "Nest eggs were being made, too, faster than the hens ever laid the common ones."

However, the accent was on modern improvements. There was a new style of "glory-hole" made of cast iron and lined with firebrick, and a new kind of pressing frame where lamps were molded, handles and all. Mr. Jarves could now experiment to his heart's content with no wry looks from disapproving directors of the Boston and Sandwich Company.

The furnace installed was modern beyond anything in the older plant, with the new Delano patent furnace feeder of which Mr. Jarves gave a glowing description. It fed the furnace by forcing up the coal at the bottom of the burning mass, thus obviating the necessity of wheeling coal on the glasshouse floor and impeding the workmen. It did away with all danger to the pots in feeding the fire. It distributed a regular and uniform heat to each pot, causing the pots to last much longer and fusing the melt better — important items to mixers. It saved from three to five tons of fuel weekly. It permitted the use of both hard and soft coal, whichever happened to be cheaper, and consumed the smoke and gas of either fuel, thus doing away with all annoyance to the neighborhood.

Once again Mr. Jarves could set himself in the place of benefactor in the eyes of the village. Not from his chimneys did the ugly clouds of sooty smoke sift down, graying the good wives' washing, dirtying clean country snow, and making all but the outlying farms not quite spick and span. While he proceeded along the new road of mechanical progress and brought more business to the town, the Boston and Sandwich Company went along in its slipshod old ways.

From the first, the success of the Cape Cod Glass Company was moderate, but assured. The cutting plant and pressing machinery were as modern and efficient as the furnace. Before long, Mr. Jarves had built a second furnace, but he never expanded as far as engraving or etching, although he sold blanks for such use to other firms. He specialized in the highest quality glass to be made — fine crystal mostly from the "shop" of Thomas Williams who had come to him from the old factory, opaque and colored glass — Sandwich alabaster, peachblow, golden ruby from formulae known only to himself and James Lloyd.

A little notebook of directions found years afterward in the abandoned building shows Deming Jarves's down-to-earth interests of this period and his relationship to his workers. There were detailed instructions for firing glass, for bedding goblets and wines in equal parts of whiting and sifted quicklime to prevent collapse under the heat, for washing out kiln and plates with whiting and water between firings, etc. He was playing no lily-fingered part around the plant. Concerning firing he noted:

Heat depends entirely on the size, thickness of kiln, quality of coal or fuel, kind of glass and color you want it. The deeper you wish it, the hotter it must be which practice and attention alone can teach. My own method, and I have tried a great many *and I seldom fail,* is partly by the eye through the holes for so doing and by placing nothing in the middle of the plate opposite the center of the door-plate and introducing an iron rod down the middle of that plate to the back of the kiln — my kiln takes about 5 or 6 hours to fire. I always fire so as to have the heat up to its right pitch about 2 hours after sunset as you can see the degree of heat better after dark and as soon as I perceive by drawing the iron rod out in a dark place that it is just red all along it, I draw the bars and take the fire away immediately, letting the kiln remain till the next evening when it will be cool enough to take the glass out without danger of its breaking.

After setting down in the notebook formulae for red stain for crown glass, orange stain, amber-yellow stain for crown glass, and yellow stain for flint glass, he adjured his workers, "These are as concise as possible, not theoretical, but the result of experiments and practice. I have no doubt you will succeed well. I trust to your honor in never divulging how you obtained these and likewise in keeping them entirely to yourself."

Here was the age-old mystery of the "batch," concocted behind locked doors and wheeled to the pots only when ingredients were mixed beyond possibility of detection. Here was the immemorial ceremony of the master initiating his associates into the secrets of his art. Sandwich was seeing side by side two distinct types of industrial enterprise — that of yesterday and today. Mr. Jarves's new Cape Cod factory followed the patriarchal form of a passing day when the owner and proprietor was a "comrade in industry" who participated directly in the business and dealt personally with the workmen whose interests were to some extent identical

with his own. The older factory represented the large corporation of the coming age with scattered absentee ownership, a hired manager, and labor considered as an impersonal
commodity to be cut down in cost as much as might be.

Less than a year after Mr. Jarves's departure, an incident
occurred which rather bore out his son James's observation
on the moral irresponsibility of American "private interest."
On January 6, 1859, there had been a serious accident at the
Boston and Sandwich factory. A boiler exploded, seriously
injuring the fireman, John Kennedy, and a laborer, John
Barry. In due time, the affair reached the newspaper in detail with "the inquest on the body of John Kennedy killed
by the explosion of a boiler at the Boston and Sandwich
works. The jury found this boiler constructed of inferior
materials and so far out of repair that it should have stopped
running, particularly when found by one of said company's
agents to have a crack quite through what should have been
sound iron."

In appearance, however, the company was still doing everything possible to foster the old paternalism. In 1859, a Mr.
Henry F. Spurr who had begun as clerk in the Boston warerooms was given as a wedding present from the company a
144-piece set of glass tableware engraved in the curtain pattern and initialed. In 1860, according to the words of the
local paper:

> Mr. George L. Fessenden, paymaster of the Boston and
> Sandwich Co., was highly complimented by the workmen in
> that manufactory by the presentation of an elegant service
> of silverware as a testimonial of their appreciation of the
> urbanity and gentlemanly courtesy which have character-
> ized his demeanor while discharging his duties in that
> capacity and for his uniformly accommodating and manly
> treatment of the operatives at all times and seasons.

This silver, bought from Bigelow Brothers and Kennard
of Boston, cost $110. The workers were limited to contribu-

tions of fifty cents each. The small sum was probably regarded by them as an investment in good will. With the apparent feud between the Jarveses and Captain William Stutson who had continued as superintendent of the old plant, the long-standing friendship of the Stutsons and the Fessendens, a native Sandwich family, was beginning to pay handsome dividends. Sewell Fessenden had risen from the factory office to the position of agent, that formerly held by Mr. Jarves himself. Now his brother, George Lafayette, was plainly being groomed to succeed old Captain Stutson as general superintendent, as is shown by the detailed "memo" compiled in 1859 and "presented to Mr. G. L. Fessenden by William Stutson." This notebook gives such intimate and vital information as the itemized coal consumption in each furnace per week, the color formulae held by the company, the usual number of pieces per "move" to the liers, the standard weight per dozen pieces, as well as the patterns then being made. Seemingly an inventory of property and methods put together after the abrupt termination of the Jarves régime, it listed the houses belonging to the Boston and Sandwich Glass Company in 1859 as twenty-one in all — a number of single houses with an average value of $400, a block of five tenements, double houses, and three tenements with a total estimated value of $9600.

Deming Jarves's assessments in the tax books for that year suggest that for awhile his own affairs and those of the Boston and Sandwich Company were considerably scrambled. They also show his fingers in the business of the town, for he had invested money in Sandwich wherever he had seen a chance to turn a penny. The list of property, all assessed at $26,405, ran "store, bake house, hammer and pattern shop, planing, saw, and grist mills, Spring Hill stave mill, building and water privileges at Upper Mill, North Sandwich, and ice-house." [3]

3 Ruth Webb Lee, *Sandwich Glass.*

To what extent his finances became disentangled from Boston and Sandwich connections is not clear, but up to the time of his death, he owned the sawmill which cut staves for the casks for Boston and Sandwich Company glass. In 1860, he was taxed for the new Cape Cod Glass factory, pot house, machine and blacksmith house, all appraised at $15,000. Later his holdings were increased by the "Herring River Iron Works upper and lower, $6500, lumber yard and planing mill, $3000, pine grove at Cohasset, cutting shop for the new Cape Cod factory, a cooper shop and new storehouse" — the total valuation, $40,000. Such was the Jarves spell over the town that there seemed to be some fear of the effect his new competitive venture might have on the old company. "Mr. Jarves is yet a stockholder of about 500 shares of Boston and Sandwich stock," was the reassuring report, "which shows that his interests are still largely involved in the success of that corporation."

If Mr. Jarves ever fancied that the Boston and Sandwich Company would wither away without him, he was sorely disappointed. The disapproving directors were almost equally chagrined to have him as an apparently permanent and prosperous thorn in the side. The hardly concealed bitterness of the rival managements reached the level of the workers in a spirit of sporting competition almost like that of two rival university teams. The Fourth of July of 1860 gave them a chance for self-expression.

This was to be, according to all accounts, the grandest and most glorious Fourth in the history of the town. Over six hundred dollars had been collected to finance the celebration. Besides the two local bands, there were to be bands from Plymouth and Nantucket in the parade. Flags and bunting festooned all buildings along the route of march from the tiniest shop to "the handsome residence of J. W. Jarves, Esq." Every store and manufacturing concern in town furnished a "float — tack manufacturers, printers, coopers, boot and shoe-makers, milliners, cabinet makers, tin-smiths, furnace pot makers, express wagons, grocers, dry-goods clothers, tailors." What a town the simple settlement of the first ten men of Saugus had grown to be!

The blacksmiths rattled by with bellows blowing. The marketmen had heaped carts of fruits and vegetables, casks and barrels of victuals topped by the motto "Man shall not live by bread alone." The climax came with the displays of the rival glass companies. The Boston and Sandwich presented a float glittering like a jewel with a display of every kind of glassware made. But the Cape Cod gaffers were the ones who dazzled the crowd by making a liberal supply of samples on the spot at a miniature horse-drawn furnace. There was no question in the minds of the onlookers that Mr. Jarves's side had won once more.

The Cape Cod Glass Works might win its minor victory, but the big Boston and Sandwich factory was still the one to reflect history. In 1860, when the presidential campaign was hot over slavery and secession, and there was a great hulla-baloo with rail-fence or zigzag marches in honor of Lincoln, the rail splitter, the factory turned out a ruby glass lantern engraved "Lincoln and Hamlin" to be borne in Sandwich's torchlight procession.

With the firing on Fort Sumter and Senator Wilson's tel-egraphed appeal for volunteers, a mass meeting was held in Sandwich Saturday evening, April 20, 1861, at only a few hours' notice, to devise ways and means to raise a company of troops for the "defense of the country." Theodore Kern, superintendent of the glasshouse, called the meeting to order. Doctor Jonathan Leonard, probably the leading cit-izen of the town, was made secretary. A committee of nine was chosen to solicit bounty money sufficient for $20 for each man who should enlist, and $626 was raised on the spot. Ac-cording to the democratic method then in vogue — a method which drove nearly mad several generations of generals from

Washington to Grant — election of officers for the new com-
pany was presided over by the town. The results were repre-
sentative enough — for captain, Charles Chipman of the old
stock; for first and second lieutenants, Charles Brady and
Henry Kern of glass-factory families. Through the years,
Sandwich and Jarvesville men side by side marched off to
war — Shadrach Swift and Louis Paganuzzi, Zenas Hoxie and
Cheserg Jean, Perez Eldredge and Ettien Morien, Naaman
Dillingham and Moses Gerrom and a long procession of
Freemans and Burgesses, Hoffmans and Rheinhardts, and
McKowens, McElneys, McDermotts, McElroys, McKennas,
McNultys, McNamaras, and McMahons.

In spite of the draining away of these workmen, business
was never better than during the war period for the Boston
and Sandwich Company. The *Acorn,* so long an eyesore to
the directors, was unloaded on the government and came to
a dramatic end in action off the Virginia Capes. Barrels of
resin bought at sixty-two cents a barrel to fuel the glory-holes
were also patriotically turned over to the government at
forty-four dollars per barrel. Glass stored in the warehouses
since the late depression was sold at the top of the market.

Moreover, discovery of oil in Pennsylvania in 1859 had
revolutionized home illumination as candlesticks and whale
oil and spirit lamps had given way to much heavier and
more ornate lamps for kerosene. Women began to be employed for the gilding and decorating of bases and shades.
The Plymouth writer, Jane Austin, in "An Eye Witness
Story of Sandwich Glass," published in the *Atlantic Monthly*
in 1864, took particular note that besides the usual number of mold and "taker-in" boys, there were "pretty little
fellows about 10 or 12 gravely engaged in blowing chimneys
for kerosene lamps and quite successfully as a large box behind a bench showed — these alone of all articles not required to pass through the liers." Far from creating a help
shortage, the war had simply taught the factories to make

use of a cheaper type of employee, and the Boston and Sandwich Glass Company actually reached its peak for all time in the number of hands employed.

The Cape Cod Glass Factory went on its unspectacular way, but the war had various effects on the individuals at 64 Boylston Street, Boston. Though Daniel Webster had been gone from the American scene for a decade, his spirit still lived in many of the Massachusetts capitalists like Deming Jarves. They honestly felt that slavery was secondary to a united and prosperous nation and might in time dwindle away through compromise without a bloody and disastrous war. Thus Mr. Jarves mildly disapproved of the state of the nation while his son James took it as a personal affront.

The New York reception of the Old Masters had been considerably cooler than he had anticipated. The American people, he began to remark wryly, know exactly what they want and will do. What they did not want and would not do was to flock to the Jarves collection, and the few who went often saw only the "ridiculous awkwardness" and "absurd anachronism" rather than the "childlike simplicity" and "profound earnestness" of the early paintings. In response to an invitation from Charles Eliot Norton and others, he brought forty of the Old Masters to present their message to his native city. With naïve optimism, he put out numbers of personal cards of admission to the gallery —"J. J. J. — not transferable." The precaution proved quite unnecessary. All he gained was a nickname among his acquaintance — "J. J. J. —not transferable!"

Sometimes, in a pet, he would threaten to take himself and his paintings to a presumably more appreciative England. The $25,000 mortgage still pressed, and his father's interests were centered in the Cape Cod Glass Company. For a while he had faint hope. The New York Historical Society, in whose galleries his collection was housed, considered the proposition at one of its meetings "to offer Mr. Jarves the sum of $50,000 for his collection." However, "as the Society had not the funds to appropriate in that way, the subject was dropped" — and the lack of funds was laid to the war.

James Jarves had been out of the country during much of the emotional frenzy that had preceded the war. Though he may have noted the Florentine publication of *Il Tio Tom*, he was much more deeply impressed with his memories of the perverse Polynesians and bore a definite grudge against the dark-skinned races. Now that the war had worked him a personal injury, he was inclined to lay it to the Negro.

"The Negro is of an inferior race in every point of view to the white," he declared. "Short-sighted individuals attribute this inferiority to the white prejudice against his color, oblivious to Nature's fact that this color is the livery of inferiority put upon him by God himself." Not that he approved of slavery in the abstract. "The white race owe it to their own moral and physical progress to get rid of slavery. It blights them by bringing them in close relations with moral and intellectual inferiority, brands manual industry as disgraceful, and adds the vices of the black to the white man."

His son Horatio, whose Hawaiian childhood had exposed him to the dark-skinned races and their culture on a somewhat different level, disagreed with his father's ideas to the point of risking his life. After a bitterness between father and son far exceeding any earlier misunderstandings between James and his own father, Horatio went off to war with his young uncle, Deming, Junior, though both might have followed the course fairly common for those of their financial and family background and paid the paltry two hundred dollars for substitute lives and limbs.

Back to Sandwich came news of native sons in battles with the homespun names of Fair Oaks, Gaines' Mills, Peach Orchard, or Savage Station. One was killed at Bull Run, another rotted away at Andersonville, a third dragged himself home to die, and so the story of heartbreak was told on Factory Street and Jarves Street, Main Street and little country lane. Young Deming, Junior, returned safe and sound, but Horatio Jarves lost a leg and died of the shock.

Yet the ultimate tragedy in the life of Deming Jarves, Senior, was not of the war's making. The burning heat of the glasshouse alternating with the chill Cape fogs which could penetrate even the brick-and-wood layers of the Victorian manse at the head of Jarves Street had finally brought upon John the fate of the Stutsons. Doctor Jonathan Leonard, the beloved physician of Sandwich, of whom the lyrical local historian reported that "his hand was soft as thistledown to the throbbing pulse and aching brow" must have found it very distressing to tell the pretty young wife, so happily secure in her life, that certain symptoms turned vague fears to dread certainty. Barring a miracle, John was doomed to go the way of his brother George and the young Stutson, Southack, and Thayer cousins.

The last, "dear Joseph," had, according to Auntie Bacon, come home from St. Louis to "take the cod liver oil" which failed to live up to its promise. Now a new "cure" offered hope. The wonderful new West which offered land and gold, adventure and fortune, was said to hold health as well. John Jarves was sent West, but the reported magic did not work. With his death, hope died in Mr. Jarves beyond any resurrection.

2

Family life in and about 64 Boylston Street was the stuff of which psychological novels are made. We see it through the eyes of Firenze Jarves — "that foreign child," as J. J. J.'s younger daughter was called by Bostonian relatives, although she had become Flora promptly upon arrival in this country to avoid being dubbed "Frenzy."

It seemed to be the United States custom to make awe-some objects of one's grandparents [she reported]. So when I went to Boylston St., I was afraid to speak in their pres-ence, but being a foreign child as I was, I looked them over and decided my grandfather was a nice person and told him so. He took me in his lap and gave me such a hug and kiss.

My father James was no kind of a father [she went on bluntly]. For long at a time, he would be so nice and take me everywhere with him, then bring me back to Boylston St., Boston, Grandfather's house, and forget all about me and go off on his art ideas.

The older daughter, Chevelita, who had adored her mother, "disliked every Stutson and Jarves on principle," but soon made a very happy marriage. During the intervals of paternal neglect, Flora's care was divided among sister, grandparents, and Aunt Anna who told her every day "how my father was a crank about pictures and spent all *their* money."

Glass-factory money! That was at the bottom of all the bickering and backbiting, jealousies and maneuverings that continually buzzed in the ears of the brokenhearted old man and his lonely little granddaughter.

James was now more hard-pressed for money than ever. The mortgage was imperiling the Old Masters, and not even a devoted mother could force or cajole enough money from the modest affairs of the Cape Cod Glass Factory to save the situation. He finally offered the collection for sale, but no one wanted to buy it in its entirety, and he "was not dis-posed to scatter a collection so valuable in its collective character." As a last resort, he sold a few separate pictures whose loss would do least damage to his carefully planned chronological sequence. If his collection was destined to be dispersed, at least he could imagine his treasures as "mis-sionaries of culture in private homes."

He was beginning, however, to despair of his mission.

"When I wrote the *Art Idea,*" he remarked ruefully, "I hoped so much of American art that now, in looking over the product of intervening time, I fear my wishes misled my judgment."

J. J. J. had usually managed an escape, either physical or spiritual, from most of the disappointments of life. Now, with scarcely a decade gone by since Perry had steamed into Uraga Bay, he itched to be the first to explore Japanese art, and he and a second wife set out for the Orient, leaving 64 Boylston Street to bicker over the bills.

"When my father was travelling in the Orient to find some wonderful picture he *must* have — and it cost something, too," his daughter reported, "my grandmother always gave him money which was no fun for Aunt Isabella or Aunt Anna."

There was some justice in the resentment of the Jarves daughters, now married, who could not help thinking of their own families as they thought they saw James gobbling up the greater part of the estate. All were exceptionally attractive women. Mary was a real beauty and a gentle person who "kept away from Boylston St. as she didn't like to fight, she said." Anna was pretty and pleasant, "also a peacemaker," in spite of the daily reminder to her little niece of J. J. J.'s money-absorbing whims. Isabella, according to her niece, was "a Tartar — handsome, very tall, and rode and drove and did everything." She was ready to battle lustily for her rights — reinforced from time to time by Deming, Junior, home on visit from New York where he was now glass sales agent.

The steady but modest profits of the Cape Cod Glass Factory simply could not satisfy all demands. Mr. Jarves now was leaving the business more and more in the hands of Mr. Lloyd and young William Kern who, after the death of John and the retirement of the Reverend Joseph Marsh, came over from the Boston and Sandwich plant to superintend opera-

tions. Only once after John's death did Mr. Jarves show a
feeble spark of interest in glassmaking. "In order to meet
the demand for information which has unexpectedly sprung
up from those interested in the manufacture of glass," as he
put it, he "enlarged into more permanent form and brought
down to the present year — 1865 — the small pamphlet of
Reminiscences of Glass-Making printed for private circulation in 1854."

One reason for the new edition seems to have been a still
smoldering desire for revenge on the Boston and Sandwich
Company. The modest early references to the factory were
unchanged — though he devoted nearly as much space to the
Cape Cod factory with its Delano patent stoker. But brief
mentions of the Boston and Sandwich works were cleverly
smothered in a praise of rivals that could not have been un-
calculated. In pressed glass, which was considered the Sandwich specialty, he declared that:

> James B. Lyon & Co. of Pittsburgh stand first. To such a
> degree of delicacy and fineness have they carried their man-
> ufacture that only experts in the trade can distinguish be-
> tween their straw stem wines and other light and beautiful
> articles made on the molds and those blown by the most
> skilled workmen. When we consider the difference in cost
> between pressed and blown ware, this rivalry of beauty of
> the former with the latter becomes all the more important
> to the public as it cheapens one of the staple necessaries of
> civilized life.

He went out of his way to pay tribute to Sandwich's chief
regional rival, the New England Glass Company of Cambridge. "Their richly cut, gilded, and ornamental glass is
considered equal to European work" and also "they execute
orders for large and heavy objects for druggists' and chemical
wares and philosophical apparatus so satisfactorily as to
secure a monopoly in them." Since these were fields also

cultivated by the Boston and Sandwich Company, the old man's lingering chagrin is only too plain.

The Boston and Sandwich Company prospered in spite of rivals or attempted revenge. So far, it had been very fortunate in its superintendents. The practical Theodore Kern, who was said to make better glass with broken pieces and old glass emptied from pots than others could make with new material, was teamed with the urbane and gentlemanly George Lafayette Fessenden — as masterly in dealing with men as Kern was with materials. Under their guidance, the factory steamed ahead, carrying the town farther and farther away from the roots of its past.

Even the farmers were leaving their old way of raising their living and squeezing out a surplus to sell for whatever their land would not yield. Now, like factories, they specialized. William Swift and his six sons, for example, were beginning the way that led to Chicago and the packing house by making big business of hogs. Every Saturday they could be seen driving their herd along the sandy road from Sagamore. The hogs had been fortified for the long dusty journey by a good feeding of dry salt bran at the farm. However, the Swifts were not heartless men. By the time their charges had worked up a good thirst, the procession had reached Town Brook. There the hogs were allowed to stop and drink their fill before being driven on, as well "watered stock," to be sold by live weight on the hoof to the glassworkers of Jarvesville.

As glassworkers and farmers both had pockets full of money, more and more native sons turned shopkeeper and outsiders saw opportunity here. Country folk for miles around flocked to Sandwich as shopping center just as the Sandwich businessmen made their pilgrimages to Boston. One night a storekeeper coming back from a business trip on the late train decided to stop in at his store before going home. As he opened the door, he was met by a cloud of smoke and the crackle of flames which soon gnawed through the flimsy wooden walls to neighboring stores. By the time a bucket brigade had gathered, it was much too late for water by the bucket.

Gone were the days of the reign of Mr. Jarves when at the first sniff of smoke, the company hand pump would come clanging out of the factory yard. The directors of the Boston and Sandwich Company had issued orders of a different sort. At any sign of fire in the town, the apparatus was to be drawn up beside the factory and kept there in readiness for the threat of flying sparks. And there fire apparatus and company firemen stayed, while half a mile away the heart of the town burned down. The spirit of Mr. Jarves had truly departed from Jarvesville.

It had been months since Mr. Jarves had visited the Cape Cod Glass Factory which was running on its own momentum under the active management of Billy Kern. Sandwich heard that the old man was ill. Sandwich heard that the old man was dying. Kern himself wrote:

> I was superintendent of the factory at the time it closed in 1869. Mr. Jarves' son John for whom chiefly he had built it was dead, and Mr. Jarves himself was seriously ill at his home in Boston. The family did not care to continue the plant in operation, and I received instructions to draw the fires on a certain date at midnight.
>
> As I was returning from the factory after attending to this last service, some boys who were congregated in the village street shouted, "There he goes; he's gone up."
>
> I paid little attention to the words at the time, but they came back to me the next morning when I received word that at the very moment when I had drawn the fires in the glass factory, Deming Jarves had passed from this world into the world beyond.

The *Boston Evening Transcript,* which had carried his marriage announcement nearly a half-century before, ran on

April 16, 1869, a similarly succinct notice of his death. "On the 15th inst. Deming Jarves Esq., 78. Funeral services will be held at 64 Boylston St. on Monday April 19th at 12 o'clock."

Just forty-four years to the day from the first breaking of ground for his "individual enterprise" in Sandwich, he was given a proper businessman's burial in Mount Auburn Cemetery — the cemetery which his son James had found "speaking too loudly of property, exclusion, and building, things of the earth instead of the symbolism of heaven."

The reading of the will was surely a shock to the heirs, not because of the terms which left all to his wife, "having in mind all I have done for my children" (Isabella and Deming, Junior, may have sniffed here) but on account of the way the supposedly inexhaustible fortune had dwindled to two hundred thousand dollars. This was certainly enough to keep the widow in respectable comfort the rest of her days, but not enough to allow even the most indulgent of mothers any great splurge in Old Masters.

James, now back from Japan, was suffering almost complete disillusionment as to his country. "The philosopher equally as well as the man who lives merely for the artistic or high-bred enjoyments of social life have as yet no real home in America."

Theodore Parker voiced the prevailing view. "The fine arts do not interest me so much as the coarse arts which feed, clothe, house, and comfort a people."

"I do not intend to disparage the motives which have led America so rapidly into civilization and power," countered J. J. J. with plaintive persistence. "They are the first great principles of social progress. But they are not enough in themselves."

He could turn his back on America more easily than he could give up his self-appointed mission to bring culture to the Americans. "Having labored so long in this cause, I am not willing to abandon it except in the last personal extremity or until convinced that Americans have no sympathy with it."

When he returned to Italy, he left his Old Masters "temporarily deposited, *not* sold as it is often stated in print" in the Yale School of Fine Arts for a period of three years as security for a loan — "one of the most irregular pieces of university finance on record and certainly one of the most brilliant," as President Porter of Yale later described it.[4] Unable to pay at the end of the interval, he permitted the collection to be sold at auction to the university, which made the only bid.

Except for brief visits, J. J. J. lived the rest of his days in Florence. With a characteristic disregard of financial sacrifice, he presented his collection of Venetian glass to the Metropolitan Museum in New York as a memorial to his father. Ironically enough, his chief tangible reward at the end of a life devoted to "the diffusion of artistic knowledge and aesthetic taste in America" was to be made Chevalier of the Order of the Crown of Italy in recognition of his work in behalf of *Italian art and artists.*

The year after Mr. Jarves's death, George's firm of Jarves and Cormerais was sold to Libbey — the name still associated with glass — and moved to New Bedford. As for Deming, Junior, his niece reported, "When he came home, he was surprised to find James and all had spent about all the money. So Deming pitched right in, out West in Detroit, and made a larger fortune himself." He dabbled briefly in glass, but as, in the spirit of the new age, his object was to make money, he turned to fertilizer and bone-black. His fortune secured, he put an ocean between himself and the stench of old bones and like his oldest brother became a gentleman expatriate.

From his château in southern France, he alone of the

4 *Dictionary of American Biography.*

Jarves brood thought back to the source of family blessings. When the town had all but forgotten its Jarves days, he left a substantial part of his library — to be selected by a native emissary sent to France with all expenses paid — to the public library at Sandwich where the books may still be seen with the Jarves personal dragon on the bookplates.

Back in Sandwich in 1868, the pretty young widow, Mary Waterman Jarves, had found comfort and new hope in a marriage with Doctor Leonard — one of those marriages of mellow affection and mature understanding between a man and woman who have both known bereavement. Thus the era of plutocratic family influence passed for Sandwich. As far as is known, no one by the name of Jarves ever walked on Jarves Street again.

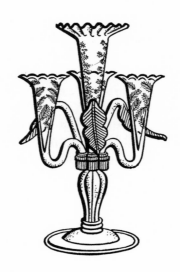

The American Way

THE CAPE COD GLASS WORKS made no more glass. For a while, there were plans. Mr. William L. Libbey, the last and most successful of the managerial partners of the Mount Washington Glass Company which Mr. Jarves had started for his son, George, had·apparently acquired some of the Jarves assets. With James Lloyd, the color genius, who also had a financial interest to protect, he planned to revive the plant. But even before reopening the factory, the two co-proprietors ended a difference of opinion with an "I'll buy you out or you buy me."

After Mr. Libbey had become sole owner, the proposition did not look good, even though this was the period when the New England states were at their zenith in glassmaking with twenty-two factories as compared to eleven in 1860. Libbey was also associated with the New England Glass Company, and a director of that company had recently come forward with the pessimistic view that it was "useless to endeavor to compete with the cheap coal and labor at the Pitts-

burgh glass works and that Pittsburgh wines offered him at
75¢ per dozen could not be made for less than $1.25 at Cam-
bridge." For that very year — 1870 — a Pittsburgh firm had
opened a Boston sales office in the heart of the market for
Sandwich and Cambridge wares.

Perhaps as a result of Mr. Libbey's disappointing connection with Sandwich, the Libbey post mortem estimate of the
late Mr. Jarves was hardly admiring. He did not

> think much of Mr. Jarves's work on glass-making [the *Rem-
> iniscences*]. Mr. Jarves established the Sandwich Glass
> Works on the mistaken idea that money would be saved by
> building a factory near the fuel, and after many expensive
> and useless experiments in the way of buildings, wharves,
> etc., he left this company and formed the Cape Cod Glass
> Company in whose works he had invested perhaps $100,000.
> The fires of those furnaces went out when Mr. Jarves died
> and have not since been lighted, and the works would not
> bring perhaps the value of the mortgage of $10,000 now rest-
> ing upon them. Mr. Jarves lived to about the age of eighty
> years and he ought to have left the glass business twenty
> years before he died. He was infatuated with the idea of
> making a success in his business, and he did not accomplish
> it, at least *not in a pecuniary way*.[1]

Mr. Libbey was less than just to the *Reminiscences*, for a
careful reading would have warned him away from the Cape
Cod works even before the director of his own company had
proved by Pittsburgh prices that building the works near the
fuel was not such a mistaken idea after all.

> There are now (1865) [Mr. Jarves had reported] in Pitts-
> burgh nine concerns manufacturing flint-glass, running 13
> furnaces and 103 pots. There are also 3 concerns at Wheel-
> ing, running 5 furnaces and 45 pots. There are also at
> Wellesville, Steubenville, and Cincinnati one or two fac-
> tories each, besides several manufactories for green glass jars

---

[1] Sterling Lanier, *A Cloth of Glass.*

and one for the making of porter bottles, one also for mineral bottles.

A home competition has sprung up, reducing prices below a fair standard — a competition the result of enterprise which will ere long regulate itself, for we fully hold to the maxim that competition honest and well-sustained is the soul of business.

"No horse so swift that he needs not another
To keep up his speed."

Mr. Jarves's stout affirmation of the American creed seems to have been a whistle in the dark, for competition between Eastern and Western glass firms was already reaching the cutthroat stage. A generation before, the cost of transporting the finished glass to market offset the advantages of building a glasshouse by a coal mine. In 1800, for example, the rate for shipping glass from Pittsburgh to Philadelphia was about ten dollars a hundredweight. By 1855, because of the railroad, the cost had gone down to forty or fifty cents. Before 1850, there had been more traffic by water than by rail. By 1860, positions of land and water transportation were reversed. Even Sandwich's position on the sea was no longer the compensating factor it once had been.

Every penny of cost came to count. There is in existence a notebook, considered the work of some spy for Western firms out to break their Eastern competitors, which lists the prevailing wage scale, names of workers and their pay, sizes of furnaces, number of pots, amount of glass made, and types of glassware with pen line drawings of patterns covering factories from Montreal, Canada, to Williamsburg, Virginia, and west to Corning, New York. It included both the Boston and Sandwich Company and the Cape Cod Glass Works, apparently visited on February 6, 1866.[2]

In the absence of definite proof as to the source of the notebook, however, there is a possibility that it may have

[2] Ruth Webb Lee, *Sandwich Glass.*

been the work of some tentative union of glassmakers. Before the day of the railroad and the universal market, glass blowers in the separate factories had always combined to control their output and wages, as Mr. Jarves had ever complained. Now there was a grouping toward larger unions to meet conditions of intersectional competition created as once local markets stretched country-wide. It is known that as the glass blowers with their strong feeling of craft brotherhood worked their way up and down the land, there was a great deal of carrying of patterns and formulae from factory to factory. There was probably underground exchange of information as to working conditions as well.

The possible distance between producer and ultimate consumer was no greater than that steadily widening between employer and employed. More and more power was coming into the grasp of those who bridged the gaps — the bankers and sales agencies that brought producer and consumer together, the factory managers who translated the wishes of corporate owners into tangible goods by means of machines and a certain number of human hands. Once, a craftsman could see a pair of shoes or piece of pottery come into being through his skill, watch it in wear or use by townsmen, and reap the reputation of work well done. Now, even in a glasshouse, he was seldom responsible for the completion of any article, only for the monotonous repetition of a certain operation which went into its making. His relations with the source of his wages were remote to the point of complete impersonality. He was losing all satisfaction in creation, hope of social self-betterment, or sense of personal worth.

So what worker could resist a union which offered a Constitution bearing on the cover clasped hands and the verse:

> "Union is strength" when hearts combine
> And make their friendship one;
> 'Tis firm where manly virtues shine
> And a power all can depend upon.

> Not all the wealth we could obtain
> Will in the future save
> If still degraded we remain,
> It forms the tyrant and the slave!"

This was the Massachusetts Flint-Glass Makers' Protective Association in 1865 whose "aims and purposes are the moral, social, and financial advancement of every man among us, the disposition to act with a spirit of justice and honest consideration between employer and employed, each willing to concede where the claims of both are put forth. The watchword of labor is the prosperity and progress of manufacture, and the watchword of capital is the safety and education of labor."

Here was an attempt to preserve the spirit which was dying with Mr. Jarves — not so much a condescending paternalism as a sense of partnership in production.

"Let us cherish good will toward each other and conduct ourselves, in the glasshouse and out, respectfully; then we shall reflect honor and dignity upon our Association and convince the most sceptical of glassmakers and manufacturers that we are combined to protect all and to injure none."

The association extended "throughout the State, divided as to factories, yet united under one government." Delegates assembled from each of the eight best established factories, including three each from the Boston and Sandwich and the Cape Cod. On the committee on the Constitution, which provided for all contingencies from the refund of dues in certain cases to the proper behavior at the funeral of a brother member, Billy Kern represented the Boston and Sandwich Company.

This was just before he left to manage production for Mr. Jarves at the Cape Cod. After the closing of the Cape Cod, he did not wish to go back as gaffer under Lafe Fessenden in the factory where his father and uncle had been superintendents before him. So he took up his tools and left the town where he had been born and lived his life and began to wander, journeyman fashion, up and down the land — South Boston and New Bedford, Philadelphia and the West.

The lone craftsman carrying his skill from town to town was the pioneer of the mass industrial migrations to escape economic constriction or chase economic promise that were to become an integral part of American life. Fewer and fewer would die in the town where they were born. Viewing life as a series of unrelated episodes with no flowing continuity between its beginning and its ending, they would little by little lose touch with elemental realities and seek machine-made lives of constant glitter and motion.

Rooted ways of living might come to be scorned by men of the future, but James Lloyd found them good. He knew that opportunity lay to the West, and several western firms had made tempting bids for his glassmaking experience and magic with color. However, he was reluctant to leave the pleasant spacious white house on Main Street in the midst of neighbors with whom he had spent a lifetime. In this opinion, he was backed up by his father-in-law, old Hiram Dilloway, the moldmaker, who abhorred the West, for all its get-rich-quick promise, as raw and ugly and unfit for decent living.

He was even more determined, however, not to go back in a full-time capacity to the Boston and Sandwich Company although he continued as color consultant to the end. He did not, he said, like the new spirit abroad there — the "union" spirit, he called it. He did not mean by this any combination of "hearts to make their friendship one" as in the Massachusetts Flint-Glass Makers' Association. He sensed the class antagonism, as yet hardly perceptible in Sandwich, growing from the separation of owner and worker and from the grind of competition which made the wage earner ever fearful of a reduction in pay.

While he was hesitating about his course, Captain Atkins, the old station agent, passed from the scene The railroad directors persuaded Mr. Lloyd to take the position while he was making up his mind what to do about going West. It seemed to Mr. Lloyd that factories might come and factories might go, but the railroad would remain. So he stayed with it, watching the flow and ebb of the life blood of the town.

2

In those days, however, most men thought the factory as timeless a part of the town as the dunes encircling the harbor where sometimes as many as thirteen schooners and a steamer would lie waiting to carry glass over the seven seas to the far corners of the earth. The railroad might bring Pittsburgh salesmen and Pittsburgh glass to Boston, but it could not carry the fame of Pittsburgh glass to Russia, Australia, and South Africa where Sandwich glass had been sent for a generation or more. Then, too, with the increased consumption brought about by the invention of the kerosene lamp and the rapid expansion of population on the seaboard states, the market for glass seemed for a while large enough to require the efforts of all who wanted to make it — provided they did not count too confidently on future profits.

In addition, the Boston and Sandwich Company was among the most progressive. Though the directors had objected to Mr. Jarves's untrammeled inventive genius, they were ever ready to receive innovations which had passed the experimental stage.

One of the innovations of this period was the process, patented by one James Napier of Glasgow, which did away with the highly paid skill formerly required for etching. "Instead of drawing patterns and figures in the glass with the use of varnish and a graver to prepare the glass for etching," as Mr. Jarves described it, "the glass is prepared by simply transferred pictures from prints which can be performed by almost any person." The picture was pasted smoothly to the glass which was given a three-minute bath in hydrofluoric acid. Then the paper was removed — and there was the picture etched on the glass. Glass that was "flashed" on the surface with another color could be treated in this way, and when a portion of the flashing or surface was removed, the picture remained in color. It was a very inexpensive and effective method which Frank Lapham of the engraving department was sent abroad to learn.

The Boston and Sandwich Company was one of the few before 1880 to replace the square, squatty annealing ovens, heated, filled with glass, and left to cool, with the liers which saved time, space, and fuel. A lier was a long tunnel-like structure through which glass was slowly drawn in iron pans hooked together like a train of cars. As the entrance of the lier was kept constantly heated while the other end was at shop temperature, glassware could be packed as soon as it came through — or within several hours instead of at least twenty-four after leaving the hands of the gaffer.

The most revolutionary change came a little too late for Mr. Jarves to record. William Leighton, formerly of the old New England Glass Company, who had been lured westward to J. H. Hobbs, Brokunier and Company of Wheeling, West Virginia, succeeded in making a beautiful crystalline glass by substituting soda lime for lead, the costliest ingredient of flint glass. The new glass did not have the weight and resonant ring of flint glass and was too brittle to be used for cutting. But the cost of lime-glass "batch" was only a third as much as that of flint glass, and in a pressed article, only those in a glass-factory town could tell the difference. Soon all the Western companies were turning out sets of cheap pressed-glass tableware to catch the market all over the country.

Caught by this competition, the old New England Company took the conservative course and decided to cater to a limited market for the high-grade cut and colored ware for which they had won some fame. The Boston and Sandwich Company simply added the production of lime glass to its established flint line. Before long, the factory was spewing out its two hundred dozen pressed lime-glass tumblers every five-hour shift, and it seemed as if expansion would be a never ending process.

In 1871, the size of the factory was doubled. New additions for cutting and decorating had made the original wooden building, once known as the "Lower House," so much an appendage of the 1840 "Upper House" that now the great new building became known in its turn as the "Lower House." The pots in the new furnaces would hold fifteen hundred pounds as against five or six hundred when Deming Jarves had melted his first "batch" more than forty-five years before. The new seventy-foot chimney sent up a thick black pillar of smoke which rose as sky mark for sleepy villages miles away and slowly settled down to begrime a typical factory town.

On Sandwich streets could be heard not only every brogue and dialect of which the English language was capable, but German and French and even stranger tongues. Newcomers had taken over the glasshouse. The lusty young men who had swum and skated and shot, the merry young men who had raised their voices in the Mozart Union were gray-bearded grandfathers now — Grandpa Lapham, Grandpa Lloyd, Grandpa Dilloway. Most of them were puttering in retirement in their neat Sandwich homes, living on tales of the good old Jarves days.

A few of a younger generation with names like Kern and Marsh and Lapham still lingered in the cutting and etching departments. Sons who had passed through their apprenticeship as blowers had, like Billy Kern, generally fared forth into a wider world. Men for the most part fresh from Europe had taken over the blowing, and in skill, they were in no way inferior to the first "shops" brought in by Mr. Jarves. By the time they learned, like the Sandwich young fry, of the larger wages paid in the West, they would be too firmly settled in Sandwich to be uprooted.

There was gentle Adolphe Bonique whose aristocratic appearance and courtly manners could make one believe that here was a descendant of one of the lords of early French glasshouses, if not something as romantic as a lost dauphin. He could spin out glass by a breath into forms as fragile as anything created by the fabulous Venetians. There was the Alsatian, Nicholas Lutz, who wove magic with glowing threads of molten color. And there was the Englishman, Bob Matthews, whose wizardry is remembered with wonder in Sandwich even today.

"All the others had their specialties, like Nick Lutz and his threaded ware," you are told, "but Bob Matthews could do them all. There wasn't anything Bob Matthews couldn't do with glass." In two shakes, Bob Matthews could transform a mere blob of glass into a miraculous penny bank in the form of a rooster for the delight of a waiting child.

More and more, the expert blowers had to depend on the impromptu bravura performance to exercise their skill. Yearly, the manufacture of glass was becoming less a craft and more a mass-production industry.

The factory influence, as ever, dominated the town. Industrial Sandwich was the only town on the south shore below Boston to have a liquor license. The five hundred glassworkers could whet their thirst at five saloons which were gallantly, if somewhat futilely, combated by Father Kinnerney and Saint Peter's Catholic Total Abstinence Society with its scientific lectures illustrated by lantern slides. There were other diversions for idle hours; Masonic doings and church doings, picnics, clam bakes, and lawn parties, road shows and visiting lecturers at town hall, rival baseball teams to revive the bragging and betting of the bygone packet races, a choral society, and two bands.

The two bands typified the social divisions which still survived. The Bay State Band was also known as "the uptown band." It has been revealingly described as composed of "both factory workers and citizens," the classifications apparently considered mutually exclusive. But there was no doubt that the Bay State Band represented the élite among the musicians and probably among the glassworkers as well. The "downtown" or Mutual Improvement Society Brass Band was wholly a glass-factory aggregation. Occasionally, members of the two joined forces. Whenever Boston and Sandwich Company directors were expected for a tour of inspection, all the factory musicians brought their instruments to work with them. Assembled at the Watch-House door, they would greet the visitors with a feudal fanfare which would nearly blow them off their feet.

Memories still quiver with the blasts of the glass blowers' bands. Lungs toughened on the blowpipe could, Sandwich was sure, out-trumpet Gabriel. Whenever a delegation fared forth to Boston on some great parade day, heads were sure to turn the length of Tremont Street.

"What band is that?"

"The glass blowers' from Sandwich." And so town fame spread.

Saturday afternoons, sidewalks were crowded to jostling with glassworkers and their families, and farmer folk from miles around come to town for excitement and shopping. After the great fire, the business district had been rebuilt and enlarged. There were grocery stores, meat markets, and drygoods stores, a drugstore, a clothing store, and stores for hardware, furniture, and wallpaper, to say nothing of tailoring establishments and the five rum shops. If anyone had any money left, there was still the Sandwich Savings Bank.

Though the glass-factory pay roll never missed a week,

and glass blowers' wages averaged two to three times those of other craftsmen — more, in fact, than the salaries of teachers or parsons — glass blowers' pockets were generally empty. Nothing was too good for the gaffers, and they mostly had their hundred-dollar overcoats and twenty-dollar high kid boots made in Boston. Besides, they were equally lavish with others, handing out royally to every cause from Fourth of July fireworks to perpetually starving Ireland.

"If you wanted anything in town," folk still say today, "you could always count on a good subscription from a glass-maker."

Sometimes, after wages had winged too speedily away, a grim-faced wife would appear to collect the fortnightly pay envelope. It took the farmers, used to storing crops for a cold and hungry season, to put away pennies as well. One Saturday in 1874, a farmer came to the bank with one hundred dollars scrimped out of months of daily needs. On Monday morning, the bank was closed.

News of the bank failure swept through town like a northeast gale. The new country-wide depression had reached out even to Sandwich. This was perhaps even more than the others a paper panic. Trade had been excellent. Everyone was earning, eating, buying clothes. But America which had always built for the future now began to bet on the future as well.

Railroads were pushed into regions which could not be expected to support them for twenty years. The money to pay for this extravagant expansion was obtained, not from the earnings of the older part of the road, but from enormous issues of bonds, mostly bought by the banks. As the railroads defaulted payments, the market for new bonds disappeared. Now all financial affairs were so intermeshed that everything crashed with the railroads — the banks that held the savings of the people and the industries which supplied their jobs.

The Sandwich Savings Bank had been gambling not on railroads, but on real estate in South Boston which proved founded in the quaking uncertainty of "made" land. It was found that the bank president, with a remarkable degree of foresight, had withdrawn his own money the week before the crash and the following year was able to adorn the town with one of the rococo Gothic mansions which were beginning to add bizarre variety to village streets. Of course, no one suspected crooked dealing — merely a canniness in saving himself to which most Yankees would give grudging admiration.

In the hard days, Sandwich was loyal to its own. Three of the Swift brothers had left the family farm for the opportunities of Chicago, and the two survivors had become middleman-merchants to convert cattle on the hoof into meat for a steadily spreading market. When the panic threatened their once prosperous business, they sent in frenzy for Sandwich aid. Farmers and storekeepers with a memory of Swift shrewdness scraped together enough money to save native sons from bankruptcy.

The Boston and Sandwich factory was not greatly affected. There were slack times when the cutters, with no company work to do, would buy spare "blanks" for themselves and cut patterns of their own design to be submitted to the superintendent. If these met with his approval, they were sent to the salesroom, and the filling of any orders from them was given to the originator of the pattern. Sometimes if officials of the company were pleased with a pattern or it became popular, the company would buy it from its designer.

To be sure, the places of workmen who died or moved to the West were not filled. Without any stoppage or layoff, the number of employees had begun to decrease — not enough to cause notice in any one year, but a steady ebbing, nevertheless.

Perhaps the suave directors on their monthly tours of inspection lost a little of their seeming imperturbability in

private talks with Mr. Fessenden at the factory or Mr. Lloyd
at the station. News from New York was not too soothing.
The International, organized by German workmen fresh
from the revolutions of Europe, was demanding from the
city (1) employment on public works at customary wages;
(2) advance of either money or food sufficient to last one
week to all in actual want; and (3) no eviction for non-pay-
ment of rent. A monster procession and mass meeting of unemployed had ended in bloody riot with the police in Tomp-
kins Square. Although most of the injured were workmen,
the incident did not seem much less unsettling.

Fortunately, since here men were at least politically equal,
the American way was to prefer the vote to violence, but
even so there were upsetting trends. In 1874, Massachusetts
had gone to the Democrats for the first time in years. Plenty
of people were laying the hard times to the gold standard
and were clamoring for a return of the silver dollar dropped
by Congress in the "crime of 1873." Crackpots who called
themselves Greenbackers were beginning to mouth the well-
worn arguments for cheap money to keep up prices and
wages.

Slowly the country once more began to pull itself out of
the depths. When the Sandwich Savings Bank liquidated,
the depositors received eighty cents on the dollar. The Swift
brothers eventually paid their debts in full. Faith renewed.
A nation which had weathered two foreign wars and one of
the greatest civil ones in history together with depressions
major and minor could look forward without fear. Minds
turned from the passing panic to the great centennial to be
held in Philadelphia.

Everybody read about it. Nearly everybody — or at least,
over nine and a half millions — went, salesmen and sea captains, honeymooners and homebodies on the adventure of
a lifetime. Never had there been such an exhibition — forty-
eight and a half acres of it, with entries from Great Britain

and Canada, New South Wales, New Zealand, Cape Colony,
Tasmania, and most of the countries of Europe. Of course,
the Boston and Sandwich Company had an exhibit. American exhibits of bottle and plate glass, window glass and cheap
pressed lime-glass tableware were many, but to compete with
foreign flint glass, crystal-clear, hand-cut in diamond-spark-
ling facets, ringing musically as a silver bell at the flip of a
thumbnail, only two domestic companies offered displays.
These were the two old rivals, the Boston and Sandwich
Company and the New England Company of Cambridge.
Since the histories of both claim medals for the "best in the
exhibition," perhaps honors were distributed as lavishly as
at the world's fairs in Paris where James Jackson Jarves had
complained that two out of every three exhibitors received
a prize. However, the company which could boast of the
crystal chandelier it had placed in the White House could
hardly have been bested.

One of the features of the Boston and Sandwich Company's exhibit was the first tumbler pressed in Sandwich a
half-century before and long since passed out of Jarves hands
into the possession of a private collector. The clumsy thick
tumbler with its crude uneven design made an effective contrast with the frosty firmness and delicacy of such new patterns as the chrysanthemum leaf. As the exhibitor was taking it from the case to pass for inspection, it slipped from
his fingers and smashed to the floor. Its end was no less final
than the break with bygone days.

Sandwich held a centennial of its own to celebrate the distance it had traveled since Sandwich men had fared forth to
fight for their country's freedom. Attics were ransacked for
great-grandparents' finery for an Old Folks' Concert at which
"ye great Horn-blowers will begine toe take in wind at early
candle lintel and ye greate chorus of menne and womene
singers will enter the Hall dressed in their meeting clothes
and att ye sound of ye spinnet will burst forth intoe sounds
of ye sweet melody."

To match the painfully determined distortions of spelling, the players and singers took such distressingly quaint names as Joshbackersham Bazzum and Hepsy Skinflax and sang "Reuben and Rachel" lustily to prove that they and their town were "rube" no longer.

It was becoming the fashion to poke a little mocking fun at the rugged simplicities of the old days — days when new churches were being built to house worshipers seeking ways closer to God. Now, empty and abandoned, they were sometimes sold for use of trade, like the Universalist church moved to replace a burned block at the head of Jarves Street. The pulpit which had once dealt out fear of sin and hope of salvation now served to hold records of man's accounts with mammon. The town had turned to ways the Founding Fathers could not have foreseen.

3

No one could live all day by the rails like Mr. Lloyd without feeling some tremors of the unrest raging over the country, and Mr. Lloyd, who had been repelled by the new spirit sensed among workers at the glass factory, must have had moments of wondering about the ultimate wisdom of his choice. The railroads which had set the pace for the slide to depression were the last to leave the bottom. An obvious means of economy was a reduction in wages. Announced cuts of ten per cent had brought strikes everywhere. Rioting railroad workers from Philadelphia to San Francisco were reinforced by missile-hurling mobs of sympathetic "producing classes" to whom the railroad with its far-reaching monopolistic power, its remote corporate ownership, symbolized all that they hated and feared in the industrial age.

Here was class war for the first time in America. For the most part, however, since a glass blower's vote was as good as a railroad president's, most American workmen preferred the ballot box. In Sandwich, the attitude had not changed although a generation had gone by since the glassworkers' naïve delight that the Reverend Joseph Marsh had been "mentioned" — if no more — for a seat in the Councils of the Country.

Political leadership of the factory workers had by now passed from Mr. Marsh to new hands — appropriately enough those of a son of Saint Peter's church. The church bell tower with its ruby glass ball had been toppled by a Cape hurricane, never to be rebuilt, but the congregation had rooted too deep to be dispersed by any Cape wind. The appointment of P. McGirr as special constable for Jarvesville had been only a first concession to the alien element. Next had come the election of one John McLaughlin as school agent for Jarvesville with the result that Miss Sarah McLaughlin was immediately appointed teacher in the District 6 school. The town could not cry nepotism too loudly in view of the long years in which all town offices had been passed back and forth among Nyes, Wings, Tobeys, Freemans, Bournes, and a few more selected families.

Back in the thirties, a letter to the *Patriot* had complained of "a class of men" who "advocate each other, and if there is any place of profit in town affairs, one of this class is sure of a place."

Though the McLaughlin clan had undoubtedly been drawn to Sandwich by the glass factory, tradition now associates it more prominently with music in town life. "They were all good musicians," you hear, and Mr. George McLaughlin became partner in the New England Organ Company, which, in the late seventies and early eighties, purveyed organs to the parlors of the more well-to-do.

In his connection with Boston, he had acquired city ways of political organization and was generally regarded as district Democratic leader for the Cape. "A little Tammany boss," was the uptown opinion, and the fact that Tammany scandals were then reaching their height added pungency to the view. "He looked after the interests of the workers," they said on the other side of the tracks.

During the period of his power, new foreigners went to Barnstable to take out citizenship papers as soon as possible and were sent to the polls with explicit instructions at every election from presidential to town meeting. McLaughlin forces never succeeded in pushing any candidate into important town office, but on town issues, where there was always some divergence of opinion, the massed McLaughlin vote carried weight. In the wider field, there was recognition of the McLaughlin efforts, and with a Democratic administration in Washington in 1884, the post office went to James Shevlin, a McLaughlin relative by marriage.

This desirable plum had always gone to a solid citizen of old Sandwich from the days of the first post riders. Matters had come to a pretty pass in the minds of many of the townspeople, especially those in the cross-Cape or Bourne section. They did not like meetings packed with McLaughlin henchmen. They felt that they were paying their taxes for Jarvesville glassworkers to spend. Eventually, they split off into the separate township of Bourne.

On a national scale, the politics of this period followed a roughly similar trend, achieving results drastic enough to scare conservatives out of their wits, but not sufficiently far-reaching to satisfy the "producing classes" themselves. In 1878, the Greenback Party had piled up more than a million votes and sent fourteen representatives to Congress. Embattled farmers, lobbying as the Patrons of Husbandry, initiated the earliest laws to curb the power of the railroads and first brought to the fore the view that the growing power of monopolistic enterprise might need regulation as well as protection.

Legislative bodies began to have a mind to industry. In 1880, a special committee of the Massachusetts legislature

visited Sandwich. The members came with the avowed purpose of "inspecting the plant and witnessing the actual operation of glassmaking." Perhaps there was an idea of inci-
dentally gathering data and enthusiasm to memorialize Congress on the desirability of protecting state industry, for the
periodic furore over the American system of tariff had
broken out anew.

They alighted at a Sandwich nearly as tranquil as in the
days of Mr. Boyden and the stagecoach. Mr. Lloyd's corner
of the railroad had kept its calm, for the nearest strike — that
against a ten per cent wage cut on the Boston and Albany —
had been lost without any fuss. To Sandwich, where farmers
were railroad stockholders and Mr. Jarves had long since
broken the monopolistic stranglehold on freight rates, it was
not the railroad, but the glass factory which stood for the
spirit of the times. Yet Mr. Lloyd's forebodings had proved
false. The genial and just Mr. Fessenden was both liked
and respected by the men and had succeeded in building an
atmosphere of good will nearly equal to that of Jarves days.
There was no word or gesture to mar the complacency of the
visiting legislators.

The smoke-grimed settlement clustered at the base of the
towering conical chimneys was the counterpart of hundreds
huddled around the brick walls of mills and factories all
over the state. The cozy low tenements built by Mr. Jarves
had been supplemented by monotonous rows of an uglier
type, but with the Jarves elms, the factory village was pret-
tier than most. There was even a little grassy, shaded public
square with a fountain which might hold water, but somehow seldom did. Guided by the monster stacks, the party of
inspection would hardly have needed Mr. Fessenden's suave
escort in the approach to the large brick building to which
others were attached like a mammoth train of cars rounding
a bend. Greeted with preternatural flourish of trumpets, they
passed through a low arch and a short passage, and came out

into a vast domed room of flashing furnaces and gnomelike workers moving among the glow of molten metal.

The detailed inspection would, of course, begin in the pothouse with its bins of soft clay, its heaps of burnt fragments of old pots ground steadily and noisily into fine powder in the wheels of a huge steam mill, its workmen treading barefoot and shaping the viscous mass with wooden knives and paddles, the finished pots seasoning their appointed days and weeks and kilned to red heat and cooled to be ready when needed.

Then the delegation was led across the breezy green-lawned yard to a dismal basement where lead was melting in ovens into silvery streams which, compounded with chemicals and baked and raked, produced the beautiful scarlet powder that was the most expensive ingredient of fine flint glass. They visited the sand room where sand shipped from the Berkshires or the Hudson, the Jersey coast or even from France, was cleansed of impurities by floods of water over a broad iron table heated from beneath by steam pipes and then was sifted in a great machine and dried to a fine glittering mass.

Hoisted to the mixing room on the platformlike elevator which usually carried the sand, they found great boxes of it together with the red lead or sparkling soda and lime and smaller quantities of strange ingredients for color combinations. Here the "batch" was compounded in secrecy behind locked doors and loaded into little covered cars to be wheeled out to the furnaces. A short flight of stone steps and a dark, windy passage led to the gloomy crypt where the coal was forced up to the furnaces overhead by grimy stokers who worked in a continual galelike draft and shower of ashes and red-hot cinders.

Up in the glass room, they saw every variation of the age-old mystery of glassmaking. Little presses were popping out bankers' inks and milky pomade jars by the hundreds. Giant presses, smoking from the kerosene oil with which they were coated before every operation, disgorged lenses with the elaborate flutings devised by the French physicist, Fresnel, to spread the light for lighthouses and ships' lanterns. Other presses were endlessly turning out coarse tumblers and de-canters (which still must be hand-shaped at the top) in ex-cessively ugly patterns.

They marveled at the ordered confusion of the mingled operations — the small boys darting to the glory-holes with pieces to be reheated for final shaping or to the liers with still-soft articles carried on forked sticks, the gaffers finishing the work of their "shops," each devoted to ware of a special-ized type. One might be making great lamp bowls of flint glass to be dipped or "flashed" in the monkey pots of golden ruby for later cutting or engraving in patterns which would show the clear flint underneath. Gaffer Kinney's shop was making electric-light globes almost as big as a barrel, while the Falstaffian Gaffer Matthews was putting the finishing touches on the tiniest of wineglasses. Gaffer Lovett worked on the thick, heavy "blanks" for deep cutting, while Gaffer Grady made the white globes in common use for gaslights.[3]

Most impressive were the solo displays of skill which now formed such a very small part of the company output. The French wizard, Adolphe Bonique, might be copying a rare imported perfume bottle for a famous actress or Nicholas Lutz might be at work on one of his famous flint-glass gypsy kettles wound around with ruby thread. As a climax, Gaffer Edward Haines, the last of the old-timers, was re-quested to make a lamp with a handle. He could still show the newcomers a thing or two. With his gatherer and mold boy working at top speed, he formed the bowl while the servitor gathered from the furnace another bit of glass which he rolled on the marver until it was about the shape and size of a very short fat snake. Blowing-iron perpendicular and

[3] Bangs Burgess, *History of Sandwich Glass.*

red-hot snake hanging down, he went up to Gaffer Haines who fastened one end to the lamp, measured the right length with his eye, and cut it off with a large pair of shears as if it had been molasses candy. With pincers he attached this end, too, to the lamp, and there was the handle. But Gaffer Haines was not done. Quick as a flash, he repeated the operation twice, and behold a unique little three-handled lamp as souvenir for the chairman of the committee. The whole process had taken just under two minutes.

After this bravura performance, the party could be expected to give only a cursory inspection to the cutting room, with the whir of the leather belt, run by steam engine below, which turned the copper disks or wire wheels for the cutters stationed beneath their conical tanks of sand and water. They probably no more than stuck their noses into the room choking with turpentine where Mr. Swann and his decorating department devised gilt curlicues and flowers brighter than ever bloomed in Sandwich gardens.

Along with their good shore dinner, they digested the pleasantly confused impressions of a brick beehive of busy men, women, and boys sheltering its clustered homes and supporting its bustling business district. Towns like this were the pride of state and country and must be protected by all possible means. There was already alarm over the flow of industry into newly developing regions which should, by all that was right and holy, contentedly go on being markets for the old manufacturing communities. The twenty-two glasshouses of Massachusetts in 1870 had by 1880 shrunk to eleven.

Mr. Fessenden could express only a cautious optimism. As far as possible, the Boston and Sandwich Company made use of the most modern methods to keep up with the growing competition, but the West had advantages which could hardly be overcome. For example, there was gas. In 1875, a Rochester tumbler works had sunk its own gas well 968 feet. By 1880, there were twenty-one furnaces burning either coal or natural gas. The cheapest grades of coal could be used for gas-producing furnaces. The cost of coal, previously about one half the cost of melting glass, could be reduced thirty to fifty per cent with gas burners. Hobbs, Brockunier and Company at Wheeling, West Virginia, in 1879 was getting slack at thirty cents per ton, or the cost of carting it from the mines to the furnace.

Natural advantages for glassmaking at least were certainly moving westward, and the railroads had done away with localized markets and made competition universal. Since tariff barriers between states were not allowed, there was not much hope that the legislative committee could offer. However, determined support of the American system of protective tariff could still save the country from floods of foreign goods.

Of course, industrial processes had always enjoyed protection in some form from the days when a Sandwich offered tax-free land by a suitable waterway "to any of the townsmen that will set up a mill." But the primitive industries so protected were granted their freedom from public charge, rights to natural resources, and monopoly privileges in return for services supposedly rendered the community. In the agricultural way of life, producer and consumer were one. The farmer both produced the corn and consumed the meal ground by the mill. The machine age, which separated producer and consumer so that most workmen did not consume the smallest part of anything they themselves produced, was creating an economy with emphasis on production.

American absorption with production was to be carried to such a degree that Mr. Jarves's ideal of putting more goods into the hands of a greater number of people would often become lost in considerations of prices, wages, and artificially controlled markets. Since the means and labor of production pertained increasingly to different classes, most wage earners mistrusted the high protective tariff as fattening a favored few — except, of course, when their own industry was involved.

Thus, whenever the Democrats offered a so-called "people's administration," tariffs and duties were reduced as nearly as possible to the point of revenue only. Tariff which originally had been a toll paid to a feudal lord for permission to cross his territory had grown into a weapon for the protection of the manufactures which had become cherished symbols of national advancement. This use Henry Clay had carried to its ultimate in his famous "American system" to "preserve, maintain, and strengthen" which he declared himself ready to "defy the South, the President, and the devil." Jackson fought for a "tariff which shall produce a reduction of the revenue to the needs of the government." Tariff policies seesawed with successive administrations.

The Civil War ended arguments for the time. In the desperate need for revenue, the average rate on dutiable articles was hoisted by degrees to 47.06 per cent, and the American system for all who clamored became a national religion. In regard to almost all protected articles, the tariffs of 1864 remained in force for twenty years without reduction. Now in 1883, with the coincidence of one more depression and a Democratic Congress, the war tariff was at last to be examined and revised. It was noted by the Congressional Committee that during these years American inventions of improvements in machinery and processes had so increased productiveness that manufacturers should be able to "compete with their foreign rivals under a substantial reduction of existing duties."

Deming Jarves had set forth a similar premise with a different conclusion. "By the perfection of our machines, double the product can be obtained, and although the glassmaker is paid at least three times the wages usually paid in Germany and France, we can in all the articles where the value of the materials predominates compete successfully with importers of foreign glass. But when the labor on glass constitutes its chief value, then glass can be imported cheaper than it can be manufactured in this country."

Of course, labor was generally the chief item in the cost of glass. And Deming Jarves certainly was not considering glass manufactured without the protective tariff which even during the Jacksonian era had been twenty per cent and at times had risen to over one hundred per cent. Glass on a free list was unthinkable. Glass had enjoyed government protection from the days of the royal Venetian glasshouses. Britain had once even offered bounties on exported glass to help the English manufacturer meet competition in foreign markets. The Massachusetts legislature had granted to Mr. Jarves's boyhood hero, Robert Hewes, license to run a lottery to raise three hundred dollars "for the purpose of building a glass-house and promoting the manufacture of crown and bottle glass in Boston." Thus, glass was always in the midst of arguments raging over tariff revision.

Those in Sandwich who had their *Boston Morning Journal* sent down by train read on Wednesday, February 20, 1884:

FREE TRADE VERSUS PROTECTION

"More Talk Before the Ways and Means Committee

"An Importer Makes Some Unfortunate Allusions to the Workingman and Is Sharply Called to Account.

"The hearing was opened by a manufacturer of glass who said that one member of the committee had admitted that the tariff ought to be fixed at a rate high enough to pay the difference between the English and American scale of wages." Now, the "unfortunate allusions" of the headline were made by an importer seeking tariff reduction who stated that "in articles of universal use, an increase or diminution of the price affects everybody practically in the United States" and "there was no sense in keeping up the tariff in order to keep up what he called the absurd scale of wages in the United States as compared with other countries."

Thereupon, the chairman of the committee "drew a graphic picture of the conditions of labor and living in Great Britain and Belgium and asked if American workingmen should be reduced to this condition." The importer could only reiterate that in his judgment, American wages were altogether too high. Another glass manufacturer countered that glassmaking was an industry "in which the product is almost wholly the result of labor. He declared that no reduction in duty could be made without reducing wages or reducing the domestic product. He then went on to compare the wages paid blowers, gatherers, cutters, laborers, etc. in American and in foreign factories, showing amounts of wages in favor of the United States 25%."

This was considerably less than the "three times the wages paid in Germany and France" of Mr. Jarves's estimate, but it was enough to give certain classes of wage earners the highest standard of living in the world. These workers were not only determined to keep their advantages, but add to them. Consequently, at times, their attitude toward the protective tariff was somewhat confused.

Whenever the tariff was advertised as an election issue, Mr. McLaughlin and other party leaders had a little trouble finding convincing logic for Democratic workmen. They could parrot as much as they pleased the stock argument that a high tariff favored the manufacturer at the expense of the worker who must consume the costly goods. That sounded very well where it concerned cloth or shoes or the product of any other industry. It made a difference when it touched Sandwich's own. Mr. McLaughlin might, as usual, herd his minions to the polls. As they marked their ballots, they thought of floods of cheap English and Continental glass wiping out their well-paid jobs. When votes were counted, it was found that dozens of Mr. McLaughlin's hitherto docile Democrats had bolted to the Republicans and the American system of tariff.

They were, however, more consistent when it came to free trade in cheap labor supplied by unrestricted immigration. To be sure, the swarms of Chinese coolies, who had even turned up as strike breakers in Massachusetts, had been stopped by the Exclusion Act as soon as Chinese manufacturers using coolie labor in California had proved able to undersell white competitors. But the worker, defending his standard of living, still was obliged to contend with such undertakings as the American Emigrant Company founded for the express purpose of importing "laborers, especially skilled laborers from Great Britain, Germany, Belgium, France, Switzerland, Norway, and Sweden for the manufacturers, railroad companies, and other employers in America." [4]

Glassworkers did not oppose the manufacturers' desire for protection against imported glass, but they decided that they needed protection against imported glassworkers. Backed by the signatures of between fifty and one hundred thousand supporters, the powerful Window Glass Workers' Union started the first labor lobby against the importation of so-called "contract" labor. Thus, almost the first restriction of America's free welcome to all who would come originated with workers determined to keep for themselves the advantages the country had given them.

Sandwich gaffers might stuff their letters back home with surplus dollars to ease the lot of those left in the old countries. Lowlier laborers might loiter of an evening around the drugstore of genial Charlie Hall until he was free to pen for them the faltering words which unaccustomed fingers could not write for themselves — words that told of good fare and pleasant living. Yet except in the case of their few

[4] John Rogers Commons, *History of Labor in the U.S.*

nearest and dearest, they had no desire to share the benefits they had found. In the midst of the most stupendous economy of production to be developed by the industrial age, the land of invitation and promise was becoming a land of increasingly strong barriers through which envious foreign eyes, heedless of city slums and submerged poverty, would vision a golden affluence of legendary proportions. The American way was changing direction with true American speed.

Ladies and Females

LOCAL PAPERS REPORTED in cozy detail the pleasant little party given by Mrs. Mary Waterman Jarves Leonard to celebrate the accomplishments of her night-blooming cereus; they failed altogether to mention the accident in which fourteen-year-old Ruthie Drody [1] nearly bled to death at the glass factory.

Ruthie was a rougher. Roughing was what we now call frosting, done with sandblast and wire brushes, on electric and gas globes, and on lamp shades as a foundation for later etching. It was one of the dirtiest, most dangerous jobs in the whole factory. The four roughers, all girls, worked in the cutting room with the men. Their work was very similar to that of the men and undoubtedly had been done by men before the Civil War. The differences now were in the men's favor. It was all cough- and rheumatism-producing labor, but an expert cutter had the pride of creative skill as he followed the pattern crayoned in red on his "blank."

[1] Some names in this and the following chapters are fictitious by request.

Of course, even the best of cutters had an occasional mishap. If there was the tiniest sand bubble in the glass, the piece would crack under the wheel and sometimes as much as twenty hours labor would be lost.

"But good glass cuts like butter," Mr. Packwood, boss of the cutting room, used to say as he lovingly fingered a "blank" clear as spring water. And Sandwich glass was good glass.

The cutters sat behind benches beneath their conical tanks of sand and water. Conveniently at hand were their wheels of different sizes and materials — copper, pumice, emery — for deep cutting or cameo-like engraving. The girl roughers were on their feet all day, standing at their benches, and they had to walk back and forth to fetch their water from the tanks of the cutters. And hour after hour, week after week, they applied the revolving brush to article after article, dozens of them all alike. The pay was by piecework and commonly came to between five dollars and six dollars a week.

The articles to be roughed were held firmly between two pieces of cork while the sand blast was applied. Every glass blower's work was known to the girls, and when a "move" to be roughed came up from a careless or sloppy workman, the girls could only pray. If a piece was the least lopsided, the cork vise would not grip it firmly. When the revolving wire wheel struck, it would fly apart in fragments as sharp as shooting knives. This was bound to happen to every girl at some time or other, but miraculously, many escaped injury. Ruthie was not lucky. An artery in the wrist was severed. In spite of a frantic running for the doctor and frenzied efforts of fellow workers to hold her arm over her head and press the wrist with handkerchiefs and strips torn from petticoats, she was drenched in blood and half dead by the time the doctor's horse galloped up to the cutting-room door.

Nevertheless, short of a coroner's inquest, nothing that

happened to a little Jarvesville rougher was important
enough to reach the columns of the newspaper. Except for
news of Saint Peter's, furnished by the aggressive Father
Clinton, affairs of the factory village seldom reached print
unless, like a glassmakers' ball or brawl, effects were felt
throughout the community. The gap between the Main
Streets and Jarvesvilles of the land was growing with the
years, and nowhere did it yawn wider than between the so-
called "females of industry" and the ladies who had, or
could give an illusion of, that leisure which had come to be
a mark of aristocracy. There were few common links between the uptown young ladies who rendered "The Storm"
or "Raindrops on the Quiet Lake" on one of Mr. McLaughlin's organs for the benefit of such swains as braved the parlor
chill, and the Jarvesville women and girls who did the dirty
and monotonous work around the Boston and Sandwich factory.

It is not known exactly when women first worked in the
Boston and Sandwich factory. Since in later days, the cleaning and oiling of the molds was always done by women, they
may have been there almost as soon as pressed glass was
made in quantity. Woman's work in the machine age was at
first generally an extension of labor she had always done,
like cleaning, sewing, or spinning, for it was the cotton mill
which had first separated woman from the home. But it was
not long before the revolutionary effect of the factory system began to be felt.

With a temptingly cheap supply of female labor on hand
everywhere for would-be capitalists, little factories sprouted
up over night in every country town. Cape Cod was dotted
with them — a shoe factory in Wellfleet with invested capital
of twenty-three thousand dollars, a shirt factory with a hundred machines at Provincetown, another shoe factory in
West Dennis housed in a "most sightly edifice" and employing one hundred and fifty hands, and two small silk factories

in Sandwich. The glass factory itself had begun to use women and girls in some numbers in the late fifties when ornate decorated lamps first came into fashion. True to its policy of importing the latest innovations, the Boston and Sandwich Company had a Mr. Bramma from England to introduce gilding, and it was found that the work of polishing the gilding with bloodstones as well as packing the lamps for shipment could be done by women at three dollars a week.

The Civil War saw even more women employed in the factory on work formerly done by men. As has been the case with wars of the industrial age, the return of the men from battle did not push the women from the work which they did more cheaply, but in the post-war expansion there was room for everyone.

In England a writer noted "a curious inversion of the proper order of things seen in the domestic economy of the cheap labor system, for women and girls were superseding men in manufacturing labor, and in consequence, their husbands had often to attend, in a shiftless and slovenly fashion, to those household duties which mothers and daughters, hard at work in the factories, were unable to fulfill."

This was not the American way. With the more immediate tradition of the man with the gun or the hoe providing the raw wherewithal of existence, there was a strong American prejudice against a married woman working outside the home. There were a few widows among the women who worked at the Boston and Sandwich factory, but no woman with husband who breathed, even if he did not move fast enough to earn a living. In that case, she took in washing or sewing for more fortunate sisters and kept up the genteel fiction of dependency on her man. It is impossible to check the exact number of women working in the glass factory at any given time, but it was generally upwards of fifty — enough to take care of the widows and spinsters and most

of the girls for their few years between childhood and marriage.

Boy or girl, few children passed through the Jarvesville
district school to the high school over in Sandwich. A Jarvesville mother might dream of having a schoolteacher daughter, but inevitably her little hope would be swallowed by the
glass factory. Children going to and from school who did
not actually have to pass the factory door could always make
excuses for walking that way. There was a fascination about
factory life for the young ones — the nicknames and special
jokes and current slang of the workers, the hints of day-to-
day drama in a mysterious adult world. It was not until
months later that those who had been sucked inside began to
feel the disillusionment of monotony and fatigue.

Fourteen-year-old Ruthie had been literally recruited
from the schoolroom. Her eighteen-year-old sister Jennie
had already been a rougher for several years when a large
rush order of electric-light bulbs came in just at school vacation.

"How about getting Ruthie in to help us out until school
opens?" Mr. Packwood, head of the cutting room, had said.

Naturally, Ruthie was eager to be grown up like her sister
and bring home a pay envelope of her own.

"If you're sure it's only for vacation," said the mother
who had seen her ambitions for her children vanish as the
factory gobbled one after another.

But it was the old story. The cutting room was just as
busy when school reopened. Mr. Packwood was persuasive.
Ruthie, never an enthusiastic student, wanted to stay, and
the money in her pay envelope had become a family habit.
Besides, she had not then had her first accident, and her sister had never been hurt. Jennie, everybody said, was lucky.
Ruthie was not.

First, she got a cut on the forearm which took seven
stitches to close. That meant over a month out of work with

no pay envelope and with doctor's bills. Then came the
bloody butchery that nearly ended her life. Scars stayed on
mind as well as arms. Over fifty-five years after the factory
closed, she could still wake up with a scream, dreaming
that a lamp shade had blown up in splinters under her
hands.

Jennie and the other girls agreed that Ruthie should try
to change her work. Few had escaped minor cuts, but no one
had had two such serious accidents in so short a time. There
were plenty of other jobs for women around the factory,
even besides cleaning the molds and packing. Since science
had reduced etching to a pasted pattern and an acid bath,
there were women etchers. Women inspectors looked over
the hundreds of dozens of lamps and tumblers and smallware
for flaws, and the so-called stopperers spent all day fitting
stoppers to bottles. There was also work on the sloar or account book, an occupation considered nearly as respectable
as schoolteaching for an uptown lady provided circumstances
made it necessary for her to work at all. Of course, Ruthie
did not have the schooling for figuring on the sloar, but she
had set her hopes high. She yearned to be one of the ladies
in Mr. Swann's decorating department.

Sandwich might consider work on the sloar more genteel.
To Jarvesville, the decorators in the lamp department were
the real female aristocracy of the factory — using the term
aristocrat in what J. J. J. had considered its American sense
as referring to one whose position is envied by his fellows.
In only two departments did the work of men and women
run along parallel lines — in the decorating shop of Mr.
Swann and the cutting room of Mr. Packwood. Both were
Englishmen who had learned their craft in the old country,
but their attitude toward their female labor was as different
as could be. To Mr. Packwood, the company was holy, and
if he found that his roughers were making too much on their
piecework, he arranged to have the rates cut. On the other

hand, everyone said that "Mr. Swann believed in high pay for his girls and got it."

Again and again, Mr. Swann succeeded in having the piece rates raised for his girls, but perhaps to avoid the effects of envy, exactly what they earned was one of the best-kept secrets of the glasshouse.

"Nobody ever knew exactly. They never would tell," is the answer usually found today. "But it was plenty. The decorators were the best dressed women in town. We all envied their beautiful gowns."

For a moment of memory, ghostly lady decorators in their basques and bustles, their satins and velvets, would haunt sleepy Sandwich streets, moving in the strong aura of turpentine which was said to scare off suitors, for few of them ever married. Perhaps, too, the lady decorators stayed spinsters because of male awe of their reputed superior financial status, for unless a man were a gaffer, he would not feel that he had much to offer.

Ruthie Drody came closest to solving the mystery. It happened at a time when there was an order for chandeliers with many frosted globes of a tricky shape that set the rates higher for the roughers. Ruthie managed to earn seven dollars — a quite alarming figure to Mr. Packwood who, so the roughers believed, tried to arrange a readjustment of rates so that they would not cost the company as much again. When Ruthie went to collect her magnificent seven dollars and the sloar book was opened to her name, she saw on the opposite page the name and pay of a decorator — fifteen dollars. As the girl had been working in the decorating department only a week or two and as pay was by piecework, the excited roughers guessed that old hands were making eighteen dollars or twenty dollars a week — a living wage for a family man, to say nothing of a lone woman.

Thereafter, when Ruthie went for her pay, the page listing the decorators was carefully covered with a sheet of blank paper, but a figure once seen was not forgotten. After her second accident, Ruthie applied to be transferred to the decorating department for a tryout.

There is a fiction prevalent today among collectors of elaborately painted lamp shades that each girl originated her own designs, that one specialized in moss roses, another in violets, and so on. The truth was that Mr. Swann, or his assistant, a German artist named Miller, created practically all of the designs.

"Pansies today," Mr. Swann would say as they trooped in at seven after the factory bell, and there on his table would be a lamp shade wreathed in pansies. Each girl would make a copy as exact as she could to take back as model to her own bench. There she would turn out pansied shades all day.

A new girl was tried out for a few days. If she did not make good in copying Mr. Swann's floral masterpieces, she was dropped. Ruthie felt sure that she could produce roses and lilies and whole garden garlands with the best of them. But Ruthie was never given her chance to try. Roughers were hard to get and were usually recruited from the families of girls already at the job, as Ruthie had been dragged in to lighten her sister's load. Mr. Packwood could not afford to lose a rougher and spoke to Mr. Swann. It was not, of course, proper for the head of one department to raid another. So Ruthie stayed with her revolving brush and sand blast, her danger and her fears.

Even for a little rougher, life glittered once a year at the glassmakers' ball — the sensation not only of Jarvesville, but of Sandwich and towns around with all the subscription tickets sold weeks in advance. The blare of the glass blowers' band could lift a body out of this world to a fairyland where ladies in gorgeous gowns glittered from hair to slipper toe with — was it diamond dust? or merely powdered glass? Then a Ruthie would dream of marrying her apprentice lad who might some day be a gaffer whose wife could wear her twenty-dollar-a-yard velvet and perhaps win the prize for the most beautiful costume at the glassmakers' ball.

It was this unquenchable hope which kept women workers from fighting to improve their lot. Few women admitted that they individually were a permanent enough part of the factory system to make the rigors of resistance worthwhile. All in all, it seemed so much easier for the majority to marry than organize — and much nearer God's order for women. The fiction that every female had or could acquire some at least partially supporting male kept women's wages below subsistence level. Women were not paid a living wage because they were not expected to live on their earnings, considered only as pin money or a supplement to an already existent family income.

In time, the trade societies of men awoke to the dangers to themselves in the situation. Since male vanity has never been able to accept the ideal of equal pay for equal work, the proposed remedies were quite ineffectual. The Constitution of the Journeyman Cordwainers provided that no woman should be allowed to work in any shop controlled by the union "except she be a member's wife or daughter." [2] There were still plenty of shops not controlled by unions. A labor convention in Philadelphia recommended that women's clubs — or more properly speaking, those societies through which ladies performed their cultural and philanthropic exercises — be urged to co-operate with the oppressed females of industry instead of supporting foreign missions. The ladies continued to find the exotic Hindu or Hottentot more to their taste than their drab sisters on the other side of the tracks.

Least of all did men want women in their own unions. Finally aroused to the danger of competition from cheap female labor, they did reach the point of resolutions "encouraging the females themselves to co-operate and form an or-

2 Norman J. Ware, *The Labor Movement in the U.S., 1860-1895.*

ganization." Uriah Stephens, founder of the Knights of Labor, even visioned "an organization that will cover the globe," including "men and women of every craft, creed, and color." When, however, the dream came to take form, stubborn male prejudice held out for the provision that women "shall have Local Associations of their own, *governed by male officers,* and that they shall *not* be entitled to full privileges of this Noble and Holy Order." As an eventual concession, a Mrs. Leonora Barry was appointed to "organize female locals," but only "where it will not conflict with more important work." When at last solidarity came to Sandwich, it was not for Ruthie, the rougher, but for those already strong.

DEMING JARVES

"Solidarity Forever!"

Ask any man in Jarvesville why he joined the American Flint Glass Workers' Union of North America, and the invariable answer was "For protection!" Yet Sandwich folk would have said that few wage earners needed protection less than the lordly gaffers of the Boston and Sandwich Company who were the moving spirits for the union in town. To be sure, the old Massachusetts Flint-Glass Makers' Protective Association, like so many of the bravely begun protective unions which had not been able to protect, had petered out in the troubled seventies. But the glass blowers still banded together in a sort of company union, as in the days of Deming Jarves, to control wages and working conditions which were essentially the same here as in the factories where the American Flint Glass Workers' Union held sway.

"Work in every department of the Boston and Sandwich glass works has been resumed after a temporary shut-down," the newspaper reported. "There is annually a six weeks' shut-down, it being the regular vacation of the glass-workers throughout the eastern states."

No longer was glass blown at all seasons except for the occasional exceptionally torrid stretch of weather. The grim contract with the workers which would automatically terminate if the fires in the furnaces went out was a matter of the past. The Boston and Sandwich Company now even had no night shift.

The only movement in town for shorter hours came from the storekeepers. The *Register* informed the public that "the subject of the early closing of the stores at 6.15 on every evening except Friday and Saturday of each week is agitated by Sandwich tradesmen."

As for the working hours of the glassmakers, the ghost of Deming Jarves haunting Jarvesville must have writhed in impotent anguish at the sight of joking, smoking glass blowers lolling around the factory door in the middle of a good glass day. They seemed to work only when they pleased and have plenty of time to turn out marvelous pieces of individual work on private order (for which the company received not a penny) — or even to blow a bright toy to catch the fancy of a passing child.

Lafayette Fessenden had gone the way of all good men after a valiant and largely successful struggle against the trends of the times. Everybody liked the new superintendent, Mr. Henry Spurr, who had the genial salesman-type personality. He had started as clerk in the Boston warerooms when he was only seventeen. Ten years later, in 1859, he had been considered important enough to receive a wedding present of tableware from the company. Thus, he had had a long record of company service, but always in sales, not production.

He seems to have had the gift of identifying himself completely with his associates of the moment, whether directors or workers, and of giving the impression that as long as all was pleasant, all was well. If Mr. Spurr had any troubles, they were well hidden from Boston officials on the monthly tour of inspection who, like a teacher coming suddenly into a classroom, found a seemingly fruitful bustle of activity. Any possible concern was equally well concealed from the workers after one of the sessions, smoothed over by his native optimism, with directors whose books had begun to show a slow, but steady loss. As for the workers, their opinion of him was expressed at a fair in Town Hall by the award of a gold-headed cane for the most popular citizen of Sandwich. And why not, since glassmakers as never before could do exactly as they wished?

If there were no particular causes of friction at the factory or material benefits to be gained, why then did the workers at Sandwich feel the need of the Flint Glass Workers' Union of North America "for protection"? The basic reason here as elsewhere in the growing urge for organization was an innate craving for the security once given by the possession of one's own bit of land. Perhaps the feeling of personal independence that went with it had gone forever. Unless an individual had unusual strength within himself, he was apt to feel that the world was becoming too vast and intricate for him to cope with alone.

"The principle of union is as natural to every man from necessity as the feeling of existence itself," the Constitution of the Massachusetts Flint-Glass Makers' Protective Association had declared in 1865.

The way of the world since then had strengthened the feeling. There was little that a man could call his very own, even the work of his hands. At the factory, he was simply one cog in an impersonal money-making machine. With the advanced subdivision of manufacturing operations, even the gaffers merely smoothed and shaped articles and did little fancy blowing. Taker-in and mold boys in many cases were child labor pure and simple and did not go on to apprenticeship. Yet the men, for all the sloppy indifference of their attitude toward the factory work, still kept their fierce creative pride as is shown in the wizardry of the articles made for private orders.

Mr. Jarves had known and encouraged each man's effort and skill. The present directors scarcely knew the men's names. In the case of one, Nathaniel Bradlee, who showed an unusual friendliness and understanding, the men responded with almost pathetic good will. For the most part, however, the workers felt that their lives were ordered by remote control and were impelled to huddle together for defense against forces they could not see or comprehend — a tendency that could lead to mass living, mass thinking, and mass dying.

With not the church but the factory as center of communal life, there had come a spiritual retrocession. The man tilling his corner of God's earth had turned to the Lord of the sun and rain and wind for help in the problems he faced. The worker for a wage saw no hope in God from the troubles brought by the man-made machine and began to summon up the primeval herd-and-hive instinct by which rootless savages, animals, and insects sought safety in their own numbers. The almost religious fervor of the surge toward solidarity was shown in the very names of growing organizations — Knights of Saint Crispin, Sons of Vulcan, Sovereigns of Industry, Patrons of Husbandry, and finally the Knights of Labor which had swelled to proportions frightening to those who wished to embalm the social structure in past ways.

Glassworkers were prominently associated with the Knights of Labor, unlike many of the other craft unions which, not realizing the danger that some machine might do away with the demand for their skills, scorned being lumped with unskilled labor. Jarvesville had followed the strikes of the Window Glass Workers, aided by the Knights who had levied an assessment of five cents a member for their support. The first strike had particular interest to Boston and Sandwich Company workers as it concerned the wage differential between East and West. A differential of twenty per cent had been allowed eastern manufacturers by the union to compensate for the cheaper fuel and resources of the West. (The differential was twenty-five per cent in flint-glass factories.) In 1882, the Window Glass Workers' Union had struck to lower their differential ten per cent. After a second strike and victory in which the Window Glass Workers gained all their points — "last years' wages (unheard of in the midst of a depression), limit of production under our control, no extra work, the apprentice system intact, and our lines unbroken" (or the closed shop), they gave all credit to the Noble and Holy Order. "Had it not been for the Knights of Labor, we would not have been successful." [1]

Sandwich, of course, was stirred over the Chicago meat packers and their eight-hour day since the Swift brothers stood for the town's success story and their company with its country-wide branches was considered a fount of opportunity for local young men. Then the shock from the Haymarket Bomb touched every little factory town, turned wage earners into a sort of sub-army against the rest of society, and made the very name of the Knights of Labor a dread thing. It was true that the May Day violence attending the eight-hour movement was incited by German revolutionaries of the International and not the Knights, whose leader, Powderly, had advised them to confine their activities to essays to be read on Washington's Birthday. It was true that the Haymarket Bomb had little or nothing to do with the eight-hour movement and only one Knight was involved. The power of the Knights could not be denied.

In 1882 and 1884, the Knights had paraded by the thousands in New York on the first Monday of September and

[1] Norman J. Ware, *op. cit.*

had declared that this day in the year should be set aside for labor's show of strength. By 1887, Sandwich folk read in their own newspaper: "The first Monday of September has been made a legal holiday in this state to be known as Labor's Holiday." Everywhere the Knights were causing shivers along conservative spines.

"Combinations, as they are called, are an objection when formed by workingmen, but called associations when formed by others, no matter what the necessity may be in either case," the Constitution of the Massachusetts Flint-Glass Makers' Protective Association had sagely stated in 1865.

This was certainly true in connection with the union movement. Yet it is a surprise to find as a matter of cold fact that, in many instances, the manufacturers' associations were formed only after growing strength of the trade unions made a united front seem desirable for defense. In the glass industry, as a matter of record, the Window Glass Workers of Pittsburgh joined the Knights of Labor in 1877 or 1878, and it was not until 1879 that the American Window Glass Manufacturers' Association took stable form.[2] The American Flint Glass Workers' Union of North America was established at a convention in Pittsburgh in 1878, and it was two years before the National Flint and Lime Association was formed. Widening markets stimulated the spreading unionization of workers and the consequent matching associations of manufacturers. By this time, Pittsburgh glass and Sandwich glass had been selling side by side for fully fifteen years in Boston and Philadelphia markets.

"Pittsburgh is the center of the glass trade," declared the Window Glass Workers to whom the Flint Glass Workers were bound by close ties of craft brotherhood and parallel working conditions, "and Pittsburgh price rules the market throughout the land. Therefore Pittsburgh brothers must have control of all the glassworkers of America." [3]

[2] Warren C. Scoville, *Growth of the American Glass Industry to 1880.*
[3] Norman J. Ware, *The Labor Movement in the U.S., 1860–1895.*

Hence, it was only a question of time before union representatives from Pittsburgh should at last reach Sandwich.
The coming of the union was not heralded by local papers.
Editors saved their excitement for more pressing concerns —
such as a proposed grand celebration of the town's "quarter
millennial," as they liked to call it, in 1889, two years hence,
in which neighboring and daughter towns were to be invited to participate. The town was still its own little
world almost as much as in the days of Deming Jarves, and
printed news was often completely out of contact with
reality.

Moreover, the town seemed prosperous and stable enough
to withstand any disturbing power. There was a new "Sandwich Co-operative Bank" for such savings as the people
could squeeze out of the times and a new and quite elegant
Casino for their pleasures. The usual smoke towered over
the town, and company directors on their monthly inspection tours outwardly wore their customary impassive and
slightly arrogant calm.

Once in a while, the railroad brought to Sandwich a faint
echo of turmoil from outside. "The Old Colony pay train
was around this week and had on board General Manager
Kendrick who was making an effort to ship men and officers to man the company's freight which was lying idle because of the strike. $28 a month and board was being offered
for deck hands. A special car will be attached to the morning train to carry those who are shipped to Fall River." But
the haranguing in Jarvesville was not yet loud enough to
reach the columns of the paper.

Human nature being as it is, the strongest stimulus to
union strength in Sandwich was company opposition. Owners had always grumbled about the tacit agreement of glass
blowers within a factory to regulate their work to the capacity of the least competent, limit apprentices, and attempt to
control factory output with an eye on the market. Spreading

solidarity was regarded with the hatred born of fear. Here was more than inter-factory or inter-regional union. In the days of groping combinations, the blowers and the cutters had functioned as separate bodies. Glass cutters had been among the first workers to be unionized, certainly among the earliest to strike for higher wages. In the Flint Glass Workers' Union of North America, blowers and cutters were combined.

Probably the union offered little or no increase in the rates of pay which seem to have been about the same as elsewhere in the East. It is known that, in the tightly organized Window Glass Workers' Union, pay rates were thirty to forty dollars a week with the exception of the very highly paid "double strength" blowers. Gaffers at Sandwich were making thirty to forty dollars a week at piece rates, the difference depending not on the skill of the worker, but the type of work done in that particular week.

The whole setup of working conditions was different from that of Jarves days. The work of the "shops" — gaffer, servitor, gatherer, and boys — had been even further subdivided into a chain of machinelike movements. Identical operations are supposed to make for efficiency, but since workers have always feared that increased productive efficiency would do away with their jobs, the glassmakers had taken very effective countermeasures. They definitely limited their day's work to two "moves," as they were called in the East — or "turns," in the West.

A "move" consisted of a certain number of pieces sent to the liers. The count ranged from about seventy in the case of large lamps to over two hundred for small pieces like salt cellars. The time involved in making a "move" depended on the condition of the glass. On the rare days when the glass was "sweet," the men full of vim, and the boys not fumble-fingered, a "move" could be made in as little as two hours. At times when the glass was "ambitty" or unmanageable or there was any accident to the batch, the men might be at the factory ten or twelve hours. A minimum of four hours' bodily presence at the factory was required by the union as apparently a sole concession to management.

There were some stormy meetings before the union men finally won the day. True, blind faith in massed force and forceful leadership give the illusion of a security of sorts — an illusion that was to be one of the most threatening dangers of the century to come. But there were still some sturdy souls who, seeing no solution for the new problem of trying to combine freedom with security, prized personal liberty above safety. Billy Kern, now working in New Bedford, was one of these. One big union seemed just an additional type of remote control over men's lives. He attributed the spreading failure of glasshouses in the East to lack of union flexibility in considering local conditions and, preferring the East at any price, declared the union — "the ruination of the whole thing. You had to do just what they told you and didn't realize anything out of it."

These were strong words from one of the original officers of the Massachusetts Flint-Glass Makers' Protective Association, but the spirit of moderation in the old union had been lost.

"There are many who object and are opposed to our organization," the Constitution of the old union had said. "We have no reproaches to heap upon them, and bear no ill feeling toward them."

The Flint Glass Workers', like the Window Glass Workers', was a strong closed-shop union and was ready with intimidation that stopped just short of murder to force all into the fold. In the end, just one ventured to hold out and call his soul his own — for could a man call his soul his own after he had delivered all phases of his material life into the custody of others? Fred Wodt, a cutter on fine crystal, had come from Germany to seek the old American ideal of freedom

as much as the new American way of life. In the face of fair
promises and dire threats, he flatly refused to join the union.

Fortunately for him, Boston and Sandwich directors had
greeted the coming of the union with a notice posted in the
Watch-House stating that the company would continue to
hire whom it pleased. In those days, there were very few
closed-shop contracts between union and management. In
general, the utmost granted was non-discrimination against
union members, and it was up to the unions to make their
own closed shop by organizing all the workers. So Fred
Wodt continued in the cutting shop, but he confided to a
merchant in the town that he did not dare to walk the streets
alone for fear of being killed.

When disturbance in the factory finally erupted into the
newspaper, however, it was not over the lone rebel or the
union. On April 19, 1887 — the sixty-third anniversary of
the breaking of ground for Mr. Jarves's "individual enterprise" — townspeople read, "A report that the employees of
the Boston and Sandwich Glass Works were out has been
denied. There is trouble there, but the workmen have
decided to continue work until General Manager Spurr
returns."

This was undoubtedly the Nicholas Black affair — the
rousing row that made such a noise in Boston and Sandwich
Company history that it has been commonly reported, to
the wrath of the surviving glassworkers, that the factory was
closed over a matter of eighty-seven cents.

The men, as has been stated, were paid by the "move" of
so many pieces sent to the liers. The liers were at one end
of the glasshouse and were filled by the taker-in boys running with the articles on their forked sticks from the gaffers
to the trains of pans moving on their chains through the
tunnel. At the other end of the lier, the annealed glass was
removed for packing by the sloarmen who checked the count
of the pieces. Nick Black was on salt cellars that day, and the

sloarmen counted his "move" enough pieces short to cut his pay eighty-seven cents.

Black swore, and he was backed up by the men in his shop, that a full count of salt cellars had gone into the "move." The sloarmen — representing the company in the eyes of the blowers — were just as emphatic in stating that the "move" had come out short. It was blowers against sloarmen in a battle that has gone down in history.

Afterwards, it was easy to see where an honest mistake might have been made. Salt cellars in the number of over two hundred all alike are not easy to count accurately. Then, too, some little taker-in boy, eager to finish the day's work and go fishing, may have jumped the count, hoping that his announced figure would get by the sloarmen without question. That had been tried before.

When Mr. Spurr returned from his Boston conference, he succeeded in smoothing over the surface of the trouble. Nick Black got his eighty-seven cents and went back to work, and the other blowers continued also. But as the sloarmen were, in a way, guardians of the company treasury, the blowers nursed a feeling that the company would trick them when it could. In this atmosphere of distrust, the factory went on busily losing money throughout the year.

Of course, no one could tell the workers that the company was losing money when they all knew that the factory had a million dollars' worth of orders. But no one tried. The directors came and went on their usual aloof monthly visits. Perhaps even they found it hard to believe that such a volume of business could not be made profitable — if only in some way they could meet the competition of Pittsburgh and cheap fuel. As was usual when a manufactory was caught between the fixed cost of raw material and the downward pressure of competitive prices, the only way to turn a profit was to reduce labor costs.

On December 24, 1887, the glass factory again crashed

into the columns of the newspaper, and the union received
its first public mention. "It is understood that the glassworkers' union held a special meeting Saturday to consider
the action taken by the manufacturers in announcing that a
new schedule of prices would take effect January 2. The
business of the town is dependent on the glass-works and the
result is anxiously watched by the people at large."

The announcement seems to have been that an increased
number of pieces per "move" would be required of the blowers at the same price — essentially what is today called the
"speed-up." Had one of the directors, like the tactful and
respected Mr. Bradlee, attended the union meeting to ex-
plain the company situation, backed by figures, the result
might have been different. At least, the men would have had
a clear idea of the issues and could have decided whether
they wished to work at reduced wages in Sandwich or to take
a chance on higher pay elsewhere. As it was, the "speed-up"
was offered bluntly on a "take-it-or-leave-it" basis with the
threat that "If the fires are drawn, they never will be re-
lighted."

(The tradition connecting this event with the old charter
of Jarves days which was automatically to expire if the fires
were allowed to go out is another bit of fiction. For some
years, as has been stated, the fires had been drawn for the
annual summer vacation.)

If the action of the directors, however irritatingly arrogant, was necessary to the continued operation of the factory,
the reaction of the workers was only natural. To be sure,
the only workers affected were the highly paid blowers who
most needed to be spurred to more efficient production and
who could best afford a cut. But the blowers during the past
half-century had slowly been losing their favored position in
comparison with other craftsmen. True, there had been a
rise of thirty-seven per cent in the ratio of their wages to
wholesale prices between 1840 and 1880, but the similar

ratio for general wages had increased by about sixty-two per cent.[4] They were sensing the trend, though they might not know the figures, and were ready to fight against any further threat to their prerogatives. As for the others, they felt that any acceptance of cut or "speed-up" would be only a beginning of more and more stringent demands. That was the way matters usually worked out. Best not to surrender an inch in the first place!

Besides, they were entirely unconvinced as to the need. All the men knew of a large order of lamps on hand for which the material was already assembled. Everyone spoke of the company's million dollars' worth of business. It is almost impossible for the man used to measuring money by the tangible pittance of his pay check to realize that a million dollars in orders is not necessarily a million in profits.

Forever and a day, the company might post notices to the effect that there was not enough profit in the business as it was run to enable them to continue and that if there was a strike, the plant would be closed. The end of the factory was as unthinkable as the end of the world.

"Bluff! It's all a bluff!" one big fellow cried. "The company can't afford to shut down."

All the workers had to do was to stand firm and call the bluff. Glassworkers, as they all knew, had had a way of winning their strikes.

Consequently, the January 7, 1888, edition of the little weekly paper carried the news: "On Monday, the employees of the Glass Factory, in consequence of the posting of new rules, left their positions and the fires are out and work suspended. Some work is going on in the decorative and packing rooms. The company say they make no essentially new requirements of the men, but desire and intend to control their own business."

For many years to come, employers were to feel that man-

4 Warren C. Scoville, *Growth of the American Glass Industry to 1880.*

to-man meetings with their workmen on terms of business equality would be beneath their dignity. On the other hand, workers were too impatient to flaunt their new strength forged of solidarity. Even Powderly of the Knights had complained, "In some places, the members refuse to arbitrate simply because they *are* strong." Now even the amiable Mr. Spurr could not bridge the gap between the coolly contemptuous notices posted in the Watch-House and the angry shouts at union meetings.

In villages half the Cape away, men missed the pillar of smoke over Sandwich and speculated with vague forebodings on the empty winter sky. The thermometer stood around zero that day, so they say. The ground was powdered with snow, wagon wheels squeaked in the frosty air, and the few people on Sandwich streets were standing as though stunned. Word had just come from Boston that — to continue from the *Register* "at a meeting of the directors of the Boston and Sandwich Glass Company Monday afternoon, it was voted to close the works. General Manager Spurr ordered the firemen not to put on more coal and the fires will be allowed to go out. The decorating, cutting, and other departments will be closed Saturday next. This industry employs about 300 men."

"Strike!" cried Sandwich. Wasn't it a strike when men refused to work, destroying not only their own livelihood, but that of innocent bystanders like Mr. Swann and his ladies of the decorating department, the non-union Fred Wodt and the girl roughers in the cutting room, and the merchants on Main and Jarves Sts.?

"Lock-out!" cries Jarvesville to this day if anyone will stop to listen. Isn't it a lock-out when a company simply issues an ultimatum and then abandons the factory without the slightest attempt to bargain with its employees?

It is a truism of labor history that any work stoppage is strike or lock-out according to which side is calling the name.

The result in any case was the same to the little storekeepers worrying over stocks and unpaid accounts, to the wives fingering the soles of their children's shoes and measuring out the daily dole of coal and flour with anxious hands, the angry and baffled men milling to and fro by a closed factory door.

2

A town, like hope, is slow in dying. The local paper did its best to hide the death pangs with a false bustle of optimism. The Grange had come to Sandwich. A creamery was soon to be started by the Grange in East Sandwich. The milk of sixty cows had already been secured. Charles Spurr, brother of the factory superintendent, had opened the Cape Cod Glass Factory as a veneering works. Business was flourishing and the machines were running day and night. Spurr's Veneer Works was now one of the large industries of the town. It employed twenty-one men.

With better intentions than tact, Senator Isaac Keith (Keith, the blacksmith, had succeeded in founding a dynasty where Jarves, the capitalist and inventor, had failed) offered to "build an almshouse on the Bourne and Sandwich line for the use of the two towns." Privately, everyone knew that there was likely to be greater need for an almshouse than ever before in town history. Not many glassmakers had saved any money. Money, unlike the farmer's grain and wool which can be tangibly gloated over as protection against hunger and cold, could more easily trickle away for the nearest want than be hoarded for future necessity. But the town delayed facing the inevitable. Though signs kept cropping up for all to read, no one wished to heed.

In March: "P. M. Crowell having closed his branch store in Sandwich, A. T. Raymond now assists in the Boston store."

Here stood the first of the blank-windowed stores, abandoned to mysterious fires.

In May: "Mr. Robert Matthews, one of the finest glass-makers in this country, left Sandwich on Saturday for New Bedford where he has accepted a position at the Mt. Washington Glass Works."

A good gaffer did not have to yield to company dictation or wait for the almshouse. He could journey with his skill, as journeymen had done from time out of mind. However, there were many glassmaking folk of the third generation in Sandwich — the Blacks and the Bradys and others who had been among the pew holders in the first little Saint Peter's in 1830. They felt that the wandering life might be very well for a lone adventurer, but the new industrial mass migration held only hardship for families rooted in a well-loved town, especially those who owned their homes.

Ten of the blowers decided that they would not be driven from town. After all, wasn't theirs the knowledge and skill that made the glass — and the money? Perhaps the closing of the factory was not a calamity, but an opportunity — an opportunity to escape the wages' system which was held to be the cause of all evil.

"Co-operation is what we want," cried the rank-and-file of the Knights of Labor when their strikes failed.

By co-operation, workers could satisfy a desire for revenge on the corporation and an urge to raise their social status from wage earner to employer. The co-operative movement had reached its peak in the preceding year, most of the enterprises, as at Sandwich, being the direct result of unsuccessful strikes. These ranged in number from twenty-two in mining to one in casket making, with glass standing at five — not counting the Cannelburg Coal Mine which was financed by the Window Glass Workers.

"We must adopt a system," Sylvis of the Iron Molders' International and Coöperative Union had said twenty years before, "which will divide the *profits* of labor among those who produce them."

So co-operation was a natural move in Sandwich, and full
of brave talk, the hopeful co-operators went into action. All
ten were Irish — Mahoney, Murray, Murphy, McNamee,
and so on — with the exception of the one German, Peter
Rosenberg. There was the big blusterer whose brogue battle
cry had sparked the strike. There was the honest craftsman,
Mike Grady, who managed to scrape together his five hundred dollars for a share because he loved glass and loved
Sandwich. For these reasons, he approached Mr. James
Lloyd at the station for his assistance with the secrets of the
"batch." And since Mr. Lloyd "felt sorry for Sandwich" —
and also a little for himself with no glass factory in which to
have a finger — he not only promised his help with formulae, but invested one thousand dollars of his money.

Others invested. Mr. George McLaughlin as usual gave
solid support to the workers' cause. Charles Brady, one of
the salesmen of the old factory, also bought a share. A study
of the co-operatives of this period shows that few developed in
pure co-operative form. The Sandwich co-operators sold
shares in their enterprise to non-producers and hired a few
employees for wages — like their clerk, young Mahoney just
out of high school, a son of one of the workers. Therefore,
strictly speaking, they were producers attempting to turn
capitalist.

The beginning was brave enough. They built a furnace in
a shack out on the sands — facetiously called the Crib by
townsfolk — and on June 10, 1888, the paper reported,
"Sandwich's new coöperative glass factory began to manufacture glass Monday and turned out a very creditable product, being flint glass of a very high grade."

There was no difficulty in disposing of their ware, which
consisted mostly of lamp shades and globes in clear flint,
white, or opalescent. The greater part went to Edward
Swann, formerly head of the decorating department in the
old factory. After building an addition on his house and

putting up a kiln, he had hired three or four of his best lady decorators and gone into business for himself. However, the Sandwich Coöperative Glass Company soon found that more than skill and will were needed to turn profits, and the Crib fell victim to the common ills of co-operatives.

Frequently, co-operative enterprises blew up in quarrels among partners. Sometimes, the effect of too many bosses on a business turned out to be as disastrous as too many cooks on the broth. In Sandwich, the active co-operators dwindled in a few months from ten to eight, but without any dramatic trouble. Peter Rosenberg died. One John Lovett lost enthusiasm for the risks of capitalism and deserted for good wages in Philadelphia.

In spite of a ready market for all glass made, the fact was that the Sandwich Coöperative Glass Company was running down for lack of capital reserve. Since orders were not paid for in advance, there were not enough funds on hand to sustain the necessary flow of raw material from outside. The workers found that, after all, capitalism had its part in production, which seemed maintained by intricate financial machinery decidedly not at the disposal of revolutionary co-operatives.

"They just didn't have enough money to keep going. There wasn't any of them of means or had very much, and they lost all they put in," is the Jarvesville obituary on the Sandwich Coöperative Glass Company.

The shack was abandoned to be beaten down by wind and weather on the dunes. With tears in his eyes, Mike Grady brought the magic recipe book back to Mr. Lloyd, begging him always to keep it as it might some day be worth a fortune — a prophecy which came true in a very moderate way when Mr. Lloyd's son sold the precious volume to the Metropolitan Museum in New York.

While the Sandwich Coöperative Glass Company blew away life's savings of workers and the spare dollars of friends, and a few virtuoso gaffers left for other parts, the rest of Jarvesville was watching the solid brick walls and towering chimneys of the old factory for signs of life and living through the summer on hope and blueberries.

"The blueberry crop in Sandwich has been nearly all gathered for this year," the paper reported in August. "It is estimated fully 15,000 quarts have been shipped to the Boston market from this town. The money derived from the sale of this fruit the past few weeks has been a very acceptable addition to the incomes of many people thrown out of employment by the shut-down of the Boston and Sandwich Glass Works."

Jarvesville folk seemed to have a way of knowing that orders were still drifting in from Africa and Australia and the ends of the earth where news of the disaster had not yet reached. It seemed impossible for them to believe that these orders would be wasted. Besides, their wishes were spurred to expectations by a line in the paper to the effect that "during the past week, there has been no little speculation concerning the plans of the Boston & Sandwich Glass Company whose works have been idle since Jan. 1."

Sandwich certainly heard of a letter from Mr. James Lloyd to Mr. Bradlee of the company regarding a plan under consideration for the possible reopening of the factory with Mr. Lloyd, a practical glass man, as manager. This letter is particularly interesting as an exposé of some of the conditions which led to the company decision to shut down.

> In compliance with your request, I give you in my opinion the best methods of running your factory [wrote Mr. Lloyd]. The following would be my way of conducting the business if the gains or loss were to be my own. — First, in running the Blowers' Department, I desire a capable man to assist me — I would prefer to have Mr. Kern. Then I wish it distinctly understood by the men that we want work made in the best possible way and that no poor work will be paid

for; no orders to be made in the factory not ordered except
by permission; and should the factory be run nights, those
who work on the night run are expected to be in place
promptly as day men — and see that the boys also are on
hand promptly to do good work. Then I should like to say
I don't think any factory can be made to pay unless run
nights — neither can men stand around outside the factory
in working hours as they have in the past.

In regard to the Cutting Shop, in other places it is run
by the day, men going in at 7 o'clock in the morning and
working till 6 at night with the exception of one hour at
dinner, and it seems a fair way to me. Here in the past they
have worked by the piece. There are advantages both ways.
Should wish to consult with you and the directors before
deciding about that. It is very desirable to have a smart
energetic man there with much ability for designing and
that will insist on good work from the men. Mr. E. J. Don-
ovan has applied for the position. But this matter can be
deferred until we know if the factory is to start.

As I view the situation, the factory must be brought to
a paying basis, and I should not advise starting it until all
these things are agreed to by the men. Every point where it
is probable there might be disagreement should be understood and settled now, and I think it would be proper for
you to frame from these suggestions what you expect from
the men and wish your manager to carry out. Then I
would suggest calling the men together and having it read
and agreed to by them.

He to whom glassmaking had always been more hobby
than livelihood went on to say that he did not think the situation warranted "such pay as you have been giving and I
am willing to work for $1500 a year if I should accept the
position of manager." But Nathaniel Bradlee died suddenly
in the midst of the planning.

The next Sandwich knew was an item copied from the
Boston Journal: "Another of the New England glass companies has yielded to the inevitable and decided to discon-

tinue operations. Labor troubles in the East and natural gas in the West both combining to place New England at a disadvantage have induced the directors of the Boston & Sandwich Glass Co. to quit the business in which they have been engaged the last sixty years. The directors voted Wednesday to wind up the affairs of the corporation and to sell off the stock and materials now on hand."

Now there was nothing to do but scramble for some sort of shelter before winter came. A few found work on the railroad or with one of the little factories in the vicinity. Ruthie Drody went out at housework for three dollars a week. The lady decorators prefer not to remember. "We did what we could."

There was a general exodus of blowers, mostly to Philadelphia or the West with the result that so much real estate thrown on the market at one time forced the prices down. About half of the home owners, when they found that they could obtain but a small part of what their property was worth, left their families in Sandwich, planning to come back during the annual summer vacation in hope of better conditions.

As was usual in hard times, especially during a presidential election year, people took to talking of political panaceas. Even the ultra-conservative little weekly took note of the fact that "several new parties have recently been launched on the scene, but how many of them will reach the port of success remains to be seen. Among them are Henry George's United Labor or Anti-Poverty Party and an old one revived, the American Party."

The latter was the old Know-Nothing, anti-foreign, anti-Catholic faction which represented the perennial reactionaries who, in the fiercely competitive industrial world, felt that the good things of life should be preserved, by force if necessary, for their own racial, religious, or social group. Henry George had set forth the theory so comforting to the

landless that private ownership of land had no more foundation in morality and reason than private ownership of air
and water.

However, in 1888, Utopia lost to Harrison and the American system of tariff. Wage earners saw no sign of promise,
or even stability, in the industrial scene. Jarvesville men
either had to part from their families or drag them from well-
loved homes to heaven knew what.

The cutters were least in the clutch of circumstance. Mr.
Nehemiah Packwood, former head of the cutting room, decided to utilize the Sandwich reputation for superlative cut
ware and the Sandwich supply of highly skilled cutters and
opened a cutting shop that was soon running day and night.
It must have seemed a sad reversal of the normal order for
Mr. Lloyd who had watched so much glass shipped out of
Sandwich to see "blanks" trickling in for Mr. Packwood's
cutting shop from Corning, New York.

Fred Wodt did not go to work for Mr. Packwood. He
started a one-man cutting shop — a little Utopia of his own
where a man could live as a man should — master of himself,
his time, his skill, his tools. Only in such a life could a man
possess his soul in freedom, unsmothered by this solidarity
which weak men craved and free men feared. Perhaps he
alone did not echo the newspaper sentiment that the year
1888 had been "a very disastrous one for the business interests of Sandwich."

The New Year opened on a further note of doom. "We
hear that the New York office of the Boston & Sandwich Glass
Company is to be discontinued."

Sandwich town meeting made a desperate attempt to cope
with fate in its motion "That whereas by closing the Boston
& Sandwich Glass Works over a year ago, general business
depression has followed, greatly crippling the town, it is the
vote of this town that the directors be requested to make
another effort to resume business, promising them all assistance and encouragement possible."

The answer was not long in coming. "The Boston & Sandwich Glass Company has sold its entire stock in trade, including molds, to Jones, Macduffie, and Stratton of Boston."

The result was soon noted in town affairs. "The school committee of Sandwich has voted to reduce the salary of the principal of the high school to $900."

It was perhaps ironical that the town chose to economize on the high-school principal when, for a short time at least, there was a possibility of more high-school pupils. Wives of glassworkers scattered from Philadelphia to Fostoria were finding consolation in ambitions for their children now that the factory door was no longer open to draw them away from school. Ruthie Drody's little sister might become a schoolteacher, her brother a clerk or accountant in a big city store, and wear their fine clothes all day long and never dirty their fingers.

So these mothers did not share the general dull dismay when Jones, Macduffie, and Stratton actually shipped off the finished stock to its wareroom, sold the precious iron molds to be melted up as scrap in the iron foundry of Senator Nye in Bourne, and abandoned the old wooden ones to dwindle away as firewood.

Under the circumstances, it was little wonder that Sandwich had to be nudged by its neighboring towns as to plans for the once anticipated celebration of the two hundred and fiftieth anniversary of its founding. "What shall be the order of proceedings of the quarter millennial of Sandwich, Yarmouth, Barnstable, and their off-shoots, Dennis and Bourne, is now the inquiry. The other towns await the initiatory proceedings of Sandwich, the mother town, so to speak."

Sandwich roused itself from the lethargy of despair long enough to put on an affair with the customary bell-ringing and band, oratory and fireworks keyed to the rather pathetic slogan: "Thankful for the Past — Hopeful for the Future."

The future offered little to justify the hope. Toward the

end of the year, there was a brief flicker of life. Sandwich men working in a Philadelphia glasshouse and dreaming ever of their "beautiful factory by the blue sea" were startled by a telegram from home. "Come back. Fires are lighted again in Sandwich."

A newspaper clipping soon explained the vent. "A special meeting of the Boston & Sandwich Glass Company was held in Boston to consider the sale of their property. The president stated an offer of $20,000 had been received, and a vote was passed authorizing the treasurer to sell. The Electrical Glass Company will probably buy the entire property."

Following the modern trend for specialization of products, this new company was to make only electric light bulbs. Noise of the excitement among Sandwich workers in the Philadelphia factory reached the ears of the superintendent. Evidently, it was a part of company labor relations to fire a man before he could leave voluntarily. While the men were making up their minds about risking a return, each received a pink slip with his pay envelope: "On account of dullness in the shade business, your services are no longer required."

So the Sandwich men went back home only to find that the new undertaking had failed and the factory was already closed again.

Twice more, fires burned in the factory furnaces. In 1895, a company started up with the fine flourish of having ninety-year-old Charles Lapham, who had blown the first piece for Deming Jarves, bless the venture with an appropriate gesture. It ran just long enough to plan a gift of tableware for Mrs. Grover Cleveland in the White House. Again about ten years later, the old glasshouse lured another enterprise, sponsored by the dauntless Mr. George McLaughlin. It lasted only until all the invested money had gone up the chimneys in smoke.

Through the years, the life blood of the town slowly oozed away as its population shrank to less than half of the four thousand of its heyday. The little factories and cutting shops died out with the men who had owned them. The stores which once had catered to most of the wants of the people dwindled to the few which supplied only the most urgent needs. The five saloons of Jarvesville and Saint Peter's Roman Catholic Total Abstinence Society faded away together, leaving the W.C.T.U. of the Main Street ladies in sole possession of the scene.

In dire financial straits, the school committee voted to close the Jarvesville school. Father Clinton of Saint Peter's, shouting discrimination, started a school of his own — a school of Murphys, McCanns, Boyles, and Gradys into which a little lone Hoxie had somehow strayed. But by the end of the year, he saw that the burden of its support was too great for his parish. Besides, the lusty Irish protests had had their effect, and the Jarvesville school was reopened until it became plain even to the most partisan that it would be better to transport the remaining handful of youngsters over into town.

For a long time yet, the great ghost chimneys towered above the screen of Jarves elms. Just as the half-deserted white churches on every village scene called ever to mind folk who had cherished the faith that, with God's help, they were building a way of life for their children after them, the abandoned factories in country towns up and down the land stood as monuments to men who had felt a mission to make the world move faster only to find that they had set in motion forces beyond their power to control.

Deming Jarves had come upon a thrifty farming settlement of some nineteen hundred souls. A century after his vision and his initial enterprise, a town of less than that number was left, and the number of self-sustaining farms could just about be counted on the fingers of a hand. Agriculture, like industry, was growing vaster in scope. With no factory to eke out the living to be squeezed from the small farms or to offer a career along other lines, there was nothing for an ambitious young person to do but leave as soon as possible for the cities which were sucking men and industries into ever larger and more intricate organizations.

Now in the old houses on their old meadows, old men played at farming to help stretch life savings. All the ancient gaffers were at rest with the early tillers of the soil. Retired schoolteacher daughters lived in their tidy homes, and fishermen and laborers were invading the factory tenements. Only a dwindling band of those who had once been glasshouse boys or girl roughers and decorators were left to shake gray heads over the freak of fancy that sent queer people scrabbling among the ruins for a hunk of slag or a shard of cullet and paying altogether crazy prices for the cheap pressed stuff — a crude little bear pomade jar or a cup plate with the pattern carelessly reversed — while a large crystal bowl with hours of hand cutting in the intricate strawberry and pineapple pattern would fetch little more than when fresh from the factory.

At last, the crumbling glasshouse was torn down to be sold and carted off, brick by brick, leaving only a flat grassy spot beside a creek, a place of haunted silence. The industrial revolution had surged in upon a town that was in its immemorial way a living organism. The industrial revolution ebbed, leaving only a charming fossil. Unlike most of the empty shells of towns abandoned by industry, Sandwich is filled with new life for just two months in the year. Even as in the days of Deming Jarves, city folk flock hither for relaxation and rest. Deer and trout are now too scanty for any extensive sport, but there are still the beauty and the peace. In the seeming stability of an outward semblance of the past, the apprehensive may for a moment ease the burden of a dread that all freedom of spirit may be crushed out in the panicky stampede for solidarity against the fear that nothing is permanent, nothing is safe — not even the world itself.

SELECTED BIBLIOGRAPHY

Abbott, Edith, *Women in Industry,* New York, 1909.

Adams, James Truslow, *History of New England,* Boston, 1927.

Austin, Jane G., "An Eye Witness's Story of Sandwich Glass," *Atlantic Monthly,* 1865.

Beard and Rogers, *5000 Years of Glass,* New York, 1937.

Bourgoin, the Rev. Raymond, *The Catholic Church in Sandwich, 1830–1930,* Boston, 1930.

Brownson, Orestes, *The Laboring Classes,* Methodist Quarterly Review, 1841.

Burbank, George E., *A Bit of Sandwich History Compiled for Use During the Tercentenary Celebration in 1939,* Sandwich, Mass., 1939.

————, *History of the Sandwich Glass Works,* A Tercentenary pamphlet, Sandwich, Mass., 1939.

Burgess, Bangs, *History of Sandwich Glass,* Yarmouthport, Mass., 1925.

Chipman, Frank W., *The Romance of Old Sandwich Glass,* Sandwich, Mass., 1932.

Commons, John Rogers, *History of Labor in the U.S.,* New York, 1926.

Constitution of the United Glassmakers of Massachusetts, Boston, 1865.

Deyo, Simeon L., *History of Barnstable County,* New York, 1890.

Freeman, Frederick, *History of Cape Cod,* Boston, 1858.

Gaffield, Thomas, *Correspondence on Glass and Glassmaking.*

————, *Essays on Glass and Glassmaking.* Ms. collection, Massachusetts Institute of Technology Library.

————, *Glass and Glassmaking.* Ms. collection, Massachusetts Institute of Technology Library.

————, *Glass Journal.* Ms. collection, Massachusetts Institute of Technology Library.

————, *Glass Pamphlets.* Ms. collection, Massachusetts Institute of Technology Library.

————, *Notes on Glass.* Ms. collection, Massachusetts Institute of Technology Library.

————, *Portfolio of Articles Relating to Glass.* Ms. collection, Massachusetts Institute of Technology Library.

————, *Scrapbook on Glass Matter.* Ms. collection, Massachusetts Institute of Technology Library.

Hamilton, Alexander, *Report on Manufactures,* communication to the House of Representatives, Dec. 5, 1791, from Alexander Hamilton, Secretary of the Treasury, on the subject of manufactures.

Hayes, Denis A., President, Glass Bottle Blowers' Association of America, "Length of the Trade Life in the Glass Bottle Industry," *Annals of the American Academy of Political and Social Science,* May, 1906.

Irwin, Frederick T., *Story of Sandwich Glass and Glassware,* Manchester, N.H., 1926.

Jarves, Deming, *Reminiscences of Glass-Making,* Boston, 1865.

Jarves, James Jackson, *Art Hints,* New York, 1855.

————, *The Art-Idea,* New York, 1864.

————, *Art Studies,* New York, 1861.

————, *Art Thoughts,* Boston, 1882.

————, *History of the Hawaiian or Sandwich Islands, Embracing Their Antiquities, Mythology, Legends, Discovery by Europeans in the Sixteenth Century, Rediscovery by Cook, With Their Civil, Religious, and Political History,* London, 1843.

————, *Italian Sights and Papal Principles Seen Through American Spectacles,* New York, 1856.

————, *Parisian Sights and French Principles Seen Through American Spectacles,* New York, 1852.

————, *Scenes and Scenery in the Sandwich Islands and a Trip Through Central America; Being Observations From My Note-book During the Years 1837–1842,* Boston, 1843.

————, *Why and What Am I? The Confessions of an Inquirer,* Boston, 1857.

Kennedy, W. S., *Wonders and Curiosities of the Railway,* Chicago, 1884.

Kingsbury, S. M., *Labor Laws and Their Enforcement,* New York, 1911.

Kittredge, Henry C., *Cape Cod, Its People and Their History,* Boston, 1930.

Lanier, Sterling, "A Cloth of Glass," *Technology Review,* April and May, 1942.

Lee, Ruth Webb, *Sandwich Glass,* Framingham, Mass., 1939.

Lord, Sexton, and Harrington, *History of the Archdiocese of Boston,* New York, 1944.

Lovejoy, Owen R., "Child Labor in the Glass Industry," *Annals of the American Academy of Political and Social Science,* March, 1906.

Maynard, Theodore, *The Story of American Catholicism,* New York, 1941.

McCullagh, W. T., *Industrial History of Free Nations,* London, 1846.

McGrane, R. C., *The Panic of 1837,* University of Chicago, 1924.

Meyer, B. H., *History of Transportation in the U.S. Before 1860,* Washington, 1917.

Newspapers:
Barnstable Patriot.
Boston Evening Record.
Boston Journal.
Yarmouth Register.

Phelps Stokes, Rose H., *The Condition of Working Women from the Working Woman's Viewpoint. Annals of the American Academy of Political and Social Science,* May, 1906.

Pratt, Ambrose E., *250th Anniversary Celebration of Sandwich and Bourne at Sandwich, Massachusetts,* Sandwich, Mass., 1899.

Scoville, Warren C., "Growth of the American Glass Industry to 1880," *Journal of Political Economy,* September, 1944.

Setzer, Dorothea, *The Sandwich Historical Society and Its Glass,* Sandwich, Mass., 1936.

Smith, Adam, *Wealth of Nations,* Edinburgh, 1908.

Stowe, Charles Messer, *The Deming Jarves Book of Designs.* Yarmouthport, Mass., 1925.

Swan, Mabel M., "Deming Jarves and His Glass Factory Village," *Antiques,* 1938.

Swift, Charles F., *Cape Cod — The Right Arm of Massachusetts,* Yarmouth, Mass., 1897.

Taussig, F. W., *The Tariff History of the United States,* New York, 1893.

Tocqueville, Alexis de, *Democracy in America*, New York, 1945.
Ware, Norman J., *The Industrial Worker 1840–1860*, Boston, 1924.
—————, *The Labor Movement in the U.S., 1860–1895*, New York, 1929.
Watkins, Lura Woodside, *Cambridge Glass*, Boston, 1930.

INDEX

INDEX

313